Women
Behaving
Badly

Also by John Stark Bellamy II:

Women Behaving Badly

*True Tales of Cleveland's
Most Ferocious Female Killers*

AN ANTHOLOGY

John Stark Bellamy II

John Stark Bellamy II

GRAY & COMPANY, PUBLISHERS
CLEVELAND

Gray & Company, Publishers
1588 E. 40th St., Cleveland, Ohio 44113
www.grayco.com

The stories in this anthology, with two exceptions, originally
appeared in the following books by John Stark Bellamy II, published
by Gray & Company, Publishers: *They Died Crawling* (1995), *The
Maniac in the Bushes* (1997), *The Corpse in the Cellar* (1999), *The Killer
in the Attic* (2002), and *Death Ride at Euclid Beach* (2004).
The stories "Bad Cinderalla" and "The Sins of the Father" are
published here for the first time.

For more information about John Stark Bellamy's works, contact him
by email at jbellamy@grayco.com.

Library of Congress Cataloging-in-Publication Data
Bellamy, John Stark.
Women behaving badly : true tales of Cleveland's most ferocious
female killers : an anthology / John Stark Bellamy II.
p. cm.   ISBN 1-59851-000-2 (hardcover)
1. Women murderers—Ohio—Cleveland—Biography. 2. Crime—
Ohio—Cleveland—History—Case studies. I. Title.
HV6517.B45 2005
364.152'3'092277132—dc22   2005023772

ISBN 1-59851-000-2

Printed in the United States of America
First Printing

With Love to my beautiful wife, Laura
Who made me love my life again

Contents

Women
Behaving
Badly

She Got Her Money's Worth

Eva Kaber, Lakewood's Lady Borgia, 1919

"Happy families are all alike," runs Tolstoy's best one-liner. "Each unhappy family is unhappy in its own peculiar way." And if you don't believe it, consider the Kaber family.

The time was July 15, 1919. The place was the Dan Kaber house, a posh, neo-Colonial showplace on fashionable Lake Avenue, several blocks west of the city of Cleveland. And the persons were the sharply disparate members of the Dan Kaber family—each desperately and uniquely unhappy.

Dan Kaber, certainly, had the most objective reasons for being unhappy. Forty-six years old and formerly a healthy, active, well-to-do printer, Dan had within the past six months become a helpless, bedridden, pain-wracked invalid. Confined most of the time to his second-floor bedroom, Dan had lost the use of all his limbs, with the pitiful exception of the index and middle finger of his left hand. His decline had begun with an apparent influenza attack during the previous November, but despite lengthy hospital stays and futile surgery for suspected cancer of the stomach and appendicitis, Dan had steadily deteriorated. His doctors muttered vaguely about "rheumatism," then "cancer" and "neuritis," but it was plain they did not have a clue as to Dan Kaber's malady. Dan Kaber was increasingly feeble, querulous, and seemingly fearful; he was apparently most fearful of his wife, Eva Kaber. Ever attentive, she insisted on personally feeding him—and quite often the soups, strawberries, and chocolates she proffered made him violently sick. Dan tried to complain to anyone who would listen that there seemed to be an awful lot of paprika in his food of late . . . but whenever he tried to tell his brother or father about his suspicions Eva would appear in the room.

Eva Kaber wasn't very happy in July 1919. Thirty-nine years old, she had struggled and schemed her way up from nothing to status as a respected Lakewood matron and the spouse of a wealthy printer's son. Born mere Catherine Brickel to parents of modest origin, she was a trial and trouble to everyone in her life from an early age. Indeed, at the age of seven "Kitty" Brickel already had a reputation as a demonic child, subject to apparently unprovoked rages in which she would assault her playmates, kicking, screaming, and sometimes even tearing both their hair and her own. A chronic juvenile runaway and thief, frequently expelled from school, she spent part of her adolescence at the Home of the Good Shepherd, her sole alternative at age 16 to a prison term for stealing $85 from an acquaintance. After working as a chambermaid at a posh East Side mansion—where she acquired a taste for expensive things— Eva was married at 17 to a barkeep, Thomas McArdle. The marriage lasted two months, and Eva subsequently disappeared—after dumping the fruit of her brief nuptials, her daughter Marion, on her long-suffering parents.

Before Dan, Eva was married again, briefly, to a barber named David Frinkle—but it is probable that Dan Kaber knew little about his wife's previous marriages. What Dan Kaber did know was that

Eva was quarrelsome, spiteful, financially demanding, and increasingly impatient with his physical deterioration. Eva was particularly upset that July because Dan was reluctant to finance another year at Smith College for her daughter, Marion McCardle. And Eva was beginning to suspect that Dan was thinking about changing his will.

Also at the Kaber home that July was Eva's mother, Mary Brickel. Sixty-seven years old, she had had a hard life; four of her eight children were already dead, and her favorite child, Charles, had frequent trouble with the law, including a short prison term for theft. Mrs. Brickel had decidedly mixed feelings toward Eva—whom she always referred to as "Mrs. Kaber"—but she nevertheless deferred to her daughter in all things. Surely not the ideal mother-in-law for poor, sick Dan Kaber.

Also there that summer of 1919 was Marion McCardle, Eva's daughter by her first marriage. Nineteen years old, Marion was mainly interested in good times, popular music, and her dream of a career as a chorus girl. And like her mother and grandmother, Marion made no secret of her hatred for her stepfather, once screaming at him during a formal dinner party: "What do you mean? I don't have to take any orders from you!" Clearly, the House of Kaber was beginning to resemble the House of Atreus more than it did your average happy family.

The Kaber case remains the greatest murder story in the history of Cleveland. Its contrivance was worthy of the Borgias, and its telling deserves the style of Edgar Allan Poe and the macabre humor of William Roughead, the greatest true-crime writer of all time. It remains the only homicide in the history of the world in which a grandmother, mother, and granddaughter were indicted for the same first-degree murder.

Sometime in mid-July 1919, Eva Kaber told her family that she was going away to visit her sister, Mrs. H. J. McGinnis, at Cedar Point. On the afternoon of Wednesday, July 16, she drove away, accompanied by her four-year-old adopted daughter, Patricia. Forty-eight hours went by.

On the evening of Friday, July 18, the residents of the Kaber house at 12537 Lake Avenue retired fairly early. Dan Kaber dozed fitfully in his spacious northeast bedroom on the second floor. Next to his room, separated by a locked door, were the sleeping quarters of stepdaughter Marion McArdle, on this night shared by Miss Anna Baehr, Marion's neighborhood school chum, who had just returned from a picture-show with Marion. Up on the third floor slept F. W. Utterback, Kaber's sixtyish male nurse. There is no reason to doubt that everyone retired to their rooms at about 10 or 10:15 P.M., with the exception of grandmother Mary Brickel, who later testified at the inquest that she carefully locked the first-floor doors and windows before retiring.

Sometime about 10:30 P.M. all hell broke loose in the Kaber household. Although Marion McArdle and Anna Baehr initially claimed that they heard nothing unusual, they eventually allowed that, well, yes, they had heard some screaming. Well, yes, actually, a lot of screaming. In fact, Marion finally said, "There was not one call for help but many screams. It will be a long time before we forget those screams!"

The screams that Marion and Anna heard were probably exactly what Kaber's male nurse heard as he was abruptly aroused from a sound sleep: "Utterback! Utterback! Murder! Come quick!"

Come quick Utterback did. Running down the stairs in his bare feet and union suit to Kaber's second-floor bedroom, he burst through the open door to discover a ghastly scene. There was a bloody knife on the floor and Dan Kaber was lying there in a pool of his own blood. Kaber was conscious, and when Utterback asked him what had happened, he replied, "A man with a cap. Look for a man with a finger almost bitten off; I bit his finger. I think there were two of them. My wife had this done!"

Pandemonium ensued. Marion, Miss Baehr, and grandmother Brickel appeared soon in the second-floor hallway and contributed loud hysterics. Doctors were summoned, the police arrived, and Dan Kaber was rushed to Lakewood Hospital, where doctors labored to save his life. It could not have been an easy task. He had been stabbed 24 times: five abdominal wounds on the left side of the navel, three wounds on the left buttock, three wounds on the right buttock, and—the unkindest cuts of all—11 stab wounds to the scrotum. Not to mention numerous scratches on the face and throat, clearly indicating that someone had held the invalid down while another wielded a very cruel knife.

Dan tried to complain to anyone who would listen that there seemed to be an awful lot of paprika in his food of late.

Dan Kaber died hard, shortly after 1 P.M. the following day. To his last breath he repeated only that his slayer had been "a man with a cap" and that his "wife had this done."

Meanwhile, where was the dead man's wife? Well, Eva returned to her home at 5:30 P.M. the following day. She expressed appropriate surprise, especially when she found silverware strewn on her dining room floor, the apparent residue of an interrupted burglary. "Robbers have taken my silver!" is probably the most accurate estimate of what she said on this occasion. She quickly posted a reward for her husband's killers, arranged for Dan's funeral, and filed his will for probate.

Eva Kaber was always good at short-term goals, and, in the short term, all she had to do was get through the inquest, which was opened by Cuyahoga County Coroner P. J. Byrne on July 23 at 10 A.M. Which she did, in stubborn, crude, typically brazen form. Repeatedly accused of lying by County Prosecutor Samuel Doerfler, Eva responded with a combination of calm denial and strategic outbursts of feminine tears. Suggestions that her relations with Dan had been less than amicable were stoutly denied, and, after all, no one could prove that Eva had been anywhere near the murder scene on the fatal night. So Eva simply "wavered and wept" until the prosecutor gave up, and it was clear even before the end of the inquest that the verdict was going to be "willful murder by unknown." That verdict was duly delivered, despite the fact that a second autopsy disclosed up to *40 grains* of arsenic in Dan's emaciated and perforated corpse. Despite heroic efforts, the source of the arsenic could not be traced, nor could it be proven just how or by whom it had been administered to Dan Kaber. And it could have been worse: one of the initial theories given attention by the police was that Dan Kaber had *committed suicide*.

And that, seemingly, was the end of it, despite the suspicions of the police. Eva Kaber cashed in her husband's insurance policies, sold the big Lake Avenue residence, and left town. It appeared at the time that she would have the last word on the subject, which was: "I can't imagine who could be guilty of such a deed. I never heard that my husband had enemies."

No one except Eva was completely satisfied with the inquest verdict, but the police and other interested parties now dropped the case for lack of evidence. Well, almost all the interested parties. One who didn't was Moses Kaber, Dan's 71-year-old father. He swore a mighty oath in July 1919 that he would spend the rest of his life and all of his considerable fortune to bring his son's murderers to justice.

There had been bad blood between the Kaber family and Eva ever since her abrupt marriage to Dan in September 1907. The Kabers were Jewish, and they apparently took a dim view of the worldly, temperamental gentile who had captivated their Dan. Nothing since the marriage had changed their stance; they knew that Eva had led Dan a dog's life, and they never doubted from the beginning that it was she who had arranged his death. So while Eva left Cleveland to enjoy her newfound widow's wealth, Moses Kaber went to talk to the Pinkerton National Detective Agency.

Moses had little choice in the matter. The police had dropped the case, and the Pinkertons were the best-known private investigative agency in the world. And there is no question that they gave Moses Kaber his money's worth during the two years that followed. Within weeks, an as-yet-unsuspicious Eva Kaber was eating, sleeping, and breathing undercover Pinkerton detectives wherever she went. She hired a milliner shortly after leaving Cleveland—the milliner was a Pinkerton. She hired a maid, too—also a Pinkerton. When she dined in restaurants, she unknowingly dined with Pinkertons. And when she went to the movies, Pinkertons sat right behind her.

The most important break for Moses Kaber and the Pinkertons was the recruitment of Mrs. Ethel Berman as an operative. Eva's former Lakewood friend had originally met Eva during her honeymoon with Dan in 1908, and Ethel had maintained her ties to Eva after the murder for old times' sake, although Ethel disapproved of much in Eva's character. Ethel had been particularly shocked to find Eva laughing on the day after Dan's funeral, when she dropped in to comfort the grieving widow. "To think that I laid him out in a dirty shirt," Eva cackled uproariously. "Dan wasn't worth a clean shirt!" Given her suspicions, it didn't take long for the Pinkertons to convince Mrs. Berman that she, and only she, could help them get the evidence to convict her friend of first-degree murder.

Next to Eva Kaber, Ethel Berman, unquestionably, is the most fascinating character in the whole Kaber story. A perfectly pleasant, respectable, handsome Lakewood matron, happily married wife and mother of an eight-year-old son, Ethel willingly left her conventional life for some months to pose as an unhappy, restless goodtime party girl to her confidante, Eva Kaber. After the Pinkertons picked up Eva's trail in New York City, Ethel got in touch with her, painting herself as an aggrieved, bitter spouse of the Eva Kaber type. This was music to Eva's ears, and she blandly promised to help Ethel get rid of *her* husband when called upon. Before long, the two were traveling around the country, sharing hotel rooms and going to movies and restaurants together. Mrs. Berman would later claim that she did the whole thing merely for the sake of justice, but there is little doubt that it must have been a great adventure for the otherwise staid Lakewood housewife. As to the morality of betraying her former friend, Ethel characterized it this way: "It was not a pleasant thing to have to betray the confidences of one who had been my friend. But if I have helped to serve the ends of justice, I am glad."

It was soon apparent to Mrs. Berman that Eva Kaber was a very troubled individual. A woman of violent temper and increasingly

---

Eva Kaber spent much of her money and a lot of her time with very strange people: fortune-tellers, clairvoyants, spirit-mediums, and petty criminals.

---

paranoid—or maybe not so paranoid—that she was being tailed by detectives, she would often ask Ethel if she thought someone nearby was a "D.T.S.," Eva's term for a Pinkerton. Paradoxically, however, she could not stop talking obsessively about her late husband's death. Eventually, she became suspicious of Ethel, particularly after Ethel questioned Eva about some words Eva had cried out in her sleep one night: "I did it! I did it! I did it!" At that time Eva confronted Mrs. Berman and demanded to know if she, too, were a "D.T.S.," but Ethel convincingly swore this mighty oath at Eva's behest: "I swear to God that I hope to go home and see my son blind before I am in with the Pinkerton people."

Shortly after this, Eva dropped Mrs. Berman as a traveling companion, but Ethel's work was not yet done. She returned to Cleveland, where she immediately ingratiated herself in similar fashion with Mary Brickel, Eva's mother. Mrs. Berman had always felt sorry for the weak-willed Mary; she had been aware for years that Eva bullied her mother to do the Kaber laundry for free—while Eva regularly took four dollars per week from her husband to pay the "laundress." Their budding friendship soon yielded the following confidence from Mrs. Brickel, conveniently uttered to Mrs. Berman at the B. F. Keith Theatre in the presence of two movie patrons behind them—who just happened to be Pinkerton detectives. "She did it and she did it for money," said Mrs. Brickel, going on to say, "If they try to put it on Charlie [Eva's brother], I'll tell all I know!"

It was now the spring of 1921. Eva had by now largely exhausted her inheritance and was running a failing millinery shop in New York City. Her daughter Marion was traveling around the United States as a member of the chorus line in *Pretty Baby*. And the Pinkertons knew, from information provided by Mrs. Berman and others, that Eva Kaber spent much of her money and a lot of her time with very strange people: fortune-tellers, clairvoyants, spirit-mediums, and petty criminals. They began to shadow these persons, too, sensing that they might have some connection to the two-year-old murder. Finally, Moses Kaber met with County Prosector Edward Stanton and Lakewood Police, and they set a trap for the end of May 1921.

It sprang perfectly on Eva's mother, Mary Brickel. Called without warning on Sunday afternoon, May 31, to the Lakewood Police Station with her son Charles, Mary was sent to sit in a room with an open door. Minutes later, she heard Prosecutor Stanton shout at Charles, "Lock this man up and charge him with the murder of Dan Kaber! He's the one who did it!" A split-second later, she heard the clang of a jail cell door.

The trick worked like magic on the 69-year-old grandmother. Within minutes Mary was singing like a canary, just as she had threatened she would "if they try to put it on Charlie." On June 1, 1919, Assistant County Prosecutor John T. Cassidy announced first-degree-murder indictments against Eva Kaber, Mary Brickel, and Marion McArdle.

Eva tried to flee prosecution but was eventually arrested at the apartment of a New York City friend on the night of Saturday, June 4. Two days later, Marion was picked up, and both were arraigned. Both stayed in character; while being led off to the Tombs, Marion whimpered to detectives: "For God's sake, don't make me testify against my mother!" Eva, never at a loss for insouciant denial, said: "Really, if the situation were not so serious it would be laughable! I have nothing to fear." Her bravado was followed within hours by two suicide attempts in her cell.

Waiving extradition, Eva and Marion were brought back to Cleveland in mid-June. William J. Corrigan, a brilliant young defense attorney, was appointed by the court to assist Francis Poulson in Eva's defense, and her trial date was set for June 28.

From beginning to end, the arrest, arraignment, and trial of Eva Kaber provided the greatest carnival of publicity and sensationalism Cleveland had ever endured or enjoyed. The Kaber case was front-page news in all three Cleveland daily newspapers from June 1 until late July, and no fact, rumor, or speculation was left unpublished. One of the magistrates even allowed a female *Press* reporter, Lewette B. Pollock, to spend a night in jail as a feigned prisoner with Mrs. Kaber and Marion. Hardly a day went by without damning headlines about Mrs. Kaber, and the flavor of unequivocal editorial condemnation was perfectly epitomized by a small headline from the *News-Leader* during the last week of the trial: *Laughing Time Is Over, Paying Time Comes Now!*

Meanwhile, the police were busy hauling in suspects from the vast subculture of mediums, fortune tellers, and outright criminals Eva Kaber had cultivated in her salad days. Within days, Cleveland police arrested several women suspects, most significantly a Mrs. Erminia Colavito, a midwife, fortune teller, and potion vendor, who was apprehended by a flying squad of police sent to Sandusky, Ohio. In mid-June Salvatore Cala, one of the alleged Kaber killers, was picked up by Cleveland detectives at his uncle's farm in New York state. By the beginning of the trial on June 28, the county prosecutor had all the threads of the story in his hands—and what a story it was.

It went something like this, allowing for all the numberless and conflicting lies that the participants in the crime told and retold: Eva Kaber had always been a superstitious soul and from a tender age had consulted fortune-tellers, mediums, and the like. When she was 17, one medium told her something she never forgot through all her years of scheming, mayhem, and treachery: *You'll always get what you want!* (Eva apparently was unaware of the medium's handwritten notes, which included these added insights: *Bold and confident, but not very smart.*) During the decade of her marriage to Dan Kaber, Eva continued to frequent practitioners of the black arts, often spending large sums of money on fortune-telling and lucky charms.

Sometime in the spring of 1918 Eva went to a Mrs. Mary Wade, a medium living on East 82nd Street. Eva painted herself as an unhappy wife and asked Mrs. Wade's spiritual intercession to persuade her first ex-husband, Thomas McArdle, to pay for daughter Marion's tuition at Smith College. Mrs. Wade agreed to do this but astutely suggested that Mrs. Kaber also make the request directly to McArdle in a letter. One can imagine Eva's jubilation when a handsome check from McArdle forthwith arrived, due no doubt to Mrs. Wade's supernatural intervention. But Eva had a bigger challenge for Mrs. Wade. She now asked the medium to use her powers to kill her husband.

Mrs. Wade, or so she later testified, immediately and piously refused her client's request, righteously telling Eva that her powers could not be used for evil purposes. But Eva Kaber was not one to give up easily. She soon got in touch with a rather hard fellow from Little Italy, Urbano Di Corpo. Like most of her acquaintances, Eva met him through a medium, a certain Mrs. Sauers who lived on East 89th Street. Sometime in late 1918, just before Dan took sick, Eva saw Di Corpo while waiting in line for tickets at the Stillman Theater on Euclid Avenue. Drawing him aside, she pointed out her husband and offered Di Corpo $5,000 to run Dan over with an automobile. Why this plot wasn't pursued is unknown, but around that same time Eva deliberately set the Kaber home on fire with gasoline, although she would later attempt to blame the arson on her pliable mother. Eva also began supplementing Dan's food with match heads and other unwholesome substances.

It was Di Corpo who introduced Eva to Erminia Colavito, mother of five, midwife, neighborhood abortionist, and general all-around hand at the black arts. In good time, Eva journeyed to Mrs. C.'s Mayfield Road home, spoke feelingly to the spiritual practitioner of Dan's supposed "objectionable practices," and begged for a "potion" to set him straight. Potions were soon forthcoming, and Dan Kaber began to suffer the mysterious decline that would climax with his violent death in July 1919. Mrs. Colavito would later claim that her potion was composed only of olive oil and ginger ale. It is worth noting that another of her potions—composed mainly of chloral hydrate—sold about the same time to a man named Pasquale Julian to cure his brother John, put the latter in the State Hospital for the Insane in Newburg.

Sometime in late June or early July 1919, Eva became impatient with the progress of Mrs. C's fluids. So Eva decided to have Dan murdered more quickly and went to the accommodating Mrs. Colavito with her problem: "Oh that devil. I could kill him! I am looking for someone to kill him! I would pay anything to have him killed!" Mrs. Colativo liked this kind of talk and soon recruited Salvatore Cala and Vittorio Pisselli, young toughs from Little Italy who could neither read nor write English. Mrs. Kaber got right to the point with them: "I want my husband killed. I have tried but not succeeded." By mid-July Eva had struck a bargain with them, an arrangement, Cala later recalled, that made Eva just "tickled pink." While she was safely away at Cedar Point, they would enter the house at night—admitted by Mrs. Brickel—and stab Dan Kaber in his bed. Cala was given a penciled map of the house, and he and Pisselli were promised that the house would be prepared so that the caper would look like a burglary gone awry. Cala and Pisselli were also promised somewhere between $3,000 and $5,000 for their night's work. And on about July 10 Eva took her mother Mary aside and said, "I want you to do some dirty work for me . . . I'm going to have Dan killed."

On July 16 Eva drove away to Cedar Point to establish her alibi. The night before, while Marion generously played the piano on the first floor to mask any noise (her performance included "I'm Always Chasing Rainbows," "Dardanella," and "Hindustan"), Eva brought the two hired killers into the house for a dry run. Marion had already jimmied the dining room bureau at Eva's command, and Eva had shrewdly taken the "stolen" silver to the house of one of her many medium friends. All was in readiness for the murder on Thursday night.

Thursday night came and went. Mary Brickel, who was supposed to be on the porch in her rocking chair after dark to let the killers in, got cold feet and kept to her room. The next morning the

---

While Marion generously played the piano, Eva brought the two hired killers into the house for a dry run.

---

killers contacted Marion and told her that if Mary didn't cooperate, they would kill her, too. Or as Cala poetically put it: "Tell the old lady we'll blow her brains out!"

The actual killing went off quite smoothly. Marion reportedly gave the signal to the murderers, either by emptying a pitcher of water out the window or flushing the toilet adjacent to her bedroom. Entering through a door left conveniently unlocked by Mary Brickel, the killers stealthily made their way up the stairs and into Dan Kaber's bedroom. There, in the dark, Cala held down the paralyzed invalid while Pisselli, wearing heavy canvas gloves, stabbed him 24 times. Cala later testified that the helpless cripple cried out, "Mercy! Mercy! What have I done to you?!" Cala, for his pains, got badly bitten on the thumb by the gutsy invalid, and Pisselli apparently dropped both his gloves and an unused razor on the way out. Minutes later they boarded an eastbound streetcar and took it to safety and the East Side.

Even before they were caught, the aftermath of the killing was not a happy time for any of the plotters involved. Eva was haunted by the murder and rightly fearful that her accomplices would either implicate or blackmail her. The only payment anyone ever received for the murder was a $500 bill, some of the "stolen silver," and Dan's Masonic ring, taken from his finger by Eva in the days before his death. The $500 bill and the ring were forwarded to Mrs.

Colavito through yet another medium friend of Eva's, Maria Matthews, who insisted on keeping the silver as her own commission in the affair. The rest of the promised $3,000 or $5,000 was never forthcoming, despite threats by Cala and Pisselli to murder everyone connected with the plot if they were not paid.

Eva's trial, a carnival of sensationalism, opened on June 28. The proceedings, held in the old county courthouse, were packed to suffocation, with rubberneckers fighting for spaces at office windows in adjacent buildings. Most of the spectators in and out of the courthouse, it is recorded, were female. By this time, both Cala and Colavito had turned state's evidence, and both Marion and Mrs. Brickel had signed confessions implicating Eva for the murder. It was going to be almost impossible to get her off—and yet the actual trial proved to be both a well-matched legal competition and an exciting juridical struggle that made legal history.

Much of the excitement was due to the forensic talents of William J. Corrigan, Eva's court-appointed lawyer. Then a young man, Corrigan was at the beginning of a career that would make him Cleveland's premier defense attorney. (His best-known case would come near the end of his long career, when he acted as the defense attorney at Sam Sheppard's infamous first trial.)

Corrigan knew that Eva was guilty and, worse than that, that she had already confessed to most of the facts of the conspiracy murder plot against her husband. Corrigan therefore concentrated on two procedural aspects of the case in a desperate effort to save his client from the electric chair. His first concern was to keep women off the jury. Sexist or not, he—and virtually everyone involved in the trial—believed that women were inclined to be more merciless in judging a member of their own sex and less inclined to sentimentality than men when sending females to the hot seat. Although his legal arguments in this regard were overruled, Corrigan managed to keep women off the jury with peremptory challenges.

Corrigan's other, more important, and ultimately successful fight was to persuade the jury that Eva Kaber was insane. The state was demanding that she die in the electric chair, but Corrigan hoped to get her off with either a plea of temporary insanity or simply insanity from birth.

Ultimately, he chose the total insanity plea, and his witnesses provided much support. The state paraded a succession of "alienists" (as psychiatrists were then termed) who solemnly testified that Eva Kaber was sane. The defense responded with several alienists who said that she wasn't. But far more convincing, doubtless, was the testimony of Eva's brother, father, and sister, who recounted many family anecdotes illustrating Eva's crazed behavior from an early age.

Eva herself eventually give dramatic support to the insanity argument. Although she managed to remain hidden behind a handkerchief, mute and pale during the early part of the trial, she became progressively and visibly upset as her father, brother, and sister appeared as witnesses to testify to her lifelong dementia. The climax came on Wednesday, July 13, the day her brother Charlie angrily denied Eva's assertion that Mrs. Brickel had been the one who had set the Kaber house on fire in October 1918. Charlie got to his feet, shouting, "That's a lie! I can prove it! She was sick at the time!" Eva went into a fit, screaming, flailing, foaming, and finally collapsing into a moaning heap. She was removed from the court and did not return until the next day. Prosecutor Stanton argued in his summation that her behavior then and afterward was feigned to support her insanity defense, but one suspects the jury believed otherwise. The best comment made about Mrs. Kaber's breakdown was to Marjorie Wilson, a *News* feature writer who covered the trial and later married William J. Corrigan, whom she met for the first time there. A fellow spectator remarked to Wilson as she walked from the courtroom that day, "If that is acting, what an Ophelia she would make!"

Hard-core sensation-mongers may have been disappointed by the Kaber trial. Some expectations raised by pretrial revelations and hints were not fulfilled. Despite a frisson of curiosity about what "objectionable practices" Dan Kaber had allegedly practiced to drive his wife to murder, the defense never produced any evidence that he mistreated her; no one seems to have believed—or perhaps cared—about Marion McArdle's assertion that Dan Kaber had once hit her mother. To the great disappointment of press and public, Eva herself never took the stand.

On July 15, 1921, the prosecution rested, and the jury went into seclusion in the early evening. Early the next morning they re-

---

Eva had been offered $50,000 for the film rights to her life story, and she schemed to use the money to engineer an escape.

---

turned a verdict of "Guilty of Murder in the First Degree—With a Recommendation of Mercy." Their verdict made Eva the second woman in Cuyahoga County ever convicted of first degree murder, but the "mercy" part meant that she would be facing life in prison rather than death in the electric chair. The reading of the verdict was delayed for two hours, as Eva had suffered yet another fit on being told by her attorneys that the jury had reached a verdict. When she was carried limp into the courtroom by two deputies, the grinding of her teeth was distinctly audible, and there was blood on her lips. There, at two minutes past 11 A.M., Eva Kaber was sentenced to the Marysville Reformatory for life, and the jury was dismissed. The verdict came just two days shy of the second anniversary of Dan Kaber's murder.

Eva's remaining years were not happy ones. "I'll be out in a year. I'll be free. Eighteen months at the least!" she bragged to reporters as she departed for Marysville Reformatory. Once incarcerated there, she was shocked to discover that she would have to give up her silk stockings and tailored suits for the regular drab prison garb. She eventually settled down to prison routine, working quietly in the prison sewing room. Alas, this proved to be yet another stratagem, and her job was replaced with solitary confinement on a diet of bread and water when prison officials intercepted a letter from Eva to her daughter Marion. It seems Eva had been offered $50,000 for the film rights to her life story, and she schemed to use the money to engineer an escape. Some of the money was to be used to bribe the prison authorities, but Eva was willing to have head matron Louise Mittendorf and her husband murdered if they proved resistant to bribery.

Eva's health began to fail in the late 1920s. A long-needed goiter operation helped some, but Eva refused treatment for a subsequent gastric tumor diagnosed in 1927, telling the doctors, "You want to kill me!" This may have been part of a deliberate strategy to win a parole for medical reasons, but it spelled slow, sure doom for Eva. After 1929 her health declined alarmingly, and she was bedridden for the last few months of her life. The end came on April 12, 1931, just as the governor of Ohio was about to act on her latest parole request. Causes of death listed included lung complications, heart disease, and the stomach tumor, which was reported to weigh a whopping 150 pounds. She was 50 years old.

And what of the others involved in Eva Kaber's satanic plot? Well, Marion McArdle was found innocent in a subsequent trial, a verdict seemingly incomprehensible to anyone having knowledge of her complicity in her stepfather's murder before, during, and after the fact. Marion's immediate response to the verdict was to go clothes shopping. She was married a year later from her aunt's home in Lakewood, and it would be churlish to pursue her personal history further, except to note that she was with her mother when she died and arranged for Eva's cremation in Portsmouth, Ohio. Grandmother Mary Brickel's indictment was quashed because of her age and her cooperation with the prosecution. Salvatore Cala received a life term, as did Vittorio Pisselli in Italy, where he was pursued and brought to justice by yet more detectives hired with Moses Kaber's money. Mrs. Colavito, improbably, was acquitted at her own trial, despite evidence introduced that her "potions" had been effective in ridding a number of woman clients of their husbands. In 1924 she was finally convicted and sentenced to prison for her part in a 1920 poisoning of an unwanted husband named Marino Costanzo. She died in Marysville 46 years later in 1972 at the age of 86. Ethel Berman was last heard of in September 1921, when she went into hiding because of death threats stemming from her Kaber testimony.

Why did Eva Kaber murder her husband? We may never really know. Whether she was a Lady Macbeth from the Cleveland slums from the start or an American Madame Bovary with a glandular disorder remains an intriguing, unanswerable question. In the end, however, you can at least say this, recalling the fate of Cala and Pisselli: Eva Kaber got her money's worth. †

Bad Cinderella

The Catherine Manz Horror, 1910

---

*My sister Catherine has been insane for several years . . .
She is the most stubborn girl I ever saw. When she decided
she would not do anything, she would not do it if they beat
her to death.*

—Joseph Manz, to a reporter, March 21, 1910

Everyone knows the fairy tale of Cinderella. At least, everyone thinks they know it. If you were born after 1950, however, what you probably know is the Disney version of the Cinderella story: the redemptive tale of an oppressed girl who triumphs over those who mistreat her and maintains her personal sweetness through all of her woes. The original Grimm Brothers' version of the story, however, is a bit more, well, grim. Like the Disney version, it ends with Cinderella marrying her prince. But that's not all: the wicked stepsisters, who have already mutilated their feet in vain attempts to make them fit the gold (not glass) slipper, are satisfyingly punished by having their eyes pecked out by pigeons in the last paragraph of the story.

To say the least, the Grimm Brothers' version is a tougher take than Disney's on the archetype of the unjustly oppressed, if ultimately triumphant, victim. But what if the reality of such a situation were even worse than that? History suggests that suffering rarely ennobles character. You don't have to come from the Balkan states or journey to the Middle East to know that those who have had it dished out to them generally do not demonstrate magnanimity and forgiveness when the wheel of fortune spins them to the top. Revenge, as novelist Robertson Davies once remarked, is the oldest story: it began with Cain in the book of Genesis and persists through today's headlines. Cinderellas may triumph, but they rarely forgive and forget. For a particularly shocking instance, consider the case of Massillon's Catherine Manz.

Catherine Manz's Massillon neighbors liked to call her "the girl who never had a chance." Maybe they were right: the cards were certainly stacked against her from birth. Born on February 16, 1894, Catherine was the last child of four sons and four daughters born to stonemason Gotthart Manz and his wife. It had long been a struggle for the family to make ends meet, and it became even harder when Gotthart's wife died of typhoid fever in 1896. Following her interment in the cemetery of St. Mary's Church, in a grave that could be seen from the Manz cottage, Gotthart broke up his family. Finding tenants for his heavily mortgaged home, he moved into a boardinghouse and placed Catherine's brothers and sisters into orphanages in Lorain and Tiffin. Catherine was temporarily taken in by Barbara Russ, a neighboring widow who had cared for Catherine's mother in her final illness. Several months later, Catherine was adopted by Mrs. Katherine Molitor, who ran the boardinghouse where Gotthart Manz dwelt.

A widow of 61, the childless Katherine Molitor had always yearned for children of her own. Now, all of her long-denied maternal feelings were put to the task of spoiling little Catherine Manz. Catherine lived with Mrs. Molitor for seven years, and the evidence suggests that she always had her way with the doting widow. Catherine demonstrated a precocious passion for clothing—and Mrs. Molitor saw to it that she always had new, fancy, and costly garments. Catherine likewise evinced an appetite for candy—and there was always candy for Catherine, who did not scruple to "charge" her purchases of sweets at Massillon confectionaries, knowing her doting guardian would pay off such unauthorized charges without a murmur.

Mrs. Molitor's feckless indulgence was not good character training for Catherine, and its effects deepened as Catherine got older. An imaginative, intelligent child, she started school before she was five, and she would say in later years that she liked school. Maybe she did, but she sure didn't like getting up and going to it in the midwestern winter cold of Massillon. Catherine dropped out of school during her first winter semester because of a cold; the next year she missed the winter term because of measles. Before she finally quit school for good, she would later recall, she had missed just about every winter term of her youthful years.

Given this background, Catherine would likely, at the very least, have matured into a spoiled, willful adolescent, if not necessarily a cold-blooded killer. But her destiny took another cruel turn in 1905, when Mrs. Molitor died suddenly. Without warning, Catherine was abruptly wrenched from her pampered, indulged existence as a virtual only child and shoved into a situation that must have been nightmarish for one with her prior experience. Gotthart Manz had reclaimed his house, and it was back into the bosom of her biological family she was now hurled. Some of Gotthart's children were still in orphanages, but son John and daughter Elizabeth were living with him and working outside of the home.

How bad was it for Catherine Manz in the "home" to which she now returned for the first time since she was less than two years old? How cruel was this unfamiliar "family," of which she had scant knowledge and no fond memories? We'll never know the whole truth. As future events would prove, Catherine Manz was a persistent and pathological liar. And by the time anyone cared to investigate just what had gone on in the Manz home on State Street, one of the principal witnesses was dead, and the two others were loathe to wash the family's dirty laundry in public.

What we do know is that Catherine's psychological condition

---

*As future events would prove,
Catherine Manz was a persistent
and pathological liar.*

---

and her behavior degenerated steadily over the next five years. Always willful and selfish, she now matured into a veritable teenage demoness. Quick to anger, she took offense easily and would instantly work herself into psychotic rages that frightened those around her. Resentful that she had to do housework and prepare meals, she grew to hate her older sister, Elizabeth, who, to Catherine, appeared to have the leisure and nice clothes that Catherine felt she deserved herself. Worse than that, Gotthart Manz had given Elizabeth a mother's authority over the sister six years her junior, and Catherine would probably have hated anyone who tried to tell her what to do. In the years after Catherine returned home, the family dynamics in the Manz household steadily degenerated until, during the last year of Elizabeth Manz's life, they turned catastrophic.

By the time her sixteenth birthday rolled around, Catherine had become some piece of work. Chronically disobedient and incorrigible, she often shirked her assigned housework and ran up unauthorized charges on her father's accounts at Massillon stores. Chafing at family prohibitions, she frequently flouted Elizabeth's demands that she stay away from strange boys and public dances. She went further, creating a number of fictitious personas, which she employed in exchanging letters with strange boys—some of whom she had never even met. Forbidden to wear Elizabeth's clothes, she

often stole them and flaunted them publicly, even when such behavior was punished with paternal whippings. Several times she
ran away, sometimes to Akron, once to Canal Dover, and once to
New Philadelphia. Massillon police chief E. M. Ertle, who knew
the Manz family well, brought her back from New Philadelphia.
Catherine constantly complained to the neighbors about her alleged mistreatment, whining repeatedly that she wanted more
"liberty." One of them, Anna Borner, would recall such conversations after Catherine became notorious:

> She used to talk with me till some trouble stopped it. She seemed
> always to be thinking of running away. She was gone all day.
> When her sister came home she was scolded. I have seen Eliza-
> beth strike her and her father whip her. But she was full of mis-
> chief, and punishment didn't seem to do any good.

More ominously, Catherine confided in yet another neighbor,
Mrs. Walter Shaidnagle, telling her she believed that "murder
blood" ran in her family. "If I ever do anything like that they'll
never get me alive," she promised the astonished Mrs. Shaidnagle.

The rages, fights, and bickering escalated during the early
months of 1910. At least two persons, Ella Hossler of Canton
and Miss Eva Young of Massillon, heard Catherine make threats
against Elizabeth Manz. After her flight to New Philadelphia resulted in a whipping from her father, Catherine warned Elizabeth,
"I'll get even with you." But by late winter of 1910, Elizabeth had
finally had enough. On March 14 she, her older sister Paulina, and
Gotthart held a family council at the Manz home. After talking
it over, they decided that Catherine's behavior had deteriorated
to the point where something drastic had to be done. Elizabeth
had already decided to visit her friend Leo Farrar in Detroit on
Monday, March 21. (She was secretly engaged to Farrar, a fact unknown to her family.) So the three decided that it would simplify
matters if Catherine were sent that same day to the Home of the
Good Shepherd in Cleveland.

As Paulina later realized, Catherine overheard that conversation. It could not have pleased her. The Home of the Good Shepherd was a well-known home for wayward girls (notorious Lakewood murderess Catherine Eva Kaber was an alumna), and Catherine knew she would have even less of the "liberty" there that she craved at home. Something had to be done.

Friday, March 18, began normally enough in the Manz household. As usual, Catherine arose at 5 A.M. and prepared breakfast for Gotthart, who had to leave for work at 6 A.M. Then she did some housework and prepared coffee for Elizabeth, who got up sometime later that morning. Around 10:30 that morning, Catherine left the house and went into downtown Massillon. She walked into the piano store in the Conrad Hotel building, where Eva Young worked. Catherine often visited Young there, but there seemed to be something different about Catherine this morning. Seeing tears in Catherine's eyes, Young said, "What's the matter?"

"Nothing," Catherine mumbled, although it was obvious she was upset. She left the store a few minutes later, only to return and stay another half hour, during which she said nothing.

Catherine must have returned home around noon, because she was there when her brother John, eighteen, came home for lunch at 12:30. He generally ate his lunch in the kitchen, but this time Catherine met him about fifteen yards from the house. "Don't go into the kitchen," she warned him, "Lizzie is sick and lying asleep on the floor in there." The incurious John docilely accepted Catherine's explanation for the absence of his older sister. He ate his lunch in the dining room and soon departed to resume his day of toil. Remarkably unobservant, John didn't even notice that the crack in the kitchen doorframe had been stuffed with newspaper to prevent anyone from seeing inside the room. Nor did he notice, when he left the house, that all of the kitchen windows had likewise been covered up with newspaper.

Ninety minutes passed after John left. At about 2:30 P.M. one of the Manz neighbors saw Catherine leaving the house. She was carrying a suitcase, and she was dressed in one of Elizabeth's fancier outfits, a red-and-white dress with an enormous feathered hat. She first walked through the adjoining St. Mary's cemetery, where she stopped by her mother's grave. Putting down her suitcase, she sat on the grave for several minutes, apparently weeping. She then got to her feet and strode toward downtown Massillon. About an hour later William Bayless, the conductor on an interurban trolley, saw a girl answering Catherine's description on his car bound for Canton: a well-dressed young woman of slender build, five feet, six inches, big blue eyes, and luxuriant light-brown hair. Sometime later that evening Joseph Burrier, the conductor on an Akron-bound interurban, saw the same young woman on his run from Canton. Catherine Manz—for it was she—got off the train in downtown Akron just as night was closing in.

Meanwhile, there were interesting developments back at her State Street home. Gotthart Manz got home from work about 5:30 P.M. Finding the back door unaccountably locked, he climbed through a dining room window into the semidarkened house. Groping his way to the kitchen door, he opened it and walked through. He immediately stepped on the body of his daughter Elizabeth.

Gotthart was not the most perceptive of mortals. Staring into the darkness, he at first thought he had stumbled upon the body of his daughter Catherine. For one thing, he expected her to be home; for another, the body was dressed in Catherine's clothes. Third, the body was almost entirely covered with a quilt. (There was a conflicting report that when he discovered the body it was completely naked—but there is no evidence to support that rumor.) Underneath her head was the embroidery frame she had been working on when death took her. Shortly after he found the body, John Manz arrived, and he summoned neighbor Walter Shaidnagle and Massillon police chief E. M. Ertle.

The body was already turning black when Chief Ertle examined it. And it was obvious that Elizabeth had died from the effects of some potent poison. The face was distorted, the corpse drawn up, offering strong evidence of violent bodily convulsions, paroxysms so powerful that one of her legs was fractured with the bone sticking out. Beside the corpse were a small, empty pillbox, a half-drunk cup of coffee, and a glass that had apparently contained water. On the kitchen table were writing materials and several recent letters.

Two of them were from Elizabeth's beau, Leo Farrar. One of them included a reference to Catherine: "I hope the Kid is behaving herself and not causing you any trouble. If she does, just give her a good licking, and if that don't do, tell her I will come down."

Chief Ertle described what he found at the Manz cottage that night as "the most puzzling case that I have had in fifteen years." Nothing at the death scene made sense to its witnesses. It initially looked like a suicide—but there was nothing known of Elizabeth Manz's personality or life to suggest that she might have taken her own life. Her letters from Leo were unremarkably pleasant and affectionate, and it was clear that he looked forward to seeing his fiancée in Detroit within the week. And if it wasn't suicide, how could someone—anyone—have forced Elizabeth to swallow a deadly poison? More puzzling still, where was Catherine Manz—and who had rifled Elizabeth's purse (supposed to have contained a substantial sum of cash) and removed virtually all of her clothing from the house? It was obvious that there was one person who might possess the answers to all these questions, and Chief Ertle immediately ordered a dragnet cast for Catherine Manz.

Chief Ertle didn't find Catherine during the next 24 hours. But he did discover some suggestive and disturbing clues to the mystery. Stark County coroner Harry A. March's preliminary examination of the corpse disclosed that Elizabeth had likely died of strychnine poisoning, indicated, in particular, by her violent death convulsions. A check with pharmacist W. B. Altland at the Massillon Drug Company revealed that Catherine Manz had purchased an ounce of chloroform there on January 21, 1910. As required, she had signed the register for it, scribbling her name as "Cath. Manz." She had told Altland (à la Lizzie Borden's famous poison purchase) that she needed it to clean clothes. Exactly a month later, on February 21, Catherine signed the register again, this time for a dram of strychnine. She told Altland she needed it to put down a dog.

Chief Ertle knew that the Manzes had not had a dog for at least eight years. By mid-afternoon Saturday, just 24 hours after Catherine disappeared, the word went out to every police force in Ohio to be on the lookout for Catherine Manz, suspected of fatally poisoning her sister.

The search for Catherine soon focused on Akron. She had been seen getting off the train there, and it was known that she had long cultivated the acquaintance of Greek confectioners and merchants there during her previous runaway adventures. On Sunday morning, it was discovered that she had left her suitcase at a Greek fruit store in downtown Akron on Saturday night. Leo Zogler, a former Massillon acquaintance of Catherine's, came forward to tell police that a friend of his had seen Catherine in front of the Akron post office on Saturday night. Fred Peckner, another of Catherine's acquaintances, saw her there about the same time. He told police that she was reading a newspaper account of the search being made for her. A few minutes later, Peckner recalled, she had discarded the newspaper and jumped on a trolley bound for the southern part of Akron.

After Catherine was found, Chief Ertle was able to reconstruct her movements after she first arrived in Akron. After dropping her suitcase off at the Greek fruit store ("to be called for later"), she went to the home of Carl Georges, an acquaintance living on Shenan Street. Georges wouldn't put her up for the night, but he sent her on to the house of another acquaintance, Harry Rosenbloom. After spending the night there, Catherine went looking for a more permanent residence.

Calling herself "Ethel Morgan" and claiming her home was in Barberton, Catherine soon found a rented room at the boardinghouse of widow F. R. Heller at 693 Rhodes Avenue. Both Mrs. Heller and Clara Waldeck, Catherine's new roommate, quickly found the new boarder a handful. After sleeping her way through most of Saturday, on the pretence that she was ill, she kept her roommate Clara awake a good deal of the night, tossing, turning, and murmuring in her sleep. Sunday morning she was up to more mischievous tricks. Boisterous, irrational, and exhibiting disquieting mood swings, she alarmed Mrs. Heller, especially when she locked her son Ray out of the house that afternoon. By the end of the day Mrs. Heller was beginning to think that she might have to eject her unruly renter.

As events evolved, Heller didn't have to make that decision. Early Monday morning Catherine left the house with Ray Heller and Clara Waldeck and went to the B. F. Goodrich plant. Heller and Waldeck both worked there, and the idea was that "Ethel Morgan" could also get a job there. The wary Catherine, however, took some new precautions. Knowing that her description had been widely broadcast, she persuaded the unsuspecting Clara to exchange cloaks with her. Catherine also exchanged her large feathered hat for a black veil and brushed her hair boyishly back behind her ears.

Catherine's stratagems were in vain. Surmising the fugitive would look for a job, Akron police detectives had staked out the most likely employers of unskilled labor. One of them was waiting as Catherine joined the line of job seekers, and he stepped forward and said, "Are you Catherine Manz?"

Catherine Manz may have been wicked, but she was no fool. Knowing the jig was up, she immediately admitted her identity and was taken to the Akron police station. Minutes later, Chief Ertle in Massillon was notified of her arrest and was soon on his way to Akron with a warrant charging her with the murder of her sister. After he arrived in Akron he and some Akron police detectives began to question Catherine Manz in earnest.

Considering that Catherine was a pathological liar, the story she told that afternoon to the police officers remained remarkably consistent throughout its many retellings over the months that followed. Denying that she had poisoned Elizabeth, she swore that she had returned home late Friday morning from her downtown Massillon jaunt to find her sister dead on the floor. She admitted purchasing the strychnine on February 21—but insisted that she had given it to a young man, whose name she refused to divulge. She had met the young man on some previous occasion, and she had been given the impression that he knew her sister Elizabeth. Sometime during the week preceding Elizabeth's death, the young man had taken the strychnine from Catherine and given her two pills. He said they were "headache tablets," and he asked her to give them to Elizabeth. Thinking that the tablets contained quinine, Catherine had thrown one of them away on Thursday night, March 17. The next morning she placed the other tablet on Elizabeth's coffee saucer before going downtown. When she returned to find her unexpectedly dead, she panicked and fled the house in

---

*There was a mob of more than
a thousand persons panting for a look
at the adolescent prisoner.*

---

fear. She unequivocally denied stealing Elizabeth's clothes—some of which she was wearing—or her money. During her interview that afternoon—as in all subsequent interrogations—Catherine displayed a complete lack of emotion or, indeed, any interest in her precarious situation.

Soon realizing he could not budge Catherine from her improbable story, Chief Ertle hustled her into an automobile and sped off for Canton. It was the small-town girl's first ride in an automobile. Ertle was particularly anxious to shield his youthful prisoner from the morbidly curious crowds already gathering in Canton, so he stopped the automobile by the Stark County Infirmary, two miles out of Canton. Transferring Catherine to a waiting limousine with drawn curtains, he drove as fast as possible to Massillon. When he arrived at the city hall–jail complex, there was a mob of more than a thousand persons panting for a look at the adolescent prisoner. Catherine was wearing Elizabeth's light-tan coat and the large feathered hat. Favoring the gawking crowd with a look of regally contemptuous indifference, Catherine was led by Chief Ertle into Massillon mayor Charles Remley's office, and the door closed behind them.

Little more was learned in the interrogation that followed. Asked if she wanted an attorney, Catherine said she didn't know.

She then reiterated her improbable tale about the young man who had given her two capsules for Elizabeth, again refusing to divulge his name. "He has been true to me, and I'll be true to him," insisted the defiant girl, although she furnished a description of him as well dressed, about 21 years of age, medium height, and wearing a diamond. Convinced that she would continue to stonewall them, Chief Ertle ended the interrogation after an hour and led Catherine away to a cell in the women's section of the Massillon jail. As she was taken away, Mayor Remley announced to the expectant newspaper reporters that Catherine Manz would be charged with first-degree murder. Before Catherine settled down in her jail cell, Chief Ertle insisted on removing her hat (with its three enormous hatpins) and her bed sheets, fearful that she might attempt suicide.

Meanwhile, the members of Catherine's family attempted to come to grips with their tragedy and to formulate a public response to Catherine's unspeakable crime. Gotthart Manz was in a state of shock, utterly convinced of Catherine's guilt and adamant that she never enter his house again. Stunned with grief, he roamed his small cottage ceaselessly, alternately weeping and shouting, and looking at least twenty years older than his 51 years. Vowing he would sue the pharmacist who had sold Catherine the strychnine, he blamed her delinquency on her reading of cheap novels and a desire for expensive clothes. His eldest son, Joseph, thirty, was more susceptible to doubt and pity. Arriving in Massillon the day Catherine was arrested, he was allowed to visit her briefly in her cell. Perhaps because he had not seen Catherine since she was four years old, he readily succumbed to the spell of her tearful, ingenuous deceits. Emerging from the Massillon jail, he admitted to reporters that his sister Catherine had been "insane for years." Recalling discussions with his sisters, he recounted anecdotes of her peculiar behavior, especially her penchant for unsettling people with her malignant stare. But he wasn't ready to accept Catherine as a cold-blooded poisoner, preferring to blame nameless foreigners:

> If Katherine did this there was an instigator back of it. The child has been with Greeks and others that she ought not to have been

with. She has always been flighty. It has all worked on her mind till I think she has been carried away by wild ideas put into her head by others.

Joseph Manz's credulity about his sister was hardheaded realism compared to other voices heard in Massillon. Denizens of the 21st century have become accustomed to child-killers, some of them much younger than Catherine Manz. But Ohioans of her era were more sentimental about the young—and their view of Catherine was best expressed by Dorothy Dale, sob-sister columnist of the *Cleveland Press*. Allowed to interview Catherine in her cell, she painted a tearful portrait of the presumably fragile teenager:

> As [her attorneys] went up [to] the door, she got up to come out. And such a little, childish-looking girl as she is. Her hair is light and fluffy as a baby's. It was tumbled back from a black velvet ribbon band. Her eyes are big and blue and her face round and dimpled. She wore her sister Elizabeth's red dress, that bagged and bulged on her slender figure.

Characterizing Catherine as "the most pitiful little figure ever connected with an Ohio murder case," Dorothy was a receptive conduit for her self-pitying prattle:

> I was so penned up. You know, a girl likes to go with other girls. When I came home from Mrs. Molitor's when I was ill. I had to begin to do housework. She was so good to me. When I went home I had to learn to cook. I don't like to cook.

Catherine spent that night in her Massillon jail cell, sleeping in the clothes she was wearing when arrested. Awakened early the next morning, she ate a breakfast described as "hearty" and was then taken back to Mayor Remley's office for more questioning. Still stonewalling on the identity of her alleged male confederate, she again repeated her improbable story that she had found Elizabeth inexplicably dead when she returned home Friday morning.

Tiring of this nonsense, Mayor Remley decided it was time to arraign her. Reading out the charge of first-degree murder, he asked Catherine how she pled to the charge. "I plead not guilty," she replied and was led back to her cell.

Later in the afternoon, the same scene was repeated in public.

Catherine was led away through
the gawking crowd, chewing gum,
her face a mask of indifference.

By that time Catherine's attorneys, former Stark County prosecutor Robert H. Day and Massillon attorney Eugene Willson, had arrived, and Massillon city solicitor Thomas Davis was concerned about the legality of her morning arraignment. After consulting with Stark County prosecutor Charles Kirchbaum, he persuaded Mayor Remley to go through it again. Waiving preliminary examination, Catherine again pled innocent to the charge and was led away through the gawking crowd, chewing gum, her face a mask of indifference. She spent the night in the women's section of the Stark County jail in Canton, her third cell in two days.

Even as Catherine endured her first arraignment that Tuesday morning, Elizabeth's obsequies went forward. Her funeral, a high mass at St. Mary's Catholic Church, within sight of the murder scene, was thronged by up to two thousand persons, mostly the morbidly curious. Six young men carried her coffin to the church: Casper Berence, Fred Gruber, Leo Englehart, Clarence Meinhart, Leo Lachner, and Clarence Paul. In his remarks on the deceased, the Reverend Michael Vollmayer avoided mention of the hideous crime that had taken her life, stressing instead her heroic character as a dutiful daughter: "If her tragic death was occasioned by her fulfilling her duties toward those placed in her charge by her father, she died a martyr. Yes, she goes from her loved ones as a sacrifice to duty."

Following the mass, Elizabeth's mourners stood in the pouring rain as her white coffin, bearing a silver plate with the inscription "Sister," was lowered into the grave next to her mother's. Elizabeth was buried with a crucifix next to her head.

Catherine Manz did not enjoy her sojourn in the Stark County jail. Built in 1879, it was, at best, a brutally utilitarian structure. Predictably, sob-sister Dorothy Dale dwelt on its horrors for the edification of her readers:

> [When] they built that old prison 41 years ago, their only idea must have been to keep prisoners from getting away. There is no evidence that they felt they were building for human beings who were innocent in the eyes of the law till they were proved guilty before a tribunal of justice. The whole prison part of the building is walled and celled with plates of sheet iron. The small windows are barred with criss-cross slats of iron, so wide that they shut out most of the air and light. Although the heat was turned off, there was not a breath of air. "They sicken after they've been up there two or three weeks," said Sheriff R. F. Wilson. "We do the best we can, but it isn't a fit place to keep a man, and as for women and children—well, that cell is the only place we have for them, no matter how many come, black or white." The woman's cell is eight by ten feet. The only window is 42 by 20 inches, with half of that covered by iron slats. The furniture is a table, a chair and a double bed. If the most hardened woman with a record of years of crime had to be jailed, she would share that bed with the little girl. If more than one was entered, the floor space would be covered with cots. Across the anteroom is the only washroom for both men and women.

Dale ended her catalog of Catherine's jail-cell discomforts and indignities with the disclosure that her first night's sleep had been interrupted by the skittering of rats in the corridor.

Whatever terrors Catherine's vile durance held, they didn't interfere with her appetite or fashion sense. She ate heartily of her breakfast and lunch on Wednesday and was modishly dressed in one of Elizabeth's dark-red suits, her hair carefully parted in the middle. She was allowed to exercise in the corridor, and her cell was unguarded, Sheriff Wilson deciding that the suicide watch maintained on her in Massillon was unnecessary. "She is quiet and not ill-natured," he remarked after meeting Catherine. "She doesn't look like the girl who would commit suicide. I'll trust her." Wilson drew the line, however, at Catherine's taste in reading material. Already too obviously enjoying her status as a notorious murderess, Catherine demanded that she be allowed to see the newspapers. When Wilson refused, she retorted that lawmen had let her read them in Massillon. "Well," Wilson responded, "this isn't Massillon."

Meanwhile, the official investigations into Elizabeth Manz's death went forward—but they never produced more evidence than had been available when her cold corpse was first found. As far as Stark County lawmen were concerned, there were three possible theories in the case. The first was the most obvious: that Catherine Manz, a resentful Cinderella, had put strychnine in Elizabeth's coffee, stolen her clothes and money, and fled the house to fabricate a new identity in Akron. The second theory was a variant of the first: that Catherine had poisoned Elizabeth because they were rivals for the same man, possible the mysterious male stranger described by Catherine. The third theory assumed that Catherine was mainly telling the truth: that the mysterious stranger, for motives unknown, had given Catherine two capsules of poison and deceived her as to their content and purpose.

By the time Catherine settled down in her Canton cell late Tuesday afternoon, virtually all Stark County officials had concluded that the "bad Cinderella" hypothesis was the true one. Chief Ertle, who knew the Manz family well, had never believed Catherine's story about a mysterious male pill-provider. By the time she left Massillon for Canton, Catherine had told police interrogators that the man was named "Murray," and a search for him was dutifully made in nearby Ohio cities and towns. But not a single corroborating detail of Murray's existence turned up, and by Wednesday even the credulous Joseph Manz had concluded that his baby sister had done her awful deed alone.

Stark County coroner Harry A. March's inquest, which finally opened on Thursday afternoon, produced little new evidence. Catherine's lawyers refused to let her testify, much to the disappointment of the sensation-hungry crowds thronging Massillon. There was as yet no conclusive evidence as to the manner of Elizabeth's death. Coroner March had performed an autopsy on her the morning after her body was discovered, and he believed he had found traces of strychnine in her stomach. But he had to be sure, so he removed the stomach and sent it off to Dr. Perry L. Hobbs, a physician on the faculty of the Western Reserve College of Medicine in Cleveland. Hobbs's report was not due until Monday, March 28, so March's inquest was devoted to examining the few witnesses in the case. Druggist W. B. Altland of the Massillon Drug Company took the stand first, telling of Catherine's purchases of chloroform and strychnine. John Manz followed him, relating the circumstances of the murder day and how Elizabeth's body was found that evening. Neighbor Walter Shaidnagle corroborated John's recollections and added details about the initial misperception that it was Catherine's body on the kitchen floor. After hearing a few more minor witnesses, March adjourned the inquest to await Dr. Hobbs's report on the contents of Elizabeth's stomach.

The legal position of Catherine Manz was a murky puzzle from the beginning. There were no useful precedents in the case, and both Stark County lawmen and Catherine's lawyers floundered for several days in their efforts to define their strategies. Both sides agreed that Catherine either had to be tried for murder or, pending a lunacy investigation, committed to an insane asylum. Prosecutor Charles Kirchbaum's initial belief was that Catherine, given her tender years, had to be tried as a juvenile and, if convicted, incarcerated in a detention home for youthful offenders. But by Friday, March 25, Kirchbaum's position had hardened, and he announced that Catherine would stand trial for her life on charges of first-degree murder. And, as the Stark County grand jury was not scheduled to meet until May, she would have to rot in the Stark County jail until then, first-degree murder not being an offense admitting bail.

As it happened, Catherine Manz stayed in the Canton jail much longer than even Kirchbaum expected or wished. Following Dr.

Newspaper photographers could count on style-conscious Catherine to be arrayed in one of her sister's stunning frocks whenever they dropped by.

Perry Hobbs's report on March 29 that Elizabeth's stomach did, indeed, contain a fatal amount of strychnine, Catherine was indicted on a first-degree murder charge in May. She remained in her cell as various legal delays pushed her trial date relentlessly forward. June, July, and August passed by, and her December 5 trial date was not even set until the fall term opened in September.

Catherine's protracted jail sojourn proved unfortunate for a number of reasons. It had been obvious from the moment of her capture on March 21 that she was a narcissistic exhibitionist who gloried in the limelight of her notoriety as a teenage murderess. Although she was prevented from reading the copious newspaper coverage of her crime, she was only too willing to preen, pose, and prattle for the numerous newspaper reporters allowed access to her. The newspaper photographers could count on style-conscious Catherine to be arrayed in one of her sister Elizabeth's stunning frocks whenever they dropped by.

Another baneful effect of Catherine's prolonged incarceration was the misplaced sympathy it engendered for her, which in turn attracted misguided, and often addled, critics of her treatment in jail. Dorothy Dale of the *Cleveland Press* was the earliest and most overwrought champion of Catherine's alleged sufferings. But

Dale's strictures on the plight of the imprisoned adolescent were soon joined by a chorus of shocked critics of Catherine's situation. M. Wilbur Dyer of Columbus was typical of the bleeding-heart mentality that hysterically arraigned Stark County officials for their alleged mistreatment of Catherine Manz. On March 25 Dyer sent a telegram to Mayor Turnbull of Canton:

> It is stated that a sixteen-year-old girl is being tortured in a steel dungeon in the town in which you are mayor. This is a state which gives us our presidents. I lift my voice in protest against this medieval barbarity and call upon the men and women of Canton to save the good name of their city by rescuing this child from further torture. I am only a commercial traveler, but there are many thousands like me in the Buckeye State.

Dyer's protests were in vain, if only because Stark County officials had no other place to put Catherine than its antiquated jail. They probably would have enthusiastically embraced the opportunity of sending her elsewhere, because her continued presence was productive of mischief, for whatever her murderous impulses and penchant for psychopathic lying, Catherine Manz did have a winning way about her. Maybe it was her youthful good looks and pathetic demeanor. Maybe it was her fine clothes, most of them a legacy from the late Elizabeth Manz. And maybe it was just that, as our forebears would say, she acted at "the instigation of the devil." Whatever it was, it was undeniable that Catherine fomented trouble as long as she remained in jail. Any number of infatuated male nutcases wrote to her or tried to visit her during her eight months in jail. Some of them even tried to contribute money to her defense. The most persistent of her suitors was Frank W. LaDue of Saginaw, Michigan. After an impassioned correspondence with Catherine, he showed up in Canton on October 19, demanding that he be allowed to visit the object of his adoration. When Sheriff Wilson denied his request, LaDue sent word to Catherine that he would buy her clothes and a ring. She artlessly replied:

I never wore ready made clothes and never will. I can't get any to fit. I always look well in blue, black and pink. Just send me the money and I will buy the goods myself. I have nothing to do but idle my time away and I live to sew. I need many new clothes and must get them soon as my trial takes place Dec. 5 and I want a nice lot of stunning clothes for the trial. No, don't send me an opal ring because I always have the worst luck when I wear an opal. Send me your picture as I am anxious to see how you look. Yes, Frank, I will always be true to you. Send me the ring, as all the boys here want to flirt with me, and as long as I have no ring I am free to flirt.

Discerning readers will not be surprised to learn that after LaDue sent her the ring, a watch, and some money, Catherine refused to communicate with him again. Undiscouraged, the smitten LaDue persisted in his unrequited attentions and eventually began uttering public threats against Catherine's uncooperative father, Gotthart Manz. Sheriff Wilson eventually ordered LaDue to leave Canton and not come back.

By the fall of 1910, Wilson himself had experienced the baneful charm of Catherine Manz. It was probably inevitable, particularly after Catherine was allowed to leave her jail cell that summer for more pleasant living quarters in Sheriff Wilson's home. An acrid scandal erupted on September 2, when Wilson fired Stark County jail warden Isaac Slusser, his brother-in-law. Charging Slusser with dereliction of duty, Wilson accused Slusser of allowing Catherine too many indiscreet privileges. Wilson was particularly piqued that Slusser had permitted Catherine to correspond with a fellow prisoner at the jail, a death-row murderer, who had been allowed to give Catherine a ring. "She is just too slick for you," said Wilson in his public dismissal of Slusser.

"She is too slick for you," riposted Slusser, who went on to accuse Wilson of taking Catherine on joyrides in his automobile.

The slow wheels of justice finally began turning in late November. No one was ever very eager to try young Catherine for first-degree murder. Prosecutor Kirchbaum himself had been looking for a way out since March, and on November 30, 1910, he found it when Common Pleas Court judge Henry W. Harter approved the formation of a lunacy commission to examine Catherine and report on her mental condition. The commission was composed of Dr. Charles Clark of the Cleveland State Hospital for the Insane, Dr. A. C. Eyman of the Massillon State Hospital for the Insane, and three Canton physicians: Drs. J. F. Marchand, A. B. Walker, and E. J. March.

The five-member commission performed a complete physical and mental examination of Catherine Manz on December 1. Although she was quite disappointed at the prospect of a lunacy hearing instead of a publicity-rich murder trial, Catherine gussied herself up for the examination, arraying herself in a particularly fetching red dress.

The lunacy commission reported its findings to Judge Harter that same afternoon. The conclusions of their examination were that Catherine Manz was insane and had been so at the time she had poisoned her sister. Terming her a "menace to society," the report further stated that she was "intellectually delinquent and normally irresponsible" and would have to be incarcerated for some years. Reflecting the primitive state of criminal psychology, the report stated that the cause of her insanity was simply "adolescent delinquency and arrested development."

Catherine received the news of their report with the same lack of emotion she had consistently demonstrated for the previous eight months. Although reluctant to comment to reporters, she graciously allowed them to take her photograph. She was wearing a red taffeta frock, red hair bow, pearl beads, three rings, a bracelet, and the watch given her by the hapless Frank LaDue. "I made this dress myself, by hand, while I have been here," she girlishly boasted. "I'd like to have a picture taken in my hat, too. I made that, too."

The lunacy commission's report was presented to Catherine's common-pleas jury on the morning of Monday, December 5. All five members of the commission testified in Judge Harter's court, and Catherine's attorneys waived any defense against the lunacy report. After deliberating for only twenty minutes, the jury returned with a verdict of insanity. Catherine took the news without any noticeable reaction, as she did Judge Harter's subsequent ruling that she be confined to the Massillon State Hospital for the Insane for an indefinite term. Dressed with her usual care, she was wearing a black serge dress (of her own making), a white Dutch collar, and a black ribbon in her hair. She was doubtless disappointed that her pretrial request to wear a spectacular black silk dress had been denied. The next day Catherine was taken to the Massillon State Hospital.

Catherine Manz virtually vanished from history the moment she entered the portals of the insane asylum. When she left it, and the character of her subsequent destiny, has not been discovered. Some months after she was incarcerated there, a female prisoner in the Stark County Jail found a short manuscript concealed in Catherine's former Massillon jail cell. It was her self-pitying autobiography, mainly devoted to a tearful menu of alleged wrongs suffered at the hands of her biological family. In its handwritten pages, she admitted no fault and did not confess to her sister's murder. How she got Elizabeth to ingest a fatal dose of strychnine has never been discovered. †

"Twelve O'Clock Girl in a Nine O'Clock Town"

The Red Rage of Velma West, 1927

To glimpse a murder from the past is to embark on a time-traveling visit to an exotic locale and to meet characters—whether victims or killers—who think, talk, and act differently from the way we do. No case illustrates the foreignness of the past better than the 1927 murder of Eddie West in Lake County.

There are lots of ways to view the West murder file. Obviously, no murder is exactly like another. Each and every killing is unique, a product of a particular place, a particular time, and a particular collision of persons inhabiting—if not always sharing—a particular culture. One could look at the gory and scandalous West ordeal as a collision between the baffled, rural America of bucolic

Lake County and the jazz-age modernity of Roaring Twenties
Cleveland. That's how sophisticated metropolitan journalists saw
it at the time: to them, Velma West's brutal hammer murder of
her staid hubby was the virtually inevitable consequence of a big-
city flapper's imprudent elopement with a small-town stuffy to the
maddening boredom of rustic Perry, Ohio. Many contemporary
refugees from small-town America agreed, no doubt, with Clarence Darrow's deterministic justification of Velma's bloody revolt
against American Gothic rectitude. He had lived in Lake County
as a young man and recalled with bitterness its cramped small-
town ways:

> It's all familiar to me. I mean the scene . . . I know the village of
> Perry. That girl was no more to blame for killing her husband
> than he was for being killed. It was a tragic mistake to take a frail
> little girl away from the life she loved and shut her away from
> the things she knew and yearned for . . . She married and went
> to live in the right-moraled, dull small town . . . Like any other
> woman who had been brought up in luxury and independence,
> she naturally reacted against every one when forced to continue
> her cramped small town life.

Cleveland Press writer Paul Packard summed up the city–country
aspect of the murder more succinctly: "Country people have little
sympathy for the mysterious blond girl who is under lock in jail
here. City people see reasons why a Twelve o'clock girl in a Nine
o'clock town might be driven to use a hammer."

You could also view the Velma West affair as a study in individual psychology. Like Lakewood's Eva Kaber, who had *her* inconvenient spouse murdered in circumstances of unspeakable cruelty in 1919, Velma West had been sickly most of her life. Velma's
defense attorneys were quite prepared to reiterate the long litany
of Velma's physical calamities when her first-degree murder trial
began in March 1928, and that dreary medical catalog included
pneumonia, diphtheria, heart disease, and suspected brain damage.

Viewed more harshly, Velma was the predictable creation of a family that spoiled her rotten every day of her first twenty years.

The most lurid and, at the same time, contemporary way of dealing with the Velma West story, however, is to treat it as an episode of anguished and misunderstood sexuality. And that is the way that society and the media in Velma's day eventually judged the matter. The shocking disclosure of Velma's "unnatural" passions at the outset of her murder trial virtually guaranteed its outcome and provided a reassuringly simple rationale for a brutal and disturbing crime.

The past *is* a foreign country, and its inhabitants do things very differently there.

It is best to begin at the beginning with the Velma West saga, because its later details are subject to uncertainty and dispute. Velma herself "confessed" to at least three distinct versions of her husband's murder, and it's clear from the conflicting details that not even she quite knew when she was lying. The tale, then, commences with the star-crossed romance of Eddie West and Velma Van Woert in the summer of 1926.

Thomas Edward West was a son of one of the oldest and most respected families in Lake County. A clan of venerable English lineage, the Wests had long lived in the Perry area and had been known for decades as the proprietors of one of the best-known horticultural nurseries in the United States. Thomas Edward, known to his family and friends as "Eddie," was born to T. B. West and his wife in 1901 and was reared to vigorous manhood in the family traditions of social stability and commercial achievement. Husky and athletic, at about 6 feet tall and 200 pounds, Eddie was fond of sports, especially baseball, and was never mistaken for the studious type at the local schools he attended in Lake County. But the ever-smiling Eddie was well liked and the special pet of his parents, his brother, and his four doting sisters. In his mid-twenties, he already exhibited welcome promise of carrying on the West family name and business. He relished heavy labor and, because of his size and enthusiasm, took on more than his share of the heavier tasks in the family nursery business.

Then in the summer of 1926 he met 20-year-old Velma Van Woert at a picnic at Perry Park.

Velma was certainly an unlikely match for the quiet Lake County nurseryman. The daughter of Bert Van Woert, a Cleveland traveling salesman, and his wife, Catherine, Velma was as completely a product of the big city as Eddie was of the bucolic countryside. Of fragile health since birth, pretty Velma had already survived several serious diseases when she developed a life-threatening ear abscess at the age of twelve. After lingering near death for a month, Velma was saved by a skull operation—though observers would later comment that the procedure seemed to transform the hitherto precociously bright Velma into an intellectually duller girl who had much subsequent trouble with her studies. After finishing her elementary grades at Rosewell School, Velma entered East Cleveland's Shaw High School but dropped out at the age of sixteen. Little else is known of her formative years, except for obvious evidence that her parents spoiled her rotten and indulged her considerable behavioral vagaries. That, plus the fact that she liked to hear and play popular music to an almost inordinate degree . . . which would become significant in due course.

Sometime in the mid-1920s Velma went to work as a clerk at Henry Rothman's notions and hardware store at 6423 Detroit Avenue. She was there for more than a year before Rothman finally felt compelled to fire her. He was particularly concerned about the unseemly rumors swirling around his still-teenaged female clerk: "I told her several times that I wouldn't permit her to do things like that [talking to boys while working], but it didn't seem to do any good. I was trying to help the girl. She wasn't bad, she was a nice young lady from a nice family and I wanted her to behave."

Velma, of course, wouldn't listen, and so Rothman let her go. The loss of her job may not have mattered to Velma, anyway, as she was already engaged to William Chapman, the 56 year-old owner of a restaurant next to Rothman's store. Velma got to know Chapman on her lunch breaks there and began going steady with the restaurateur old enough to be her grandfather. Eventually, their relationship was formalized with Chapman giving her a diamond ring and setting a date for their wedding in July 1926.

The May-December marriage was not to be. Scant weeks before her scheduled wedding to Chapman, Velma met handsome, friendly

---

The shocking disclosure of Velma's "unnatural" passions at the outset of her murder trial virtually guaranteed its outcome

---

Eddie West at that fateful Perry Park picnic. A whirlwind courtship followed, and Velma and Eddie stunned family and friends by eloping to Ripley, New York, on July 4, 1926. The engagement ring was subsequently returned to a stunned Chapman by Velma's father.

Love is blind. What attracted Eddie West to Velma Van Woert remains a mystery. Her mother would later claim that, initially, Velma fiercely resisted marrying Eddie, fearing that she was too delicate to be the wife of such a sturdy physical specimen. But marry him she did, and it should have soon been obvious to both Eddie and Velma—as it was to virtually everyone else—that theirs was a marriage made in hell from the start. They had virtually nothing in common except for their mutual attraction, and, not surprisingly, storm clouds began to gather almost from the moment of their vows. Days after the wedding, a crestfallen Eddie returned to Lake County and was seen begging friends to lend him money. His story was that Velma had thrown him out when they ran out of money on the honeymoon, and she had ordered him to obtain more cash before he returned to her arms. Eddie's parents eventually came up with the money, the honeymoon was resumed, and Eddie and his new bride eventually came home to a Lake County welcome.

Although both Velma's and her husband's families appear to have tried hard, it was a frosty encounter from the start. Giddy, nervous, and often silly, Velma's behavior, with its aura of sinful, big-city temptation and corrupted, frivolous womanhood was a red flag to the staid rural folk of Perry—a mere village of 250 souls—and particularly to the Wests, who were a notably religious family. A *Cleveland Press* journalist later summarized the collision between city and country ways: "There was 'a marked tightening of the lips of the village social censors' after their initial exposure to the irrepressible Velma."

Worse yet, Velma smoked—*in public!*—an enormity almost unknown for women in Lake County and an action liable to stop traffic even in Painesville, the nearby county seat. Under the headline VELMA SMOKED—AND PAINESVILLE IS SHOCKED, *Press* writer W. R. Crowell put his finger on the obvious moral declension such a vile habit in a woman suggested—just what you could expect from a big-city girl who was not fit to be a wife:

> Velma Van Woert West, bridge-playing husband slayer, doubtless will have her day in court . . . Today, however, Main Street was sitting in judgement on her. While the grosser phases of this case in time may come to rank with Lake County's classic [the incredible Mentor Marsh Murder of 1922] . . . for the present at least street corner gossip hinges on one thing: "Velma smoked a cigarette." . . . What were [the] outside signs the girl displayed that boded ill, reporters questioned. "Why she—she smoked," was the shocked reply.

The connection between the moral depravity of Velma's cigarette smoking and her corresponding wifely deficiencies was further elaborated by a tobacco-chewing deputy sheriff:

> My grandmother smoked a pipe of clay but set a table that would knock your eye out. If Ed had lived he sure would have had to go to the neighbors for his breakfast. The only victuals in the place was a piece of pie and it was sour. Cigarette-smokin' city gals don't have no time for keeping house as a woman should. Ed's wife smoked.

Sob-sister *Cleveland News* columnist Nina S. Donberg echoed the deputy sheriff's strictures, albeit more grammatically: "Even her house tells [the] story. She didn't take a housewifely pride in it. There was no thoughtfully planned, well-filled larder, no boxes of cereal, no can of coffee and tea."

It was soon evident to the newlyweds' families and friends that there was a lot more to the West marital discord than incompatible backgrounds and Velma's notorious defects as a housekeeper. Velma was restless and edgy and craved the nightlife of Cleveland, 35 miles away. Ensconced in a modest white bungalow on the edge of the West family estate (adjacent to the dwellings of both Eddie's parents and his brother James), Eddie and Velma settled down to a routine of slovenly housekeeping and acrid bickering, punctuated two or three times a week with frantic jaunts to Cleveland. Eddie often unwillingly accompanied Velma on these trips, but it was only too clear that he wanted to settle down—and the sooner the better—to a domestic life of family, children, and work. It was equally evident, within weeks of their hasty nuptials, that these were the very goals and values that Velma most despised.

Somehow, a year went by, and the unhappy marriage lurched along. The young couple didn't have much money—Eddie's salary in the family business was at most 25 dollars a week, supplemented by free use of the bungalow—and Velma increasingly pouted and pined for the luxuries, great and small, she had known as the petted and indulged daughter of Mr. and Mrs. B. L. Van Woert. Local residents thought maybe Velma was finally settling in when she was seen for some weeks at work in the West family vineyards in the summer of 1927. But her grape-picking stint was only to pay for a desperately desired fur coat, the very accessory Velma needed for her frequent trips to enjoy the high life of Cleveland.

Something had to give, and it started giving in the summer of 1927. Miss Mabel Young, 23, of 2111 Willowdale Avenue in Cleveland, came to visit some friends in the Perry vicinity, and Velma met Mabel soon afterwards at some social function. The two women hit it off, and very soon Velma was penning passionate letters to Mabel, pledging her undying love. So passionate, indeed, was the correspondence that Velma soon cautioned Mabel to route her own letters through the address of a cooperative friend in Perry. Eddie, it seems, was showing symptoms of jealousy about her female friendships, and Velma became so upset about Eddie's resentment that she complained to Lake County Sheriff Edward ("Big Ed")

Eddie and Velma settled down to a routine of slovenly housekeeping and acrid bickering, punctuated with frantic jaunts to Cleveland.

Rasmussen about Eddie opening her mail. A well-meaning individual who flattered himself—with some justice—on being a kind of father figure and confidant to young marrieds in the county, "Big Ed" had a chat with both Velma and Eddie that autumn of 1927 and assumed that the matter was resolved.

It was not. Sometime in late October 1927, Velma left Eddie for several days and returned to her parents' apartment in East Cleveland. She said that her marriage was over, but Bert and Catherine persuaded her to return to her husband. Then, on November 23, the day before Thanksgiving, Velma showed up again in Cleveland. Stopping at a barber shop at West 65th and Detroit Avenue to get her hair bobbed, she retailed her marital woes to barber Valentino Del Fino: "My husband strikes me . . . he scolds me all the time and over the littlest thing that's wrong around the house. Only this morning we had another quarrel, and he struck me."

Philip Manacapilli, sitting in the chair next to Velma, subsequently heard Velma telephone Mabel Young from the shop and heard her tell Mabel that Eddie had hit her. Minutes later, at the Gordon Square Pharmacy, the chatty Velma told pharmacist Albert Edelstein that her husband mistreated her and had hit her several times. But once more, the marital fences were mended, and Velma unhappily returned to life with Eddie in the white bungalow.

Only a husband and wife know the real truth about their marriage. And it is likewise true, as newspaper writer Paul Packard argued, that "just what took place in the bedroom of the little West bungalow no one will ever know." But something terrible and fatal to Eddie West indubitably occurred there, and what follows is the fullest account that can be garnered of what transpired:

Sometime on the afternoon of Tuesday, December 6, Eddie and Velma got into their green Hupmobile roadster, and Velma drove them to Painesville to see Eddie's doctor about his chronic rheumatism. They argued bitterly all the way to the doctor's office and left when the wait there proved intolerable. After eating a late lunch at Mrs. J. B. Well's roadside hot dog stand, they returned to the doctor's and got some medicine. They were seen about 5:30 P.M. at a Painesville bank, and Velma later claimed that they argued all the way back home, where they arrived shortly before 6:00. E. I. Skinner, a nearby neighbor, saw a car pull in their drive about that time and then some lights flash on in the house. Skinner could not, however, identify either the car or who was in it.

Exactly what happened next is the big question. We know that Velma and Eddie were still arguing when they got to their second-floor bedroom and that Eddie changed into his pajamas, as if getting ready for bed. Maybe it was something he said, perhaps something nasty about her suspicious friendship with Mabel Young— something that, as Velma later insisted, "Riled me, it cut me to the bone." Maybe it was just his adamant refusal to give her the car keys. Maybe he even threatened to divorce and disgrace her. Maybe he hit her, maybe not. In some versions of her story, Velma said she slapped him and that he gave her a bloody nose. In another Velma version, she confessed that she said something insulting and that Eddie, uttering dire threats, started toward her . . .

Whatever words, threats, or actions sparked Velma's rage, we do know what resulted. Velma picked up a hammer, just brought from the basement or fetched previously for a window repair, and hit Eddie in the head with it. She hit him hard, and he probably fell down on the floor, enraged and groping blindly as blood gushed from a terrible wound in his skull. Velma's first confession was her bluntest statement on what happened: "I hit him and he dropped." Eddie probably tried to get up again at least once, perhaps as many as five times. Velma's chief defense attorney, Francis Poulson, would later cross-examine Dr. R. H. Spence, a doctor who examined Velma in jail, in an effort to prove that Eddie was still in a position to retaliate murderously against Velma's continued hammer blows. Poulson's interrogation couldn't have helped his client much:

Poulson: Did she tell you that after he went down for the
           fourth time he was still struggling?
Spence: No, not exactly. It was the fifth time that he was
           still struggling.

In any case, the evidence on Eddie West's corpse was unmistakable: Velma hit him at least six, perhaps eight, times in the front of his head with a heavy clawhammer. After he ceased trying to get up, she pulled a pillowcase over his head and bashed him some more with the hammer; the pillowcase was to cut down on the amount of blood sprayed. Then she rolled the body over and beat Eddie's skull again for a while with a leg from a broken bedroom table. She later said she kept beating him even after he stopped moving because she was afraid he would kill her if he regained consciousness and got up again. Given her state, which she variously characterized as a "red rage," "blind rage," and "wild rage," Velma probably couldn't even remember exactly when and why she did what she did.

Her next actions, however, revealed cautious and sober cunning. Fetching a ball of nursery binding twine, Velma tied Eddie's wrists and legs together tightly. (Her initial claim was that she wanted to make sure he couldn't hurt her, but she eventually confessed she wanted to make the scene look like a burglary gone awry.) She then dragged some of the bloody bedclothes down to the cellar, thoroughly smearing the walls and floors with Eddie's blood along the way. Down in the cellar, Velma burned the bloody linens in the furnace, along with her own gore-encrusted garments. She then walked outside and smoked several cigarettes. Returning to the bedroom, Velma fished the car keys (with great difficulty) out of the pockets of her husband's trussed corpse and went downstairs. Leaving the back door wide open, she got into the green Hupmobile and drove thirty-five miles to Cleveland to the house of her friend, Mabel Young.

It was a gala night at Mabel's house. All the members of the Semper Fidelis Club, a group of West Commerce High School alumnae, were gathered there for a bridge party, and many of the members had been anticipating the arrival of Velma West, who was said to be a lot of fun, the life of the party. Which she soon proved to be. Arriving about 8:30 P.M. at the Young residence, Velma went upstairs to freshen up. A horrified Mabel Young later recalled Velma's entrance:

> Velma never seemed in better spirits than when she arrived at our home Tuesday evening. The vibrant personality that made her easily the most popular among the younger married girls in our set was never more in evidence. She greeted me at the door with a laugh and went immediately upstairs to "fix up" for the party. If I had known her mission was not so much to use a lipstick as to wash from her hands the blood of Eddie West, what a different party it would have been.

A different party, indeed. Velma joined a bridge game in progress and, although new to the pastime, won every hand she played and was high scorer at her table that evening. She probably would have been the highest scorer at the party, except that she periodically interrupted her game to go to the piano. There she regaled her impressed audience with a medley of popular "blues" tunes of the day—songs like "So Blue," "Tired and Lonely for Home," and, most movingly, "Just Like a Butterfly Caught in the Rain":

> Here I am lonely, tired and lonely
> Crying for home in vain.
> Longing for flowers, dreaming of hours, back in the
>   sun-kissed lane.

I know that all of the world is cheery, outside that old cottage
    door.
Why are my wings so weary, that I can't fly home any more.
Here I am praying, brokenly saying, "Give me the sun
    again."
Just like a butterfly caught in the rain.

Although, later, with her daughter facing a first-degree-murder
rap, Velma's mother would insist that Velma was actually withdrawn and quiet at the Young bridge party, the girls present all
agreed—and testified—that Velma was the heart and soul of the
fete and that her plaintive, bluesy singing was the hit of the evening. The party broke up about 11:30 P.M., and Velma spent the
night at the Young house.

Velma arose the next morning, ate a breakfast inevitably described by the newspapers as "hearty," and left Mabel's house at
about 9:30. Velma took the streetcar to her mother's apartment in
East Cleveland, and then the two of them took the trolley to Public
Square. They had long planned a mother-daughter outing to buy
Christmas presents, and they sampled the sights, sounds, and mer-
chandise of downtown Cleveland stores like Higbee's and Halle's
until mid-afternoon. Velma bought a dozen handkerchiefs "for Eddie" and longingly ogled a scarf "that Eddie would just love" but
did not purchase it. Catherine Van Woert and Velma then returned
on the streetcar to the Van Woert residence at 1727 Page Avenue.

Lake County sheriff Rasmussen and the East Cleveland police
were waiting there for them. Taken into custody as they were walking up the drive, they were taken to the Lake County jail in Painesville for interrogation by Rasmussen and Lake County prosecutor
Seth Paulin. They were soon joined by Mabel Young, also picked
up for questioning, and Bert Van Woert, who got off a train in
Ashtabula when he read the shocking news about his son-in-law
Eddie in an afternoon newspaper.

Eddie West had been found beaten to death in the cottage on
Narrows Road in Perry. Eddie had not shown up for his 10:00 A.M.

nursery shift on Wednesday morning, an uncharacteristic lapse that soon brought his brother James to the front door of the white bungalow. The door was locked, but the back door was wide open and most of the electric lights were blazing. James eventually made his way upstairs, where he started back in horror at the sight he found. His brother Eddie was lying on the floor of the bedroom, with his shoes off and his head beaten in. Some of the bloody bedclothes were wrapped around his body, there was a bandanna around his head, and his hands and feet were tied with twine. James West immediately called Sheriff Rasmussen and Dr. W. R. Carle. Eddie's corpse was removed from the house, a guard was posted to prevent anyone from going inside, and a search was begun for the murdered man's missing wife.

Velma held up well during the first three hours of interrogation. She remained calm, even after being told of her husband's grisly death, and she steadfastly insisted that she had left him in good health the night before and knew nothing about his murder. She remembered Eddie cranking the Hupmobile for her when she left for Mabel's party and then kissing her good-bye. Sheriff Rasmussen, who conducted most of the questioning, was baffled, both by her smooth story and her incredible sangfroid. Finally he said, "I know you're telling me the truth. But why did you leave the back door open?" Velma suddenly slumped forward, recovered, and then said, "All right. I'll tell you the whole truth. I killed him after a quarrel." She then wrote out and signed a 200-word statement, admitting her guilt.

That statement was the basis of the first-degree-murder charge eventually brought against Velma, although she added other details—many of them conflicting—in subsequent conversations with the avuncular Sheriff Rasmussen. And, allowing for some differences in language and detail, the story was pretty much the same: They quarreled, Eddie hit her or threatened to hit her, and she hit him with a hammer a number of times. Whatever quibbling Velma did about the details, however, the crux of her intended defense was clear from the beginning. She was an abused woman who killed her husband for fear of losing her own life at his hands. EDDIE HIT ME, WIFE CRIES, screamed the headline of the next day's *Cleveland News*.

The disclosures of the next seven days furnished material for a first-class orgy of sensationalism, and Cleveland's newspapers did not disappoint. While the *Plain Dealer*, a deliberately staid sheet, concentrated on the details and discrepancies of the investigation, the *Press* and the *News* focused on what their readers really wanted: lurid facts and bizarre psychology. The *Press* obliged with voluminous baiting of the Lake County hicks, whose presumed bucolic folkways and cow-pie culture had driven sophisticated Velma around the bend. After dwelling on the horror caused by Velma's public smoking and bad housekeeping, *Press* scribes caricatured Eddie West as a rude rube, resentful of his wife's polish ("He'd rather play 'Hearts' in the village store than bridge in a Cleveland mansion"). They then dwelt with unconcealed, prurient relish on the girlish garments on display in Velma's Painesville jail cell, in a feature, "Pretties in Velma's Cell":

A blue and gray steamer rug plaided in red has been used to cover the bare wooden bench. Soft silk pajamas of delicate pink are thrown casually on the lower bunk, and there are the other dainty underthings of a modern, luxury-loving girl . . . An apple green felt hat with a rhinestone pin, obviously chosen because of the becoming contrast with the gold blond hair, lay on the desk.

The *News* relied on the considerable sob-sister talents of Nina Donberg from the beginning, and her editors weren't disappointed. Donberg wrung every last tear out of the story, and at the same time satisfied her readers' sense of retributive justice with a stance of unrelenting, bullying scorn toward the accused murderess:

Will the spoiled-child little girl face of Velma West save her from the consequences of her revolting crime? . . . It is not a sweet face, nor is it a pleasing, friendly one. Neither has it the shadows that indicate depths of character. The eyes are a restless blue and look out under droopy lids that make Velma appear sleepy and sullen in spite of her nervous glances. The childish snub nose gives a petulant willful look to the face and the pouting lips over white teeth speak of intolerance and angry moods . . . Daddy's girl has let her temper get the best of her once too often and now she stands accused of the murder of her husband and it is up to daddy to summon all of his life to protect her from her own folly.

For those desiring the veneer of science spread over their prejudices, Cleveland newspapers offered a smorgasbord of half-baked psychologizing and pseudoscience about the alleged killer's personality. As noted above, Clarence Darrow, whose opinion was solicited by the *Cleveland Press,* weighed in with a defense sympathizing with Velma's revulsion to small-town life, virtually excusing it as an understandable incitement to murder. And only a day after Eddie's body was found, David Dietz of the *Press* found a Cleveland psychiatrist, Dr. Daniel A. Huebsch, to natter learnedly, if unconvincingly, about Velma's presumed mental state:

She is suffering from an infantile fixation which in its turn, led to a split personality . . . To her unconscious mind her husband represented the obstacle which prevented her from returning to babyhood. He was the symbol of present-day reality which cut her off from her dreams. Her unconscious mind had control when she killed him.

Homer Croy, a prominent American novelist, was also recruited by the *Press* to analyze Velma, and his take on her echoed Darrow's disdain for the presumed hatefulness of small-town life. Velma wasn't trying to kill Eddie, Croy argued, she was simply striking out at "everything that tortured her in Perry." It was the inevitable consequence of a husband's trying to constrain his wife's lifestyle with psychological chains. Such repression could only have one result: "But when he first clamps [the chains] on, it certainly means trouble. Pretty soon, the girl finds some sort of hammer. She is not hitting the boy—she is cracking her chains."

Best of all was Dr. H. Del Spence of Painesville, whose statements must have increased contemporary popular contempt for alienists a great deal. When Nina Donberg of the *News* asked if Velma was insane, Del Spence delivered the goods: "Define insanity for me and I will answer your question . . . Insanity is geographic. Her insanity means non-conformity to the beliefs and habits of her community. Perhaps 200 or 300 years from now or possibly sooner, we will not punish such people as Velma West, but we will treat them as we do the physically sick."

It's a good guess that for most Cleveland newspaper readers, there was probably far more resonance to the antifeminist sentiments of "Mrs. E. P.," whose letter published in the *News* drew from the Velma West parable the clear, if ungrammatical, lesson that a woman, "once married, should consider their husband and not pleasure."

Those inclined to give Velma the benefit of the doubt were not aided by Catherine Van Woert, whose appeal for sympathy in the December 13 edition of the *News* painted an unnuanced picture of a spoiled-rotten adult child:

> But even after her marriage, I couldn't think of her as anything but her mother's little baby girl. I tried too hard to make everything easy for her . . . She visited me frequently and wanted me to go with her. She wanted me to join with her mood and play with her. But I was too busy . . . I [have] told her that as soon as the world hears her whole story that they will know she never meant to commit a crime . . . What more could any mother do?

Velma wept copiously, smoked many cigarettes, and read the voluminous newspaper coverage of her crime in her jail cell. Meanwhile, her father began to organize her defense. Initially recruiting attorney H. T. Nolan and his son Eugene, B. L. Van Woert soon turned the case over to Richard Bostwick, the twenty-seven-year-old Geauga County prosecutor. Bostwick, the son of the previous county prosecutor, was well known in Northeast Ohio as a "dude," celebrated for his long fur coat and derby hat, and he honed his public persona with comments like: "I always mean to play the lone wolf in my practice." He soon made it clear, in a comment to a

---

"Cigarette-smokin' city gals don't have no time for keeping house as a woman should," said a deputy sheriff.

Press reporter, that he was going to use a self-defense strategy with Velma: "a physically weak girl-wife who accidentally killed defending herself from a beating she expected and feared from a brutal, husky young husband." Bostwick was soon relegated to second place, however, by the recruitment of Francis W. Poulson to head the defense team. Famous for having helped save Eva Kaber from the electric chair in 1921, Poulson struck a pose of unalloyed bravado from the outset. Asked if he would move for a change of venue, he told reporters, "No, I will be perfectly willing, even, to try the case as I see it now with a member of the West family on the jury." It was noised about for awhile that William J. Corrigan, Poulson's associate in the Kaber trial, was also coming aboard, but that proved just a rumor.

The judicial process ground into action on December 8 with a preliminary hearing before Judge Marvin H. Helter at the Painesville Town Hall. After testimony by police officials and witnesses, Velma was charged with first-degree murder and sent back to jail. She maintained her eerie calm until the photographers began to flash their bulbs at her, when she became hysterical, fainted, and fell to the floor. Helped to her feet by Sheriff Rasmussen, she made it to the town hall steps before swooning anew, screaming as she fell, "Oh God! Oh God!" Velma's teary travails didn't impress

Nina Donberg one bit: "When she left the courtroom she decided to have a tantrum on the stairs and fell to the floor."

Two days later, Velma's late husband was buried after a memorial at the T. B. West residence. There were also services at the Perry Methodist Episcopal Church before interment in the little Perry cemetery near by. Throughout this family ordeal, Eddie's relatives conducted themselves with remarkable dignity, maintaining an almost perfect public silence—except to say that it would have been worse for them if they had been in the present position of Velma's family. Mrs. Van Woert, who apparently didn't know when to keep her mouth shut, commented to reporters that same day that Velma was "lonely" and had wanted to attend Eddie's funeral.

Even as Eddie West was lowered into the Perry graveyard, Richard Bostwick began to drop hints that the Velma West defense might use an insanity plea in addition to the claim of self defense. However gay her behavior in jail—reports were that Velma laughed much, smoked prodigiously, and read a lot of *True Story* magazines—Bostwick gravely described to reporters the fragile mental state of his client at the time of her rash act: "Mrs. West was ill when this murder was committed. She was exceptionally nervous and distracted. She was abnormally irritable."

Velma returned to the Lake County Court on December 12 for another hearing before Judge Helter. Poulson made a motion that the charge be reduced, thereby making Velma eligible for bail, but Helter refused. When Velma heard his decision, she started screaming, "Let me alone! Let me alone!" She screamed and fainted again when she saw the crowd waiting outside the courtroom. It was later explained that she reacted so violently because she was under the impression that Judge Helter had just sentenced her to the electric chair. The deciding factor in Helter's decision to deny bail was probably Lake County coroner O. O. Hausch's description of the wounds on Eddie West's corpse. There was a deep gash on the forehead and another terrible blow that destroyed one eye; either blow would have been sufficient to cause death, but there were also numerous additional injuries all over the face and skull. Meanwhile, at the jail, the theatrical Sheriff Rasmussen gave unsolicited demonstrations of Velma's probable murder technique to female visitors, realistically waving the murder hammer in the air and pretending to fall under its blows.

It was a lengthy interval between Velma's arrest and her eventual trial, but Velma whiled away the time as best she could with cigarettes, magazines, and endless chattering to the jail matrons and "Big Ed." Within seven days of her arrest, she was already receiving hundreds of letters, mostly supportive, from correspondents, mostly female, from around the country. One woman wrote that she was "thoroughly familiar with the life of an oppressed wife and didn't much blame one for rebelling, even with a clawhammer." It was soon reported in the newspapers, however, perhaps after diplomatic hints from her defense team, that Velma was reading the Bible and thinking pious thoughts. In any case, it is a fact that she was baptized into the Perry Methodist Episcopal Church on January 23 by the Reverend E. P. Wykoff, who had conducted her husband's obsequies only two weeks earlier.

There were still a few tidbits left for sensation addicts as Velma's arraignment neared. Scott E. Leslie, a reputed handwriting expert, analyzed Velma's scrawl and found it childish, indicating "a restless and inconsistent nature." The ever-reliable Dr. Daniel A. Huebsch also examined Velma's handwriting and found that it—surprise!—gave evidence of a "split personality." And there was a persistent rumor that Eddie West had still been alive when Velma departed in a huff to Cleveland on that fatal December evening. The gossip whispered around Lake County was that local bootleggers, angry at Eddie's enthusiastic cooperation with the efforts of local authorities to enforce the Volstead Act, had either assassinated him that night or rather fortuitously came upon the half-dead Eddie after Velma was done with him—and finished the job.

Fifty-one witnesses came before a Lake County grand jury on January 9, 1928, to give evidence in the case. Almost a dozen of them reiterated that Velma was the veritable life of Mabel Young's party the night she killed her husband. Velma's lawyers were very upset that they were not allowed to examine the death bungalow, but Judge Helter's decision stood and would not be overturned. A first-degree-murder indictment was duly handed down, and trial was set for March 5. Velma's lawyers refused to plead her at a hearing on January 23 before Judge A. G. Reynolds, and so a legally mandated plea of "not guilty" was entered for her.

Velma's long-anticipated trial opened at 10:00 A.M. on March 5 before a packed courtroom audience (estimated at 75 percent female). But rumors were already rampant that her lawyers were trying to plea-bargain her case down to a second-degree-murder charge. A new element in the case, long hinted at, had finally surfaced during the previous weekend. Suddenly, the two traumatized families involved in the impending trial discovered a common interest in halting the case. Over the weekend of March 3–4, Mabel Young submitted an eight-page deposition to Sheriff Rasmussen. The prosecution was prepared to introduce it as evidence.

Elicited from Young by Rasmussen during a three-hour questioning session between 5:30 and 8:30 P.M. on March 3, Young's statement confirmed in detail what had long been suspected and hinted at behind the scenes in the Velma West mystery: Velma West was a lesbian, and it was more than probable that her unconventional sexual tendencies had figured in her husband's terrible death.

Of course Mabel Young's matter-of-fact revelations caused a sensation in the newspapers. Female homosexuality was a big deal in 1920s Cleveland, a very big deal in ways that cannot be imagined by contemporary readers habituated to more public disclosures of, if not always more tolerant views on, alternative sexuality. The *News* editors were so stunned that they refused to name Velma's sin in public, coyly alluding only to "abnormal sex proclivities similar to those portrayed in the French play 'The Captive.'" But the *Press* spoke for a shocked Cleveland public on March 5 when it stated: "The abnormal love that the state charged to Velma West may go unnoticed in some parts of the world, but in Lake County it was strange."

Mabel Young's eight-page statement was a sad document, and

probably every word of it was true. It told of the friendship that had sprung up between Mabel and Velma that summer and Mabel's disquiet when she learned that Velma's affection for her was "not the friendship of woman for woman, girl for girl." It went on to testify to Mabel's genuine feeling for the unhappy Velma, and Mabel's hope that Velma's sexual passions could be straightened out by exposure to Mabel's wholesome social set. (Hence, Velma's inclusion at Mabel's bridge party on the night of December 6.) Young's statement documented further Velma's blizzard of letters to Mabel, each one pledging steadfast love.

The assertions of Young's statement, when put together with other facts known about Velma or divulged by her to Sheriff Rasmussen while in jail, coalesced to create a portrait of a sexually tormented and very confused young woman. Apparently seduced some years previously by an older woman, Velma had begun dressing up frequently in male attire several years before she met Eddie West. She liked to have her photograph taken in such attire—it was known to Velma's lawyers that the prosecution had photographs and was willing to introduce them—and Velma insisted that Mabel address her as "Val," a sobriquet Velma thought more masculine than her given name. The whole situation was a recipe for tragedy, as Velma's unrequited physical passion for Mabel added a dangerously explosive element to her increasingly unhappy marriage to Eddie West. No one will ever know what went on between Velma and Eddie behind closed doors, but their relations, emotional and physical, could not have been happy ones. It is even possible that the triggering incident occurred when Eddie himself began to show an interest in Mabel Young. Velma admitted that she saw Eddie kiss Mabel on several occasions, but Velma insisted that the kisses were at her own request. Velma, in any case, denounced Mabel Young's statement as "lies, all lies!" and swore that she would never forgive her erstwhile friend.

Late on the afternoon of March 5, the prosecution, led by Seth Paulin and Homer Harper, and the defense, represented by Bostwick and Poulson, cut a deal. Velma would plead guilty to second-degree murder, and none of the evidence would be released to the public. Each side continued to posture that it had the winning case, but Poulson was probably right when he argued that the prosecution's intended introduction of a motive based on Velma's alleged lesbianism (that Eddie's death was a murder of removal, so Velma could concentrate on Mabel) would actually have helped his client, because "no alienist could deny Velma was insane if the reported accusations in Miss Young's statements were true." In other words, female homosexuality was considered open-and-shut evidence of insanity in 1920s America, and Poulson knew that the introduction of such exhibits as the photographs of Velma in "mannish attire" would instantly get his client off on an insanity plea.

So the deal was made, although everyone involved, except for presiding judge Jesse D. Barnes, kept up a barrage of belittling remarks. Poulson, who had actually threatened to sue anyone who suggested that he was ready to plea-bargain and had characterized initial reports of Mabel Young's statement as "mere muck," publicly praised the successful plea bargain as a compassionate compromise that spared the reputations that would have been wrecked by the exposures of a trial. Prosecutor Paulin scoffed at Poulson's claims, sneering, "Compromise? This is no compromise. Second degree was all I expected to get, anyway, and why not take the quickest and cheapest way?" To which rejoinder canny Richard Bostwick riposted with the perfect squelch, "You really had a perfect first-degree case." Sheriff Rasmussen, who perhaps had been anxious to reenact his popular pantomime of the murder struggle in court, confessed himself "heartbroken" at the decision, insisting they had the evidence to send Velma to the chair. Velma's parents were indiscreet and ungracious to the last: Catherine Van Woert let it be known that she was very unhappy with the verdict, and her husband delivered himself of one final blast of spleen against the country village that had rejected his petted daughter: "Of course I'm not satisfied. What parent would be? The village is not satisfied either. The people wanted to hear all the dirt and filth of a trial."

Wearing a felt hat, black satin dress, and black shoes and stockings ("an ensemble which proved becoming to the young widow with her pale complexion, slightly reddened lips, blue eyes and golden hair"), Velma stood before Judge Barnes on March 6 to receive her sentence. Permitted to speak, Velma replied, "I have nothing to say." Speaking to the trial principals, the venire of 46 unused jurors, and 200 avid spectators, Judge Barnes noted the weaknesses in the evidence for first-degree murder: "It isn't even an argumentative question. The state couldn't hope for a conviction of anything higher than second-degree." He then turned to Velma and said: "I don't think this is the time for talking. The mandate of the law is the most potent lecture that can be given. This was a horrible, and unthinkable thing. This staid old community has been stirred . . . I have never before been called upon to sentence a woman for an offense of this kind."

Barnes continued, "It is the sentence of this court you spend the rest of your natural life in the Women's Reformatory at Marysville." Velma burst into tears. Judge Barnes's words came exactly three months to the day after Velma took a hammer to her husband's head.

And so what Prosecutor Paulin so drolly and repeatedly referred to as that "little transaction at Perry" came to an end.

Velma left for Marysville the next day after a tearful farewell with her mother. Her last words to Francis Poulson were a plea to put in a good word for her at parole time; Velma had high hopes of getting out when she first became eligible in 1938 at the age of 31. The car taking her to Marysville followed much of the same route she had taken on her last drive to Mabel Young's house the previous December. As the car approached the reformatory gates, Velma seized Nina Donberg's hand—the *News* columnist had been allowed to share the last ride—and whimpered, "Hold my hand, hold it tightly, please!" (Donberg later reported that Velma had been having nightmares for weeks, during which she repeatedly cried out, "Ed, don't!") When she arrived at Marysville, she was greeted by Superintendant Louise Mittendorf, and she piously vowed to start a new life, saying, "I am going to get in with the right sort of girls." Perhaps Velma was inspired by the well-known words on the sign at the Marysville entrance:

> When you entered here you left your past behind you.
> We do not wish to have you ever refer to it.
> Your FUTURE is our concern—to determine that, you are
>   here.

Alas, Velma didn't follow through on her resolutions very well. Many days of her early years at Marysville as Prisoner no. 3181 were spent in solitary confinement, owing to her refusal to live by the rules. In violation of regulations, Velma continued to keep her hair mannishly short, using shards of broken glass from electric lightbulbs and other objects to cut it on the sly. She was eventually allowed some duties in the prison art classes—but lost them when she showed an unwelcome interest in one of the other female prisoners. She was often in trouble, too, for smoking, which Superintendant Mittendorf banned for two reasons: "The first is that it is dangerous here. The second is simply that they are women and I don't approve." When interviewed by *Press* reporter Walter Morrow in November 1930, Velma seemed dispirited and gave only listless replies to his questions. Prison officials told Morrow that Velma had admitted to them that she had participated in a "love cult" before her marriage and that she had married Eddie partly to prevent her mother from suspecting her true proclivities. Velma's behavior, they added, had gone downhill after the disastrous Cleveland Clinic fire in May 1929. She told Louise Mittendorf that one of her friends had died there, commenting, "What have I to live for now?"

By the time *Cleveland News* reporter Howard Beaufait interviewed Velma five years later, she had settled down considerably. She was still disobediently cutting her hair but seemed healthier from a regime of working outdoors in the flower gardens, vegetable patches, and hayfields of the reformatory. She was interested in news of the outside world, especially Cleveland's newly built Terminal Tower, which she had never seen, and still cherished hopes of getting a parole in 1938.

But 1938 came and went, and there was no parole for still-notorious "hammer murderess" Velma West. Although by now a valued "trustee" at the prison, Velma had begun to lose hope,

---

Please don't let them talk too awfully bad about me after this. I'm not bad— just frightfully unlucky in life.

---

and her anxiety was increased by mounting fears about her health, especially a heart condition. She also complained of a constant noise in her ears, "like an airplane." In the early morning hours of June 19, 1939, Velma escaped from Marysville with three other inmates, passing through three supposedly locked doors to freedom outside. She left a letter for the new superintendant, Marguerite Reilley, pledging affection and justifying her betrayal:

> Because I must have one little adventure in this dull life of mine—Because I am so tortured with pain in this body of mine that it drives me almost crazy. Because I have lost hope of getting out as I would like to get out . . . Please don't let them talk too awfully bad about me after this. I'm not bad—just frightfully unlucky in life.

Although Reilley initially professed mystification at how Velma had passed through so many locked doors, the superintendent eventually admitted that Velma had been trusted enough to have access to some of the master keys at Marysville.

A month later Velma was captured in Dallas. When picked up by the police there, Velma was allegedly on the way to her room with a man, although, as Marguerite Reilley commented, "That doesn't sound like Velma." Velma first swore at the Dallas police and refused to talk but reverted to the chatty self of her erstwhile Painesville jail days when offered a pack of cigarettes by a friendly reporter.

While insisting that her fling had been worth it, Velma confessed that life on the outside had been pretty hard. It was apparent that the three fugitives had been able to get so far away only by hitchhiking and selling their bodies in the most squalid of circumstances. And when Velma's two companions rolled a customer for his wallet in Tennessee, the bloody results made squeamish Velma faint. On her return to Marysville, Velma lost her hard-won privileges and was put in solitary confinement for a few weeks. Her only reference to Eddie West, her first since coming to prison, was a heartless one: "He couldn't take it. I hit him playfully on the head with a hammer one night and that was that."

But the years went by, and Velma began to mellow at last. Sometime before her father died in 1944, Velma got religion and entered the Roman Catholic faith. During the last decade and a half of her life, she often entertained her fellow inmates at Marysville, singing and writing her own, often gospel-based, compositions. These included tunes like "Careless Kisses," My Secret Dream," and "Won't You Spare One Little Prayer for a Sinner Like Me?"

About her faith and Eddie, she said, "It may sound corny but this is true. We pray more for others than ourselves. Every time I say communion it is for my husband. If his soul can't be saved, I don't want mine to be saved."

Velma's last years were difficult ones, as she was troubled by health problems, including the heart condition that eventually caused paralysis of her arms. Although considered for parole several times, it was obvious that she had nowhere else to go. She died of heart disease on October 24, 1959, at 8:15 A.M., after wasting away to 86 pounds. She was 53. In her declining years, she was known to tell fellow prisoners: "Go straight when you get out. There's still a lot of good you can do in this world." †

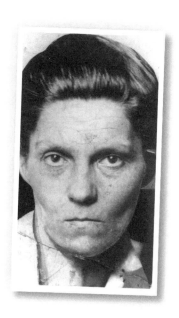

Medina's Not-So-Merry Widow

Martha Wise's Deadly Crying Game, 1925

It is well that the meek shall inherit this earth, because a lot of them sure get kicked around here initially. Most never get a chance to kick back. Sometimes, though, they do, and their revenge, taken to occasional extremes, constitutes a fascinating, if discordant, element in what Thomas Gray so justly termed the "short and simple annals of the poor." Martha Wise's vengeance on the world that mistreated and malformed her is just such a tale and is likely to breed disquieting chills of horror and guilty gratification in even the most jaded breast.

It was not so very long ago, and hardly far away. But it might as well have been, for Medina County in 1925 was a world far distant from the bustle of big-city Cleveland, 23 miles removed from its largely rural fastness. And Hardscrabble, a hamlet of modest farms in the center of Medina's Liverpool Township, was probably as far away from the Forest City's metropolitan sophistication as you could get. Newspaper accounts of the Wise tragedy invariably characterized Hardscrabble as "mud-bound" or "muddy," as assuredly it must have been—especially in a rainy spring season—thanks to its largely unpaved roads. But the same accounts hinted at something darker and more uncivilized lurking in Hardscrabble: an almost feral population of neolithic life forms oozing out of the "forsaken mud and slime crossroads where the black death of the Dark Ages comes . . ." So was modest Hardscrabble viewed by Cleveland's Roaring Twenties sophisticates when the curtain rose in late 1924 on the series of deeds that would bring notoriety to miserable, misbegotten Martha Wise.

Even by Hardscrabble standards, Martha Wise had lived an unfortunate life. Forty years old in 1924, she had been born Martha Hasel to a family of unpretentious farming folk, Wilhelm and Sophie Gienke Hasel, in 1884. From the beginning, Martha was slow, sickly, markedly morbid, and vulnerable to the contempt and bullying of those around her, especially her family. It would later be said that her youthful mental and emotional precariousness worsened noticeably after a dog bit her, but other evidence suggests her psychological and physical fragility stemmed from chronic, undiagnosed epilepsy and a severe adolescent bout with spinal meningitis. The latter ordeal, townsfolk remembered, left Martha with a "cluttered brain." Suffice it to say that Martha Wise came of age at the turn of the century as a hysteric with a notorious enjoyment of funerals—especially the weeping—and a full-fledged hypochondriac.

Given the limited entertainment available in 1920s Hardscrabble, Martha's appetite for funerals seems a likely and innocent-enough diversion, from a modern perspective. As Walter Morrow, a *Cleveland Press* writer of the 1930s, explained, the emotional delights of funeral obsequies opened up a hitherto blocked channel of release in Martha's unhappy, difficult, and stunted life:

There was music and there were flowers. The children were clean and dressed in their best. And from nowhere, almost, there appeared the usual association of bearded ladies who hover about the homes where death has visited to offer consolation and solace. Martha became a regular attendant at funerals, She came to love them. Dressed in her weeds she attended all within reach, her sobs and lamentations rising above the smothered tide of keening by the bereaved women. Weeping became sheer joy to her.

Morrow, no doubt a hopeless romantic, liked to think that Martha first discovered the pleasures of public grief at her husband Albert's 1923 funeral—an event occasioned by Martha's poisoning him with arsenic—but the fact is that Martha was already notorious by 1924 as one who had not missed an area funeral for twenty years.

She was equally well known by that date for a galloping case of hypochondria and its concomitant need for medical attention and sympathy. There is ample evidence that Martha Wise had an unfortunate medical history, but her legitimate physiological complaints were not enough for her as she grew to middle age in "American Gothic" Medina. Dr. Henry John Abele of Lakewood would eventually admit at Martha's trial for first-degree murder that he had been treating her for a variety of "imaginary ailments" since 1898, when Martha was fourteen. On one occasion she had come to him with a "sore" arm. When he removed the medical dressing she had contrived, Dr. Abele discovered an arm obviously "bruised" with Easter-egg dyes. On another occasion, she came to his office with severe blistering on her arm, clearly caused by the turpentine she had deliberately rubbed into it.

Martha left school at the age of fourteen. Such an abbreviated education was not uncommon for a farm girl of her time and place, but there were additional reasons for Martha to forsake her lessons. As her teacher, Mrs. Elma Reisenger, remembered, Martha was clearly mentally retarded, even as a child; as Reisenger put it, "She couldn't learn. She was queer and erratic. She was not a nor-

mal child." Her education ending in the fifth grade, Martha spent
some years working as a kitchen girl in various Medina homes.
Then, at 24, she met Albert Wise—and her life took a turn for the
even worse.

Albert Wise's family had come into the Rocky River valley,
where Hardscrabble lay, sometime in the early twentieth century.
Why he married Martha Wise is not known, but we know that the
subsequent fifteen years of marriage produced five children and a
decade and a half of misery and joyless toil for Martha Wise. Albert
Wise, even by the unsentimental standards of a rough-hewn farming community, was a hard case. He set the tone for their union at
the outset by refusing to buy Martha a wedding ring, and she soon
became his thankless drudge and victim. Beating her frequently,
Albert made her toil like a common field hand on their 100-acre
Hardscrabble farm as day followed day in year after endless year
of backbreaking labor. The morning after her first child was born,
he sent her out to work in the fields. She became notorious—to her
tearful shame—as the only woman in Medina who had to slop the
hogs. George Hammond, who worked briefly for Albert Wise as
a farmhand, later testified at Martha's trial that he left after three
days because the work demanded was too heavy. Small wonder
that Martha Wise took increasing comfort in funerals and in complaining to doctors.

And, apparently, in fantasies of revenge. No one knows exactly
when or why the worm turned, but it probably revolved decisively
in 1923. It was in that year that Martha apparently poisoned Albert
Wise, a murder never proven—the official cause was an "infected
arm"—and not even suspected for some years and an act that must
have suggested a way out of further difficulties and heartaches.
It must have seemed to unhappy Martha Wise, with her circum-
scribed existence, that her Hardscrabble world of tribulation and
tears was opening up at last.

As Lady Macbeth found in like circumstances, her triumph was
not to be. In 1923, the same year she disposed of Albert Wise, Martha started really going off the rails. Hitherto known as "queer"
and abnormal, she raised community eyebrows yet further with

increasingly bizarre behavior. She took to roaming the Medina countryside after dark, appearing unexpectedly and sometimes foaming at the mouth, rolling her eyes, or even barking like a dog, symptoms indicative of both her probable epilepsy and a mind giving way under an unprecedented strain. To her family of siblings

---

Given the limited entertainment available in 1920s Hardscrabble, Martha's appetite for funerals seems a likely and innocent-enough diversion.

---

and in-laws, she admitted having frequent hallucinations, including visitations by angels and white doves. What she didn't tell her relatives was that she had also taken to burning down the barns of her Medina neighbors and stealing their jewelry and farm implements. At least ten mysterious fires would eventually be linked to Martha's activities, and she herself eventually confessed as much:

> Some of the fires I started at night. Some of them I started in the daytime after the devil had told me at night to do it. I was afraid to go out at night—I always saw him when I did and he always told me something new to do. I didn't think about the fires killing anybody at first, but later I knew they might—that's when I started out to set them at night, so I could surprise people. I never stayed at the fires—no. I slipped away to a hiding place and watched them blaze and crackle and burn.

Love, as poets and popular songs remind us, oft takes us by surprise, and so it apparently astonished Martha Wise that same year after her husband died. We shall never know the truth about any of her alleged liaisons; she was rumored to have at least three different "sweethearts" and ultimately confessed one amour in particularly intimate detail to avid reporters. What we do know, though, is that

Martha, at least, believed that one of her swains seriously wished to marry her. It must have seemed like an unlooked-for happy ending at last for the Widow Wise, socially forlorn and with a brood of four young children to raise (one had died as an infant). As a later commentator put it, she was at last within reach of a "protector and love she had not known when her first husband was living and work, work, work was her song of love."

It was not to be. On catching wind of Martha's nuptial hopes, her family, especially mother, Sophie, and uncle Fred Gienke, put the collective family foot down. They had not been amused by Martha's carryings-on and erratic behavior since Albert Wise's demise, and they were dead set against her choice of a second mate. The man in question, Walter Johns—who for the historical record ever after denied being more than Martha's platonic friend—was reputedly of a different religious creed. The Gienke-Hasel clan, moreover, was quite upset about the gossip that swirled about Martha's head in the close-knit Hardscrabble community. Much of that gossip, reputedly, had its source in the women of the Ladies of Aid Zion Lutheran Church in nearby Valley City, which organization had for some months furnished the Widow Wise with the bread of charity in the form of vegetables and clothing. Rumor was that the victuals of this ecclesiastical charity were being shared by Martha's unworthy male friends, and the ensuing discomfort of the Ladies of Aid had reached the sensitive ears of Sophie Hasel, who forbade Martha to marry. Actually, she did more than forbid it: She threatened to cut Martha out of her will and publicly disown her in the bargain.

It can only be imagined what such a threat must have meant to an individual so marginal as Martha, in a community so close and conservative as Hardscrabble. Already publicly reviled and teased as a moron, made a figure of fun for her epileptic symptoms, and scorned as an object of public charity, Martha Wise was now threatened with what was—in the black hole of Hardscrabble—social death. She wept, she ranted, she raved, and finally, apparently, she gave in.

But the "postman always rings twice," and those who kill once will likely kill again. The Gienkes and the Hasels didn't fear that truism because they did not realize that Albert Wise's death had been an unnatural one. But Martha knew it, and an already proven path out of her difficulties led her now to the pharmacy of Medina druggist W. H. Weber on November 24, 1924. There she purchased two ounces of arsenic, which she signed for with her own name, as required by law, in the poison register. She told Weber she needed it to kill rats. Several days later, she went to her mother's house, a double dwelling that Sophie shared with Martha's brother Fred Hasel, for Thanksgiving dinner. Sometime during her visit on this family holiday, Martha contrived to put a potent pinch of arsenic into the water bucket in Sophie Hasel's kitchen. Several days later, she repeated the dose at a stronger level, having replenished her supplies at Weber's store to the tune of another ounce.

The results weren't long in coming. There were minor stomach complaints for those who attended Thanksgiving dinner at the Hasel residence. And then, in early December, Sophie Hasel came down with terrible abdominal pains and weakness in her legs. She didn't linger long: after several days of nonstop agony, she succumbed on December 13 to what her doctors were pleased to describe as "influenza and inflammation of the stomach." On her deathbed, Sophie Hasel called her daughter Emma to her side and tearfully begged Emma, with her final words, to look after her troubled sister: "See that Martha is taken care of; she needs your help."

Martha didn't need as much help as Sophie thought. Everyone would later remember how Martha carried on at Sophie's funeral, sobbing and shrieking in paroxysms of grief: "My dear mother, who was so good to me; why didn't God take me and leave mother? How are we ever going to get along without her? She suffered awful. I want them to sing 'All the Way My Savior Leads Me,' it was her favorite hymn." And then, at a gathering at the Hasel house after Sophie's funeral, two days after her death, Martha's brother Fred, his wife, his son Edwin, and two other relatives, Paul and Henry Hasel, became violently ill after drinking coffee and water.

As with Sophie's death, no questions were raised about this untoward event at the time. And why should they have been? As the county prosecutor, Joseph Seymour, would later characterize the situation, there was at the time no reason to think anyone had it out for the Hasel or Gienke families: "There is no apparent motive for the crime. The family is highly respected in their community.

"Mother told us never to drink the water
when we went to the Gienkes."

There are no known enemies. There was no domestic trouble. No one is under suspicion."

It is unknown what tortured sequence or rationale in the mind of Martha Wise led to her next lethal acts. There was speculation— after the fact—that she thought her uncle, Fred Gienke (Sophie Hasel's brother), suspected her hand in his sister's sudden death. Hardscrabble gossip would later depict Fred Gienke approaching Martha after her mother's funeral, picking her up, shaking her violently, and telling her to mend her ways.

We can be certain that Martha Wise didn't mend her ways, and we can be equally sure that giving up pinching arsenic into her relatives' water supply was not one of her 1925 New Year's resolutions, for that is exactly what she did during a New Year's Day dinner at Fred Gienke's house. It must have been an impressive quantity, for Fred Gienke; his wife, Lillian; daughter, Marie, 26; and sons Fred Jr., 24, Rudolph, 17, and Walter, 8, as well as Fred Hasel and his son Edwin, became violently ill within twenty minutes of eating the festive dinner of pork stew, washed down with water and coffee. It was reported in later press accounts that a Mrs. Martha Wise had also experienced gastric discomfort, but no mention was made of her four children, who also attended the happy New Year's Day family reunion. No doubt—as Lester Wise, 14, Martha's eldest child, remembered—this was because of Martha's repeated maternal advice to her offspring: "Mother told us never to drink the water when we went to the Gienkes."

Arsenic poisoning is not a nice way to die. Lillian Gienke writhed in agony for three days, wracked by the tortures characteristic of heavy-metal poisoning—stomach pains and stiffening in the leg muscles—before expiring in a house full of family almost as sick unto death as she. She died on January 4 and soon joined her sister-in-law, Sophie, in the Gienke-Hasel plot in nearby Myrtle Hill Cemetery.

The dramatic results of Martha's activities had not gone completely unremarked by the authorities. The physician who attended Lillian Gienke in her death throes notified Medina County coroner E. L. Crum and County Health Commissioner H. H. Biggs about his suspicions. He was subsequently informed that there was nothing to investigate.

If Martha Wise had ceased her homicidal activities at this point, she probably would have gotten away with murder. Sophie Hasel and Lillian Gienke were dead, but her other victims were recovering. But Martha just couldn't stop herself, and the Gienke family physician's suspicions became further inflamed by a new series of attacks on January 16. These were even more virulent than the others, and soon Fred Gienke Sr. and his children, Rudolph, Marie, Herman, and Richard, plus Lillian's sister, Rose, were felled with the mysterious symptoms that had brought death to Sophie and Lillian. By February, Rudolph and Marie were in Elyria Hospital, soon to be joined by Fred Sr. In the meantime, a Cleveland nurse, Rose Kohli, had become ill after making coffee at the Gienke house but soon recovered. Fred Sr. died on February 8, 1925, in Elyria Hospital after days of excruciating agony. The listed cause of death was "inflammation of the stomach."

The second wave of Gienke poisonings had at last sufficiently aroused the police powers of Medina County. Health Commissioner Biggs ran tests on the victims of the late January poisonings—but these turned up negative. A subsequent test on the contents of Fred Gienke Sr.'s stomach was not completed because of the illness of Elyria city chemist E. G. Curtis. But Elyria Hospital doctors were convinced something was terribly amiss with patients Rudolph and Marie Gienke, and doctors W. H. Hull and

A. G. Appleby insisted that they be thoroughly tested. By February 12 Medina county prosecutor Joseph A. Seymour had the results—and they showed a lot of unexplained arsenic in the bodies of Rudolph and Marie Gienke.

The newspapers later reported that Prosecutor Seymour subsequently conducted a "secret" investigation into the source of the Hardscrabble poisonings. It must have been very secret, indeed, for little word of it leaked out to the wider world until March 13, when the story suddenly burst into lurid tabloid bloom on the pages of the *Plain Dealer,* the *Press,* and the *News.* It soon became an obsession with all three papers and remains to this day a terrific period piece in the annals of sensationalistic journalism.

It was a story that had everything for urban Clevelanders hungry for lurid thrills. It had an exotic locale: remote Hardscrabble peopled by beings caricatured by disdainful urban journalists as ignorant, sweaty rubes inhabiting a region unimaginably remote and primitive to a city dweller. As a *Plain Dealer* reporter with a penchant for the picturesque put it: "This is a rubber boot country. An almost impossible mud road—Methodist road on a surveyor's map—leads to the house."

It had gothic, inexplicable violence, too. Backward and forward, with repeated relish, Cleveland's three newspapers recited the list of victims—three dead and fourteen sick (including Martha)— and wondered when next an unknown, demonic poisoner would strike. Or as Dick Williams of the *Press* put it, in words that would not have pleased any local chamber of commerce: "The ghost of a series of wanton murders, apparently directed at the extermination of a peace-loving and industrious family, today arose from the mud and slime of Hardscrabble to add its ghostly name to Ohio's record of crime."

And it had mystery. Whence, why, and by what unknown hand had these homicides come? Virtually every possible theory—and some impossible ones—came into play in the minds and column inches of fevered journalists. The original assumption that the New Year's Day mass sickness at the Gienke-Hasel homestead had been due to ptomaine poisoning was shunted aside with a flourish as the *Press* trumpeted the hue and cry of "Super-Killer Hunted in Medina-Co." ("a super-murderer who kills for the mere joy of killing"). Not everyone agreed. Rival newspapers discussed the possibility that the arsenic could have originated in chemical sprays used on Hardscrabble apple trees, carbide gas used for cooking purposes in the Gienke kitchen, or even, somehow, in the metal finish of the Gienke coffeepot. And the *News*, either to mock *Press* speculation or with impressive prescience, simply stated that a "moron" was being sought as the probable poisoner.

By March 14 the investigation was in high gear and moving closer to the trial that would make Martha Wise's name a feared byword in Northeast Ohio. Martha Wise's signature had already been found by the police in druggist Weber's register, and there was evidence that her signature for a subsequent arsenic purchase had been badly scribbled in a clumsy attempt to disguise her identity. The authorities, led by Seymour and Medina County sheriff Fred Roshon, were already suspicious of Martha. She was just the kind of local eccentric to fall under a cloud of suspicion at such a time—in medieval times she probably would have long since been burned as a witch—and it was clear that she had enjoyed sufficient access to the Gienke-Hasel house and—more significantly—to the Gienke-Hasel food supplies.

Suspicions about Martha intensified over the weekend of March 14–15. Richard and Fred Gienke had nourished some doubts about Martha since the beginning of their family troubles, and Richard voiced his growing suspicions in an interview published in the March 16 *Press*:

This woman [identified as a "woman crazed by hallucinations"] threatened to get us. We heard about that, but didn't pay attention to it . . . After mother and dad died we began to wonder about the poison, but didn't think of the threats. But when the rest of us kept getting sick, we remembered them.

And just to ensure that the cops didn't miss the point, some kind soul sent a letter, postmarked Valley City, to Prosecutor Seymour that read: "I just want to make a suggestion. See if you can find out if there was any ill feeling between Martha Wise and Lilly Gienke. She claims to have been sick, too, but that may be a lie."

On Wednesday, March 18, the body of Lillian Gienke was exhumed from its grave in the Myrtle Hill Cemetery. The stomach was removed and sent to Elyria for a postmortem, which was conducted by Coroner Crum and doctors A. H. Woods and H. P. Robinson. Elyria city chemist E. G. Curtis's final report would show enough poison to kill three persons; the stomach and intestines were thoroughly saturated with arsenic, which had almost totally destroyed the major tissues of the bowels. Plans to exhume the corpses of Sophie Hasel and Fred Gienke Sr. were considered but eventually dropped.

Meanwhile, the net was closing in on hapless Martha. On Monday and Tuesday, March 16–17, Cleveland newspaper accounts of the poison investigation included coy references to the dragnet for an "unknown woman" and a "mysterious poisoner." But Martha was no longer mysterious to Medina County sheriff Fred Roshon, who motored up to Fairview Park Hospital on Cleveland's West Side on Wednesday. Martha Wise had also come to Fairview Park that afternoon to have an arm infection treated, and it was in the hospital waiting room that Roshon arrested Martha and asked her leave to take her back to Medina for questioning.

Martha agreed to come with disarming cooperativeness, despite the fact that Roshon had not brought a subpoena and had no legal power to compel her return. *Cleveland Press* writer Dick Williams was allowed to accompany Martha and Roshon on the ride back, and to Williams Martha expressed seemingly heartfelt sympathy and shock for her recent victims:

> My heart bleeds for them. It must have been a monster that would kill them, and my poor, innocent old mother, why did they kill her? It was terrible. I sometimes think they were poisoned by accident. Because I can't imagine anyone being so terrible.

With compelling evidence of Martha's guilt already in hand,

Sheriff Roshon could easily imagine someone in particular being so terrible, and when they returned to Medina, he and Martha repaired to Prosecutor Joseph Seymour's office for an official interrogation. Also present at Martha's questioning were Coroner E. L. Crum, Roshon's wife, Ethel, and stenographer Nell McCarrier.

As Dick Williams later re-created the scene (he may have been allowed to be present by the cooperative Sheriff Roshon), Martha stonewalled her questioners for two hours with repeated cries of "No, no, no! I didn't, I didn't, I didn't!" She eventually cracked, however, owing to the sympathetic manner of Ethel Roshon, who invoked Mother Nature's aid in eliciting Martha's confession. It had been raining all afternoon, as Dick Williams melodramatically recounted:

> "Listen to that rain," said Mrs. Roshon. "Do you know what it is saying, Martha? It is saying, 'You did it, you did it.' It is the voice of God, telling you to tell the truth."
>
> Widow Wise half rose from her chair. "I didn't, I didn't, I didn't," she screamed out as the raindrops chanted Mrs. Roshon's words: "You did it, you did it, you did it." Widow Wise's face blanched.
>
> "Listen to it, Martha," said Mrs. Roshon. "See how it says 'You did it, you did it, you did it.'"
>
> "Oh, my God," the harassed woman cried, "maybe I did."
>
> "No, not maybe," said Mrs. Roshon, "not maybe, Martha. It says, 'You did it.'"
>
> Widow Wise listened. "Oh, God, yes, I did it," she shouted. "The devil told me to."

Martha's official confession followed, and she never altered its details afterward. As she remembered it, she had gotten the first dose of arsenic from druggist Weber in late November. Although she told Weber she was going to "pound it into meat and put it into the cellar to catch rats," she instead put "just a pinch" in her mother's water bucket on Thanksgiving Day and continued doing so until Sophie Hasel was dead. Her second round of killing began

New Year's Day, when she came to the Gienkes' for milk (Fred Gienke had been letting her use his cow ever since her own had gone dry) and began dosing the Gienkes' kitchen water bucket.

All in all, Martha's confession was a straightforward piece of work, although it was stronger on mechanics than motivation. All she could say as to her purpose was: "I don't know why I did it. I just couldn't help it. The devil was in me . . . Something seemed to make me do it. I lost my mind. My mind wasn't right . . . it has been working on me since last summer."

While thus plainly admitting her horrifying deeds, Martha could not disguise her relief at discharging the terrible burden of fear and guilt that had weighed on her mind for months:

> After I did it, it bothered me and worried me. I worried about it all the time. I feel better now . . . I feel better since I have told you all about it . . . It is the Lord's will that I should be punished and I know I must be.

That same night, Martha further elaborated on her fatal decision-making process to *Press* reporter Alene Sumner:

> The Devil made me do it. He came to me in my kitchen when I baked my bread and he said, "Do it!" He came to me when I walked the fields in the cold days and nights and said, "Do it!" Everywhere I turned I saw him grinning and pointing and talking. I couldn't eat. I couldn't sleep. I could only talk and listen to the devil. Then I did it!

Needless to say, Martha Wise was a cynical city editor's dream. The same *Cleveland Press* story that disclosed Martha's guilt trumpeted a compelling, if woefully distorted, portrait of the pitiful Martha and her methods with the screaming headline: WIDOW CONFESSES SHE POISONED THREE THRU CRAZE FOR FUNERALS. And Dick Williams's accompanying text delivered the goods promised by the label of a woman gone berserk for sheer lust of public grief:

People didn't die often enough in Hardscrabble to satisfy Widow Wise's morbid appetite. So Widow Wise made her own funerals. She killed her mother, her aunt and her uncle, and almost wiped out their families. Widow Wise walked miles to attend a funeral. She had not missed a funeral in 20 years in her home town.

Meanwhile, following her confession and incarceration in the Medina jail, Prosecutor Seymour had Martha examined by doctors and began preparing for Medina's first capital poison case in 35 years.

If Seymour had enjoyed his druthers, Martha would simply have endured a lunacy hearing and been committed to Lima State Hospital for life as an insane person. But public opinion, greatly inflamed by media coverage, demanded a murder trial, and the psychiatric testimony of the physicians who examined Martha excluded any alternative. Doctors H. H. Drysdale and Joseph S. Tierney both interviewed Martha and judged her fit to stand trial on a charge of first-degree murder. As Tierney put it: "She is of an inferior constitution and mental grade, but she is not insane, nor was she insane prior to or at the time of her acts. If she killed to attend funerals, it wouldn't make her insane. It would only show a greater degree of moral turpitude."

Tierney concluded his examination with the informal observation that Martha was "the most wretched bit of humanity I have ever seen in a criminal action." Tierney's conjecture was that her criminal actions were the result of long-repressed emotions stemming from the many years of mistreatment suffered at the hands of her dead husband. Meanwhile, Martha languished in the Medina county jail, longing for her children and worrying about the possibility of the electric chair. She was indicted for first-degree murder on April 7, with fourteen witnesses appearing before the grand jury, and her trial was set for May.

Martha's trial opened on May 4 in the Medina County Courthouse and, as anticipated, proved to be the social event of the decade. Hundreds of spectators, mostly farmers and their wives, showed up hours before the 9:00 A.M. starting time to procure good seats. It was estimated that women outnumbered men by a ratio of forty to one. Many spectators brought their lunches with them, lest the demands of Nature cost them their coveted seats. A local

---

"People didn't die often enough in Hardscrabble to satisfy Widow Wise's morbid appetite. So Widow Wise made her own funerals."

---

undertaker had provided extra folding chairs. When Judge N. H. McClure finally gaveled the proceedings to order, there were almost two hundred people in the courtroom, with as many more standing outside. And if press accounts are to be believed, no one present was disappointed by the appearance of the "super-killer" as she was led into the courtroom by Ethel Roshon:

> Her face was drawn, her eyes downcast. There were lines about her eyes and mouth, testifying to the mental suffering thru which she has passed during the months that she has been in jail. Her hair was combed straight back from her wrinkled and yellow forehead. Her eyes were weird, dark caverns, deep-sunk behind her steel-rimmed glasses. When she was arrested her hair showed few traces of gray. Today it is thickly streaked with white . . . The woman walked like one very tired. Her shoulders sagged. Her head dropped on a sunken chest. Her clothes were clean, but ill-fitting over her gaunt form. Her hands hung listlessly at her sides, one clutching, claw-like, a small blue handkerchief.

As always, in that heyday of yellow journalism, the media did not skimp in descriptions of the accused's attire: "Mrs. Wise was simply dressed and wore no hat over her piled black hair. A tan coat covered her dress of blue and reached to her new patent leather shoes. From time to time she fingered a necklace of imitation pearls or adjusted her gold rimmed glasses."

Considering the state of Medina County public opinion, Martha Wise received a reasonably fair trial. Although in the entire venire of more than 140 persons called for possible jury duty, no one could be found who hadn't formed an opinion, eventually seven women and five men were selected after they testified they were capable of putting their opinions aside in evaluating the evidence. Martha's defense attorney, Joseph Pritchard of Cleveland, and County Prosecutor Seymour, assisted by Special Prosecutor Arthur Van Epps, then began calling their witnesses to the stand.

The trial lasted ten days and proved something of an anticlimax. Prosecutor Seymour announced at the outset that he would not seek the death penalty for Martha, so the ensuing legal contest was a mere battle to decide whether Martha was insane or not.

Joseph Pritchard did not dispute the facts in the case. He could not challenge Martha's confession because the state did not introduce it as direct evidence, although Ethel Roshon was allowed to testify about the multiple oral confessions made to her by the talkative Martha. Nor could he challenge the results of his client's actions, which were made painfully evident when a still-paralyzed Fred Gienke Jr. limped into the courtroom, and when his sister, Marie, crippled for life, was brought from Elyria Hospital on a stretcher to give her tortured testimony in evidence. The effect of her sufferings on the jury can be imagined, as attorney Van Epps asked her what it felt like to ingest arsenic. "It nearly tore my heart out," Marie said. Martha couldn't even bear to look as another of her victims, cousin Herman Gienke, limped into the courtroom on a cane. And even as it was, the state's case against Martha was almost halfheartedly argued: the only charge legally brought against her was the murder of Lillian Gienke.

Defense attorney Pritchard had subpoenaed 139 witnesses, and 52 of them actually took the stand to paint a consistent portrait of Martha Wise as a congenital half-wit and pathetic village eccentric extraordinaire. Martha tried to keep up a steely front, but she broke down and cried when one of her former male friends testified that she had barked like a dog and foamed at the mouth. Indeed, it was obvious to all spectators that by the time her witnesses finished describing her as a murderer, arsonist, thief, hypochondriac, and moron, Martha Wise was a totally shattered woman. Attorney Pritchard's summation was a concise precis of their portrait of an almost incredibly sick and distressed woman: "Pyromania, plus kleptomania, plus epilepsy, plus spinal meningitis equals insanity." It is said that Pritchard wept aloud as he pleaded with the jury to find Martha insane.

The state's case was simple and to the point. Druggist Weber came forward to swear that Martha Wise had purchased 960 grains of arsenic from him, and Elyria city chemist Curtis testified that he found five of those grains in Lillian Gienke's corpse. And Seymour's summation rebutted the defense's picture of a bewildered idiot with an alternative portrait of a cunning killer:

> Slipping into the Gienke home when no one was watching, pinching arsenic into their water pail, returning twice to add further poison—that's not the manner in which insane people kill. She bought enough arsenic to kill every one in the Hardscrabble district where she lived. She came to the Gienkes when they all were ill and told their doctor she thought their illness was influenza. That's not the act of an insane woman.

Joseph Pritchard's most promising defense strategy eventually blew up in his face. He was aware that Edith Hasel, the wife of Martha's brother Fred, had lately been troubled by delusions that it was *she*—not Martha—who had poisoned the Gienke and Hasel families. Aware that Pritchard might put her on the stand in an effort to portray his client as harassed by similar hallucinations, Edith slashed her own throat with a paring knife on May 6, necessitating a delay in the trial while the Gienke-Hasel clan made preparations for yet another unexpected funeral. In fairness to Pritchard, though, it should be stated that Hardscrabble gossip had it that Edith had killed herself because of morbid guilt stemming from an old family feud with Martha. On May 13 the state rested its case with a plea for a guilty verdict with a recommendation of mercy. In his final words, Prosecutor Van Epps sounded the note of awestruck pity for Martha that was seemingly shared by everyone in the courtroom: "I, like every man, woman and child in the courtroom have nothing but the deepest respect for Mrs. Martha Wise. It is natural for us all to feel sorry for her in her predicament."

But, Van Epps continued, justice warranted a response sterner than sympathy, and it was telling that the defense had not had enough faith in its client to allow her to take the stand. The case went to the jury at 10:21 A.M. on May 13. The seven women (six of them housewives) and five men (three of them farmers) returned in little more than an hour later with a verdict of guilty of murder in the first degree—with a recommendation of mercy. The deliberations had taken only 58 minutes, and a second ballot had been taken only to confirm the unanimity of the first. On hearing her fate, Martha said, "I am satisfied. They did their duty," and left the courtroom with Mrs. Roshon. Subsequently sentenced to a life term at Marysville, she told Judge McClure, "Thank you for your kindness."

There remained some unfinished business yet in the case. Attorney Pritchard had been badgering Prosecutor Seymour with allegations that someone had helped persuade Martha to kill her family, and the Medina authorities now pursued that notion. Lester Wise, Martha's eldest son, came forward to testify that he had been with his mother in early November when he heard her talking with a man about poisons. When the couple became aware of Lester's presence, they told him to leave. But the matter had preyed on Lester's mind, and he finally broke down and told his uncle Paul Hasel about the conversation. The upshot was the arrest on May 16 of Walter Johns on a charge of first-degree murder.

The truth about the Wise-Johns relationship will never be known. But if hell hath no fury like a woman scorned, Martha Wise now certainly came forward to play the part of a scorned female. She was now as anxious to justify her behavior as she was to incriminate her alleged former sweetheart: "I would have carried this to the grave. I never intended to tell. But now that everybody is talking about it, I can't hold my tongue any longer. He never came to see me in the jail and at the trial he never looked at me, although he was there every day."

At the same time, Martha now was willing to let Satan off the hook: "Walter Johns told me to do it. It wasn't the devil—it was Walter Johns. They didn't want me to get married. He said to get Mother out of the way, and I did."

Confronted by a seemingly shocked Johns at the Medina jail on May 18, Martha elaborated further: "He made me do it! He put me up to it! He kept at me to do it! He told me I should get the arsenic and get rid of my mother, and then I'd be free and happy . . . I took my punishment. You scorned me. Now I tell."

Subsequently ensconced in a nearby jail cell, Johns could only repeat the same denial over and over: "She lies. I don't know anything about this."

The case against Johns collapsed almost as quickly as it had inflated. A father of five and a steady worker employed by a Cleveland firm, Johns had a good reputation, and there was little evidence to support Martha's claim that he had been her lover. There was no way the state would ever take the risk of putting Martha on the stand in a criminal trial, and the testimony of Lester Wise was considered insufficient to support a convincing case.

Inevitably, Johns was finally released for lack of evidence on May 21 and returned to his family in Cleveland, no doubt a chastened man. For her part, Martha calmed down and was soon taking an almost jocular, baiting tone in her jailhouse conversations with Ethel Roshon: "It's a good thing you caught me when you did. Why didn't you catch me sooner? I'm glad you did get me and I know I have to be punished."

The two-month Medina sensation slowly dissipated. Efforts went forward to place Martha's children—Lester, 14, Everett, 11, Gertrude, 10, and Kenneth, 7—in adoptive homes. Martha's estate was pitiful, consisting only of her eighteen-acre farm and a $1,800 bank account. And the latter asset would have been significantly diminished by court-assessed witness fees had not Judge McClure taken pity on Martha and reversed his own ruling.

The rest of Martha's life at Marysville Reformatory was a long anticlimax and probably happier than the years that had preceded

---

"It's a good thing you caught me when you did. Why didn't you catch me sooner?"

---

her incarceration there. Experts predicted that Martha would be crazier than a bedbug within eighteen months of her arrival, but she confounded them by making a good adjustment to the routine of prison life. Put in charge of the chickens and ducks, she developed a real liking for the animals. She was eventually celebrated as Marysville's best laundress ever. There were some bad moments for her, as she confessed to an interviewer in 1930: "I see ghosts. Every night they come and sit on the edge of my bed in their graveclothes. They point their fingers at me."

She was still relatively calm five years later when *Cleveland News* reporter Howard Beaufait called on her, although she wistfully confessed to him, "I want my freedom. I pray to God for it."

In a macabre miscarriage of judicial clemency and executive procedure, Martha almost got her wish—but only after she had ceased desiring it. Denied parole in 1946, 1951, and 1956, Martha finally had her first-degree murder conviction commuted to a second-degree charge by Governor Michael DiSalle on December 26, 1962. This had come about through the efforts of a Lutheran group interested in her situation, and the same group soon succeeded in securing Martha's parole, which was announced on January 30, 1962.

It was all a horrible mistake. Seemingly older than her 79 years and suffering multiple physical ills, Martha was in no shape or mood to take up whatever vestige of "normal life" would have been possible for this eternally unhappy woman, whose total assets were $570. As her children expressed no desire to take her in, the state had made arrangements to have Martha board, at a state-paid fee of eighty-five dollars per month, at a private nursing home run by a woman in Blanchester, Ohio. (It was alleged by cynical-minded parties that the state of Ohio's intention was to simply "dump" Martha Wise, owing to her rising medical expenses, but there is no solid evidence as to that charge.) The callous denouement came on February 2, when Parole Officer Helen Nicholson drove a weeping, fearful, and disoriented Martha Wise to her presumed new home. On their arrival, the woman who had agreed to board her came out to the car and abruptly announced the deal was off: "Oh, my God, no. She can't come into our house. I'm a food caterer. This is a very small town. People would talk. What do you think would happen to my business?"

Nicholson drove Martha to her own house, where they spent the night, and Martha returned home to Marysville for good the next day. Martha died at the age of 87 on June 28, 1971, at 4:40 P.M., and was buried at Marysville. †

The Incredible
Vanishing Killer
Cleveland's Nameless "Black Widow," 1922

Black Widow. The two words provoke several images, none of them cheery. Most people are aware, at least by repute, of the female black widow spider, the most lethal arachnid native to America, notorious for occasionally dining on her male partner after mating. Some, too, are familiar with the archetype of the female serial-killer spouse, memorably rendered in a number of films, most recently by Theresa Russell in *Black Widow* (1987). Few Clevelanders realize, however, that almost four score years ago their city riveted the attention of the nation for almost a fortnight with sensational news of a serial husband murderess. They should probably be readily forgiven for not knowing: the "Black Widow" story came out of nowhere, burned fiercely in the public mind for two weeks, and then, just as suddenly, disappeared forever.

Edward C. Stanton was probably the most interesting, aggressive, and effective prosecutor in Cuyahoga County history. During his tenure as county prosecutor (1921–29), Stanton sent eight men to the electric chair and earned a deserved reputation as a publicity-savvy, cunning, and relentless lawman. Propelled into office by his avidity in prosecuting the alleged May Day rioters of 1919, Stanton quickly gained the public's favor with his unexpected conviction of municipal judge William H. McGannon for perjury, for his dramatic pursuit and prosecution of those involved in the infamous murder-for-hire demise of Lakewood printer Dan

Kaber, and for the long-awaited guilty verdict that ended the chilling criminal career of Cleveland's Public Enemy No. 1, George "Jiggs" Losteiner. (All of these trials are covered in the pages of *They Died Crawling*, 1995.) Stanton's zealous efforts also sent three men to the electric chair for their role in the brutal payroll robbery and murder of businessmen Wilfred C. Sly and George K. Fanner on the last day of 1920. (The Sly-Fanner murders are chronicled in *The Maniac in the Bushes*, 1997.) It is likely, however, that none of Stanton's celebrated cases was more bizarre, more chilling and yet paradoxically inconclusive than the ephemeral "Black Widow" phenomenon of 1922.

The story erupted on May 1, when Stanton announced that a 37-year-old Cleveland woman was under investigation on suspicion of multiple murder. Held in the county jail on an unrelated larceny charge, she was suspected, Stanton told reporters, of having poisoned two of her four children and perhaps as many as three of her five husbands in order to collect on various substantial insurance policies. The next day's newspaper headlines left nothing to the reader's imagination. The *Plain Dealer* blared, SUSPECT WOMAN KILLED HUSBANDS FOR INSURANCE, while the *Press* shouted, BODY EXHUMED IN POISON PLOT. Interestingly, neither Stanton nor the newspapers revealed—then or ever—the identity of the accused distaff Borgia.

Stanton, as usual, was in deadly earnest. Early the very next day, county coroner A. P. Hammond showed up at staid Lake View Cemetery to oversee the exhumation of the suspected poisoner's fifth husband, a machinist who died in May 1921. After removing the corpse to the county morgue on Lakeside, Hammond's physicians quickly extracted the vital organs and turned them over to city chemists Harold J. Knapp and George Voerg for analysis. Pursuant to Stanton's orders, they were looking for signs of metallic poisons: Stanton publicly vowed a murder indictment should so little as even a tenth of a grain of arsenic show up in the cadaver.

Meanwhile, the background story luridly unfolded in the pages of Cleveland's three daily newspapers. And what a story it was. The woman, it seems, had originally come to Stanton's notice a year before, when she sought his aid in collecting on her recently deceased husband's insurance. Her sad story to Stanton was that her late spouse was a World War I veteran whose health had been fatally ruined by poison gas in the trenches of France and that the heartless United States government had refused to pay off on his $5,000 war risk insurance. Stanton couldn't help her, but he turned her over to the Cleveland offices of the American Red Cross.

This proved an imprudent move for the grieving widow. Not only did the Red Cross fail to expedite her insurance problem—it seems that Husband No. 5 had been remiss in his premium payments—but Red Cross official Esther Knowles became suspicious as she learned more and more details of the high-living widow's lifestyle. Several months later, in April 1922, the widow would be arrested on unrelated larceny charges, and Esther would renew their acquaintance when the Red Cross took over care of the woman's two teenage daughters. After talking with the daughters, Esther went to Stanton, and he went to the media on May 1.

Over the next week, the strange saga of the "Black Widow" unfolded in the newspapers. Her trail led back to Pittsburgh, where nearly 20 years before she had wed her first husband and produced two daughters. They did not last long: the heavily insured girls died after eating "poison tablets" in what was assumed to be an unfortunate household "accident." The Black Widow soon divorced and married Husband No. 2, a Pittsburgh druggist. That marriage produced another two daughters, born in 1907 and 1908 but, alas, not nuptial felicity: the couple divorced during World War I. Husband No. 2 survived his experience with the Black Widow, but he would later recall that she did seem to have "a mania for collecting insurance."

The pace of her marital adventures now picked up steam. She married Husband No. 3 in Pittsburgh, and she and her daughters moved with him to Cleveland, where he had found a splendid job opportunity. Indeed, it was so good that it even included a free $1,200 insurance policy as an employee benefit. Unfortunately, No. 3 didn't stick around to enjoy it, as he died very unexpectedly only a week after it took effect. Described as in "perfect health," he nonetheless fainted at work one afternoon and was dead within 24 hours. After cashing in his policy, the Black Widow took her family back to Pittsburgh.

There, she wasn't lonely for long. Within the year she had snared Husband No. 4, a wealthy man likewise described as being in "perfect health." Shortly after the nuptials were celebrated, however, he began to fail alarmingly and died in May 1919. The Black Widow had by now begun to attract the attention of local lawmen, and an autopsy was conducted on her late No. 4. Robert Brauh, the Allegheny County chief of detectives, was not surprised when the autopsy turned up traces of arsenic in the stomach. But nothing further was done, because Husband No. 4's physician testified that he had prescribed medicines for the deceased containing the potent metallic powder. The late No. 4 left $5,000 to his stricken widow, who now shifted her base of operations back to Cleveland.

As ever, the new widow did not pine long. Seven months after No. 4 shuffled off his mortal coil, she met Husband No. 5, an ex-soldier just returned after the Armistice. After a whirlwind courtship, which was by now her wont, the newlyweds settled down to marital bliss in an expensive flat on East 40th Street.

Probably more is known about the corpse of Husband No. 5 than about the living man, but it is fair to surmise that his brief married life was not a felicitous idyll. Unlike his immediate predecessor in the Black Widow's mercurial affections, Husband No. 5—known to inquiring newspaper readers only as "Joe"—was not a wealthy man, and his machinist's wages were not adequate to underwrite the lifestyle to which his spouse had become accustomed. Sad to say, very soon after tying the knot, his wife took to wistfully voicing her discontent aloud to her bosom friend, Jessie Burns. It began with subtle wishes, modest daydreaming hints like: "Wouldn't it be nice if Joe died? Think of the fun and parties we could have if Joe died." Within a few more weeks, as the 25-year-old Jessie later reminisced, the Black Widow's coy remarks became more direct and concrete: "I would like to get rid of him. I would like to give him arsenic."

But all was not Lady Bluebeard gloom-and-doom at the East

40th Street love nest. Various roomers who sublet premises from the couple would later testify that Joe's wife not only insisted on cooking all of his food herself but was shrewishly insistent that not a tasty morsel go to waste, often screaming profanely, "—— —— you, eat that food. I'm not going to cook for you and have you leave everything!"

Perhaps more ominously for Joe, there were increasing hints that his wife had not lost her "mania for collecting insurance." He complained to friends that she was constantly nagging him to join lodges that offered insurance benefits, and she attempted, unsuccessfully, in the weeks just before his death, to get his veteran's insurance raised from $5,000 to $10,000. And to friends to whom she owed money, she promised that she was just about to come into an "expected windfall" of $5,000—the exact amount of Joe's G. I. death benefit.

Although the Black Widow would later claim that Joe's abrupt demise stemmed from longstanding health problems caused by his gassing in France, neither War Department records nor the recollections of Joe's brothers supported her assertion. Indeed, Joe's fatal crisis must have come unexpectedly. The couple's only remaining roomer would recall leaving Joe in perfect health on a May day in 1921—and returning only three days later to find him laid out in a casket.

For her friends, who remarked that the new widow seemed rather jolly under the circumstances, the Black Widow had a ready explanation, encrusted with convincingly mundane detail: "Joe ate a hearty meal last night and drank six bottles of loganberry juice. At about 10 P.M., he went to take a hot bath. Eating, drinking and the hot water must have affected his heart, I guess, because when I got up the next morning I found him dead on the bathroom floor."

Perhaps custom by now had steeled Joe's widow to the familiar pain. But it is likely that she had already realized ready cash from his unexpected departure, as a mere 48 hours after her spouse's funeral she was throwing parties and spending her substance in what a disapproving Stanton later characterized as "riotous living."

Moving to a luxurious East Side apartment, the Black Widow decorated it with expensive furniture, splurged $1,400 on diamonds, and bought herself a new car.

Also pampering her aesthetic side, she acquired a piano and, along with it, a new beau. His name was L. P. Farrell, a widowed 53-year-old, and he met the Black Widow when he delivered the piano to her new digs. They had a few drinks and struck up a conversation that soon developed, he would ruefully recall, into her "making violent love" to him after she discovered he was a man of some property. Over the next few months she wooed Farrell assiduously. The result was a wedding date set for April 24, 1922.

That problematic union never came off. The Black Widow was arrested that very morning on multiple charges of larceny brought by her neighbors, who connected her with the recent disappearance of their cherished valuables. After she was taken to the county jail, her children were turned over to the Red Cross, leading ultimately to Esther Knowles's fateful conversation with Edward Stanton and the ensuing nationwide sensation.

The story peaked on May 5. That afternoon, Stanton announced that the autopsy of Husband No. 5 had turned up traces of both morphine and arsenic in the vital organs. Simultaneously, word came from Pittsburgh authorities that they had been trying to build a murder case against the Black Widow for three years. There was talk of impending murder indictments and the possibility of digging up husbands No. 3 and No. 4 and her two dead children from their graveyard homes. Yet another talkative friend came forward to tell police of an additional, now vanished child the accused had given birth to. A search of East Side drugstore records disclosed two purchases of arsenic in the spring of 1921 that bore her surname. The discovery of a cache of suggestive newspaper clippings at the Black Widow's flat further inflamed police and public suspicions. One was a report of a judge's charge to a jury, which seemed to have a lurid bearing on her present predicament: "Bear in mind that suspicion was an entirely different thing from legal proof, and it was in accordance with proofs and not suspicion that their verdict must be given."

A second item provided a juicy rationale for the much-married suspect's alleged modus operandi: "As to loving more than once, it certainly can be done. No love is so great that no one else can come along and take the place of the former love."

What more did the authorities need to hear?—except, perhaps, this remark from the widow, kindly recalled by one of her friends: "Wasn't Mrs. Kaber foolish to have her husband stabbed? Why didn't she give him ground glass instead of poison?"

Excited Clevelanders didn't know it, but the sensational story of the Black Widow was about to implode and disappear. Within five days it would vanish from the newspapers, Cuyahoga County coroner's files, and police records forever. Almost everything known after May 5 consists of negative facts: We know that the supposedly infamous Black Widow was never indicted, never brought to trial, and never publicly exonerated from the terrible charges made against her. What happened?

In the absence of documented fact, conjecture rules—but it's a pretty good guess that Stanton's impressive case against the Black Widow was not so impressive after all. After the initial stories about the finding of arsenic in the corpse of No. 5, word leaked out that the amount was laughably insignificant. In fact, city chemist George Voerg at first reported that he could find no arsenic at all. Ordered to take a more scrupulous look, he eventually found the sought-for poison—at a concentration of one per three million parts in the dead man's vital organs. This was considerably less that Edward Stanton's indictment threshold of a tenth of a grain, so the body of No. 5 was once again dug up from Lake View Cemetery on the morning of May 6. Apparently, nothing more was found.

Nothing has been heard of the Black Widow since May 10, 1922, when Cuyahoga County authorities promised reporters that there would soon be "startling developments" in the flagging investigation. It is not known where she went, and whether she recovered her two daughters—whom the Red Cross had placed in foster homes—when she was finally let out of jail. Whether she was just a crass, unlucky gold digger or a fiendishly heartless serial killer remains an open question. It is only fair, however, to let her have the last word, considering the unproved charges against her. When she was first arrested, reporters could hear the Black Widow screaming from Stanton's interrogation room, "It's a lie! It's a lie! I won't answer another of your questions!" Her final word on her situation was issued through her attorney, G. W. Gurney, on May 8:

> I am the unnamed woman in County Jail. Much has been said unfavorable to me. I know the public wishes to know the truth . . . I am here because of false charges. It has been intimated that I may have poisoned my husband. The desire of public officials to gain applause for themselves soon opened the floodgates. If any of my accusers had any evidence that I had poisoned my husband, they kept it to themselves for nearly a year . . .
>
> I did not murder my husband. He died of natural causes. I loved him dearly . . . I have had many offers to marry since his death and some of the offers have come from wealthy men. If my business is to marry and kill for the love of gold, is it not a bit strange that I should have allowed a year to pass without any further pursuit of my profession? . . . There is no evidence of my guilt, for I am innocent. The county officials are merely trying to weave a chain of circumstances in my life that might make it possible for me to have poisoned the man I loved. How much easier it would be for them to weave a dozen chains to prove my innocence. My innocence would not please them. Meanwhile I must suffer . . . My greatest solace is that there must be someone who will believe me innocent, at least until some real evidence of my guilt has been discovered.

Whatever her guilt or innocence, that "someone" was certainly not her one-time fiancé, piano mover L. P. Farrell. On learning of the charges against her, he replied, "When I read of her arrest, my blood turned cold. I am a lucky man to have escaped her . . . I had a feeling that I would meet a terrible end." †

The Wickedest Stepmother
The Mary Garrett Tragedy, 1887

Stepmother. There are few words in the English language—perhaps none denoting relationship—with more negative overtones. It's one of those unfortunate nouns that unfailingly arrives with the explicit or implied modifier of *wicked* attached. And, whether brought to unquiet mind by the indelible archetype of Hansel and Gretel's nemesis or the Disneyfied image of Snow White's witch/queen, the mere word itself—*stepmother*—seems to have the evil power to evoke shudder-inducing stereotypes and irrational judgments. The next time you hear the word, though, you'll likely consider the tragic tale of Mary Garrett and her unlucky stepdaughters. Maybe Mary Garrett was the wickedest stepmother in Medina County history. Maybe she was as bad as the judge, jury, and public thought she was—and she was probably pretty bad. But one

can't help concluding, after sifting the bizarre evidence, that Mary
Garrett came chillingly close to an Ohio hangman's noose really
because of that fatal word—*stepmother*—which clung to her like a
bad smell.

There seems little to be known about Mary Garrett until the
mid-1880s, when the then Mary Heffelfinger, a fortyish widow
from Tiffin, Ohio, met and married Alonzo Garrett, a 63-year-old
widower and farmer from Carlisle Township, Lorain County. The
daughter of a Kentucky slaveholder, the plump and prepossessing Mrs. Heffelfinger brought two daughters from her first marriage to her new union: Anna, 16, and Elnora, 11. Alonzo, for his
part, brought a grown son and daughter, neither living at home,
and, more important, two imbecile daughters. The elder daughter, Anna, 44, was at least several years older than her new stepmother, and her younger sister, Eva, was about 28. Although both
Anna and Eva had been institutionalized in state facilities for the
feeble-minded at various times, they were both living with Alonzo
at the time of his remarriage and had kept house for him for several years. Mary Garrett, astonishingly, would later claim that she
did not know of the existence of Anna and Eva until the day she
married Alonzo. If her assertion was true, she probably also didn't
know that Alonzo's first marriage, to his cousin, almost 50 years
before, had produced yet another imbecile daughter who died in
infancy. In any case, whatever she knew and whenever she knew
it, two years after Mary and Alonzo's marriage in September 1885,
the six members of the Garrett family moved to a 101-acre farm
in Spencer Center, Medina County, just a half-mile south of Dun-
lock's crossing on the Wheeling and Lake Erie Railroad.

The Garretts' neighbors in Spencer soon sensed that all was
not harmonious with the new family living on the old Kramer
homestead. Mrs. Garrett made it brutally clear even to strangers,
neighbors, and hired hands that she could not abide her adult stepdaughters, Anna and Eva. The two girls were constantly belittled
by their father's new wife: put to work at incessant manual chores
like chopping firewood, toting water, and digging garden plots;
prohibited from eating at the family dinner table; forced to live on

slops; and made to wear clothes that amounted to little more than filthy rags. Restricted to sleeping in a small 7-by-13-foot room, a converted kitchen at the back of the house, Anna and Eva were denied shoes even when at their gardening tasks, as evidenced by the ugly scars the metal shovel left on their feet. And when they weren't slaving away at menial household work, they were often forced to stay in their bedroom from 3 or 4 in the afternoon until 9 or 10 in the morning. More ominously, as the summer of 1887 waned toward autumn, Mary Garrett could more and more often be heard saying things like, "I would give a nice colt to anyone who would help me get rid of these girls," or even, after Alonzo apparently reneged on a promise to send the girls away, "If the old man goes back on me there will be another corpse in the home before night." As November arrived, tensions in the Garrett household had clearly achieved critical mass—and on the night of Tuesday, November 1, that mass exploded in terrible tragedy.

The Garrett mystery proper began at 11:30 P.M., when W. D. Dimock, the Garretts' nearest neighbor, on a farm about 1,000 feet away, was awakened by shouts. Peering out the window, he saw Anna and Elnora Heffelfinger. They screamed something about their house being on fire and disappeared into the night. Pulling his clothes on, Dimock awakened his adopted son, Harry Warner, and the hired man, Anthony Nicholas, and the three men rushed to the Garrett house. As they departed, Dimock's wife, Annie, was already ringing their heavy farm bell to spread the fire alarm throughout the Medina countryside.

The scene Dimock and his companions found at the Garrett place was a strange one. Although they could smell smoke, there was little visible flame coming from the one-and-a-half-story house, and Dimock and his companions were astonished to find most of the heavy furnishings and household goods—tables, chairs, a stove, a melodeon, a sewing machine, a new rug, and numerous other items—neatly piled on the front lawn. Indeed, while Alonzo ineffectually wept, raved, and wrung his hands, Mary and her daughter Anna were bringing yet more items out. Taking in the scene, Dimock shouted, "Where's the fire?" The elderly Alonzo was hysterical and could only reply, "Put out the fire! Put out the fire!" But Mary, altogether self-possessed, pointed to the small southeast bedroom at the rear of the house and said, "I am afraid that those girls are smothering in that room." Staring at Mary with her hands full of household items, Dimock sen-

---

Mrs. Garrett made it brutally clear even to strangers, neighbors, and hired hands that she could not abide her adult stepdaughters, Anna and Eva.

---

sibly replied, "My God, save the girls and let the house go to the devil." Then, dashing through the front door, Dimock got to the rear bedroom and pounded frantically on the door. Finding that it was locked from the inside, he tried to kick it in. His first kick smashed the lower panels, and his second knocked the door right off its hinges. Running inside, he quickly emerged with the lifeless body of Anna Garrett. Seconds later, Anthony Nicholas brought Eva's corpse out, and the two bodies were laid on the grass outside. The fire, such as it was, was soon extinguished with a surprisingly small amount of water.

There were many oddities to that horrific midnight scene at the Garrett house, and everyone present seems to have remembered them vividly at the eventual trial. One peculiarity was the odd farrago of items on the lawn, virtually all the heavy furniture and most prized belongings of the Garrett household. Another odd thing was the fatal fire room itself: the blaze had burned very little of the walls or floor. More suspiciously, there appeared to be a quantity of kerosene spilt on one corner of the floor and a great mass of rubbish strewn about the room: leaves, rags, lint, newspaper, broken boards, dirt, and a pile of partially burnt paper.

The story that Mary Garrett told her neighbors that night was the story her lawyers repeated in court and the same story she stuck to for the rest of her life. She claimed she had been awakened about 11:30 P.M. by a noise coming from the barn. Thinking it was the mischief of a fractious horse, she dressed herself and went out to investigate. Finding nothing amiss at the barn, she decided to return by way of the back garden fence to check on some clothes left there on a clothesline. (In November?) It was then that she smelled and saw smoke coming from the window of Anna and Eva's back bedroom. She pounded on the window, but it was locked. Getting no response, Mary rushed inside the front door of the house, only to find the inner back bedroom door likewise locked. Rousing Alonzo and her own daughters, she sent Anna to spread the alarm, and she and Alonzo began throwing small buckets of water at the outside bedroom wall. To anyone who asked why she had not persisted in trying to save her trapped stepdaughters, she insisted that she thought they had already escaped from the burning bedroom.

Neither her neighbors nor the Medina County authorities liked Mary Garrett's story very much. The evidence of flammable litter and kerosene in the bedroom strongly suggested arson, and the presence of the household valuables on the lawn—apparently placed there before the fire started—suggested criminal premeditation.

Only one more piece of evidence was needed to put Mary Garrett in a murderer's cell, and it came when the bodies of the two dead girls were closely examined by Mr. Dimock and B. F. Lewis, another Garrett neighbor who had arrived to put out the fire. Both stepdaughters had died of suffocation, specifically carbon monoxide inhalation, and Anna's lower body was badly scalded, so much so that the burned skin came away at a touch. In addition, Anna had a terrible bruise on her forehead and another one on her side. Most shocking, however, was the appearance of her throat: Clearly visible around her neck were the finger marks of two hands, indicating that she had been strangled before the fire started. Before daylight on November 2, Lewis and Dimock telegraphed Justice Lyman Daugherty in Medina and requested that he come to hold an inquest into the suspicious deaths. It began at 10 A.M. the same day with six jurymen, two doctors, a crowd of witnesses, and Justice Daugherty presiding. At its conclusion 24 hours later, Mary Garrett was arrested on charges of arson and murder.

After an official, painstaking postmortem examination of the girls on Thursday afternoon and a brief funeral service held for them at the house on Friday morning, November 4, the girls' remains were taken back to La Porte, Ohio, for burial in the Garrett family plot. Meanwhile, at the jammed Spencer Town Hall, Mary Garrett, to the audible pleasure of the "suffocating" crowd, was arraigned on counts of first-degree murder and arson and ordered away to the county jail in Medina. Her request for bail was abruptly brushed aside by Justice Daugherty, who replied with this bit of rural folk wisdom to a *Cleveland Press* reporter's query: "This affordavit sez murder in the first degree and I ain't goin to go agin' it. The appropriate court can tend to the bail matter." Mary was spirited out of the courtroom immediately, in part because of rumors that a lynching would be attempted by the unruly, partisan crowd. Her dignified composure broke only once, as she realized, while leaving the courtroom, that her husband, Alonzo, shared the popular conviction that she was guilty. Laying her head on his shoulder, she murmured, "Did you agree to this, husband?" Receiving no answer, she entered a plea of "not guilty" and was led away. To a *Cleveland Press* reporter who inquired as to his thoughts on his wife's guilt, Alonzo said, "Oh, I can't say, I can't say. But I have my opinions." In a move perhaps more eloquent, Alonzo advertised his farm and goods for sale a few days later. Meanwhile, Spencer residents were left to reflect and to recover from the unprecedented crowds and attention the Garrett tragedy had brought to their modest town. Justice Daugherty probably spoke for all with his characteristically folksy comment, "Well, that's the blamedest, everlastin'est, most amazin' crowd I ever see. Why, boys, I'll bet a dollar there were more'n 400 people in that little room. Beats all, don't it?"

After several weeks of delay and maneuvering, Mary's trial was scheduled for the May term of 1888. By then she had secured seemingly astute legal representation in the persons of E. G. Johnson of Elyria (already famous throughout Ohio for his 1887 defense of "Blinky" Morgan), J. H. Dickson of Wellington, and the firm of

Bostwick & Barnard of Medina. A further delay, however, became unavoidable when it was discovered that the accused murderess was in a "delicate condition." Delivered of a healthy baby boy in July, the new mother was sufficiently recovered to allow for the opening of her trial on Monday, September 17, 1888. Opposing her defense team were prosecutors J. W. Seymour, John C. Hale, and Frank Health, with Judge G. W. Lewis presiding.

The state's case against Mary Garrett was simple and directly presented, with a large cast of talkative supporting players. A parade of eyewitnesses described the strange goings-on at the Garrett home on the night of November 1, with particular emphasis on the localized scope of the fire, the presence of the household goods on the lawn, and Mrs. Garrett's eerily calm demeanor throughout the excitement. More witnesses, many of them neighbors and friends of the family, testified to Mary's hatred and ill treatment of her stepdaughters from the moment they came into her life and to the many occasions on which she had expressed a fervent desire to be rid of them. Various witnesses detailed the repeated attempts she had made over the two-year period of her marriage to have divers state, county, and private charitable institutions take the girls off her hands. One such scheme involved a veritable abduction of the witless girls to the county poorhouse during the previous summer while their father was away. Another was Mary's mendacious attempt to place Anna at the Home of the Good Shepherd in Cleveland (later the temporary abode of "Lakewood's Lady Borgia," Eva Kaber, during her erring adolescent years) on the premise that Anna, then in her forties, was a "fallen" girl likely to again go astray. It was an awful picture of perverted maternal treatment and neglect painted by the prosecutors. The defense did little to counter it, other than call a couple of witnesses to deny that they had personally seen any maltreatment.

The cumulative and disturbing details of Mary's systematic cruelty to Eva and Anna no doubt told heavily with the jury. But, after all, the state's charge was not that Mary Garrett was a bad stepmother but that she had maliciously and with premeditation committed "arson, strangulation, scalding, and suffocation" as a means of ridding herself of the girls. The evidence on record, however, shows that the state did a lousy job of proving that any of those acts occurred, much less presenting any direct evidence that Mary Garrett planned and perpetrated them. The jury, for example, never even visited the scene of the alleged murder. If they had, they might have laid more emphasis on the fact that the death-room door and windows could be locked only from the inside. How could Mary Garrett have set the fire and then escaped through the door or window? The prosecution never addressed the issue, relying on Mary's heavily documented and unspeakable conduct toward the girls to carry its case forward.

The evidence of the dead girls' corpses, moreover, added little strength to the state's case, despite an exhumation and second autopsy performed in December 1887. As the defense claimed, the scalding below Anna's hips was likely caused by the action of the fire on the water that Alonzo and Mary were throwing at the blaze. Anna's two bruises were inconclusive as to their origin, and as for the finger marks on her throat (as Mary's attorneys attempted to prove with expert testimony by Dr. E. G. Hard), they could well have been the marks of Anna's own hands, the result of her death struggle as she frantically fought to get air into her lungs. The fire itself, attorney Johnson argued, was started by the girls themselves, who had locked the door and window in order to play with matches unobserved. Although they were not allowed to have a lamp in their room, he reasoned, they must have smuggled in some kerosene without the knowledge of their stepmother. The leaves, which had done much to feed the fire, were explained as Anna and Eva's attempt to make a bed for their cat.

There was that suspicious matter of the furniture on the lawn, which the trial testimony did little to explain. Some of the witnesses claimed that it had been removed to the lawn prior to the fire to facilitate housecleaning; others claimed that Mary and her children spent most of their time on that fatal night moving out more furniture rather than trying to save Anna and Eva. Even if the latter was the case, it would support only a charge of criminal indifference, rather than premeditated murder.

The state rested on Wednesday, September 26, and Judge Lewis soberly and carefully charged the jury of 12 men, mostly farmers. Lewis properly dwelt at length on the question of what constituted premeditation and on the need to afford Mrs. Garrett "the benefit of every reasonable doubt." He was also appropriately cautionary

---

Witnesses claimed that Mary spent most of that fatal night moving furniture rather than trying to save Anna and Eva.

---

about the enormous volume and value of the hearsay testimony that had done superb service in the blackening of Mary Garrett's character during the trial: "no class of testimony is more unreliable, and a more frequent cause of error in courts of justice than the narration of conversations real or pretended."

Mary's jury retired at 3 P.M. the same day and returned after only five hours with a verdict of guilty on both the murder and arson counts. A week later, on October 4, Judge Lewis sentenced Mary to death by hanging. As ever, Mary maintained her remarkable composure through both her verdict and sentencing ordeals and during her subsequent journey to the Ohio Penitentiary in Columbus to await execution. In the privacy of her cell there, however, she unburdened herself by letter to her estranged husband:

> God only knows I am clear. I ain't afraid to die. I pity my family, poor husband lonely and no one to care as I did. I want him to look for the children . . . I am going to meet those I did not abuse . . . I can stand all. God is my strength, help in all. I glory in his name. I am wronged here. I am rewarded in heaven, I feel it.

Several weeks later, Alonzo Garrett filed for divorce.

The date set for Mary's execution was January 24, 1889, but

no one ever expected her to actually hang. Only one woman had ever been executed by the state of Ohio, so no one was surprised when Governor Joseph Foraker commuted her sentence to life imprisonment in late January. Typically, because it was a capital case involving a woman, the petition for executive clemency was signed by Judge Lewis, the prosecuting attorneys, and all 12 of her jurors. By this time Mary had settled pretty well into the rhythms of life on death row, the same special annex in the Ohio Penitentiary where Blinky Morgan had spent his final days, and she was so taken with Warden E. G. Coffin that she named her baby boy, christened Warden Garrett, after him. (This despite the fact that Coffin was quoted in print characterizing Mary as "a dangerous and wicked woman," and expressing his opinion that "she was no doubt guilty.") Following the commutation of her sentence, Mary was removed to the female prison wing and began her fight to win freedom and clear her name. Her son, Warden, was returned to his father's custody in Medina County in January 1890, after more than a year of life in prison with his mother.

Mary's "life imprisonment" lasted but 12 years. After her lawyers' motion for a new trial was denied by the circuit court, she and her few supporters began a vigorous campaign to obtain an executive pardon. Their ranks gradually swelled, and by 1895 even ex-warden Coffin was working on behalf of Mary Garrett's release. She won that release in December 1899, when the governor of Ohio granted her a pardon as a Christmas present, and she returned to a life of obscurity and, one hopes, happiness.

So, the question remains: Did Mary Garrett do the deed—did she deliberately set her stepdaughters' bedroom on fire as a means of getting rid of the unwanted girls—or did she not? Well, there's no question that, whatever the varying veracity of the many gossipy witnesses at her trial, Mary Garrett never would have been named Medina's Mother of the Year. Beyond the shadow of a reasonable or unreasonable doubt, she treated her stepdaughters worse than animals, greatly assisted and enabled, it should be mentioned, by the doormat complicity of her doddering mate, Alonzo. But it's very improbable that she murdered them with malice aforethought. Harriet L. Adams of Cleveland, who worked mightily in the successful campaign to free Mrs. Garrett, put the case for her innocence persuasively in a letter to the *Cleveland Leader* published just after Mary's release from prison. Commenting on the circumstances of the fire, Adams noted:

> As the room was small and the one door and one window closely fastened, there was not sufficient air for the fire to burn readily, but it finally charred a space about three feet long and one and a half feet wide on the floor and burned through the baseboard, thus getting between the walls and burning a few small holes in the siding outside. That was the entire extent of the fire . . . To be brief, no human agency could have set this fire but the girls themselves. The door was securely fastened from within by sliding bolt and the window by shutters with drop catches on the inside . . . I am confident, from an interview with the foreman of the jury in the case, that had the defendant's counsel taken the jury to the scene of the supposed murder there never would have been a conviction.

Two minor points are worth mentioning before bidding adieu to the story of Medina's worst stepmother. The first is that we don't know just how "feeble-minded" or retarded Anna and Eva Garrett really were. Mary herself termed them impossibly "idiotic" and "imbecile" and claimed they were incorrigible, untrainable, and virtually unhousebroken. Her martyred comment to a *Cleveland Leader* and *Herald* reporter was, "God alone knows what a trial those girls were to me, with their terrible tempers and vicious habits. Language cannot describe it." The testimony of the Garrett neighbors at Mary's trial, however, consistently portrayed the unfortunate girls as "slow," "stammering," and "fluttering" but tractable and of mild disposition. The other matter is the reason Mary Garrett claimed she barred the girls from the family dinner table: Like many superstitious people of her time, the pregnant Mary believed that her coming child might turn out "ugly" if its mother were continually exposed to the faces of her "ugly" stepdaughters while in her delicate condition. But whatever the true nature of the doomed girls or the complexity of Mary Garrett's maternal motives, it is hard to protest the fate that brought her 12 years behind bars after everything she did to her suffering stepdaughters. She may not have been an actual murderess, but it seems she got what was coming to her anyway. †

"Step aside, Daddy, and I'll fill him full of lead!"

The Insouciant Mabel Champion, 1922

We don't even know who she really was. History knows her as Mabel Champion—but that name is just a convenience for chroniclers and criminologists; how else to treat the tale of a female who changed the details of her biography and antecedents as often and capriciously as some women change their earrings? Her husband, Ausley—if he was her husband, and if his name was really Ausley Champion—sometimes called her Mabel but also "Mary," "Inez," "Clara," "Teddy," and "May." Cleveland's newspapers called her "the Sphinx." County Prosecutor Edward Stanton called her a cold-blooded, "cunning, clever" murderess. Alternatively, Walter D. Meals, her defense attorney, called Mabel a "perfectly ladylike little girl" and pleaded that she was not only innocent of murder but had "never been guilty of any vices or even taken a drink of liquor." But call her what you will: Mabel Champion made quite an impression on Jazz-Age Clevelanders by the time her personal comet had appeared, blazed, and faded before the eyes of those who followed her remarkable, daring adventures.

Mabel's improbable saga began on the night of July 26, 1922, when a flashy, late-model beige Cadillac pulled up to the curb in front of Downing's Restaurant at 1798 Euclid Avenue. It was almost midnight, and Playhouse Square was thronged with hundreds of play- and movie-goers exiting from the newly constructed and luxurious theaters across the street. Shocking to say, it was also crowded with lawbreakers—lawbreakers who flaunted their illegal acts before the indifferent eyes of blasé Cleveland policemen. After only two-and-a-half years, Prohibition was already a dead letter in the Forest City, and by all accounts Playhouse Square's sidewalks and restaurants that night were crowded with Clevelanders tossing down drinks as fast as they could be poured. And among them were the people in the Cadillac: driver Ausley Champion, his 22-year-old wife, Mabel, and their guests for the evening, Mr. and Mrs. Guy Williams.

It's a good guess that Ausley, at least, was already rather drunk when he brought the Cadillac to the curb. Pausing for a few moments, he pulled out a large bottle of hooch and shared it with the others in the car before reaching for the door handle. As he did so, he was accosted by a man named Thomas Albert O'Connell. Just minutes before, O'Connell, a 29-year-old carnival promoter known to his friends as "Eddie," had been seen drinking pure alcohol in Steiner's Cafe a few doors away. But he was still thirsty, it seems, and, spying the bottle in Ausley's hand, lurched up to the Cadillac and belligerently demanded a drink. There were some words between Ausley and O'Connell, but Ausley grudgingly handed over the bottle; O'Connell took a long pull and returned it. Ausley, Mabel, and Mr. and Mrs. Williams went into Downing's Restaurant, and that seemed the end of this sour, if minor, encounter.

It wasn't. Shortly after Downing's night manager, William

Conklin, seated Ausley's party, O'Connell came through the front door. Muttering "I'm going to get a drink from that man," he pushed his way through the crowded restaurant to the Champion party. Slamming his fist down on the table so hard that flatware was knocked to the floor, he confronted Ausley and demanded another drink. Ausley refused, but when O'Connell started threatening him, Mabel told Ausley to let him have one for the sake of peace. So Ausley fished out his bottle, and O'Connell poured a stiff one and drained it down. Unsurprisingly, O'Connell now demanded yet another drink, and Ausley again refused. This time he surely meant it, but what happened next is a subject of unsettled debate. Ausley would forever after assert that the ensuing violence was triggered by O'Connell making unchivalrous slurs about women in general and Mabel in particular, shouting that the women at the table—and all women, for that matter—were "whores." Other voices, however, would later be heard to insist that the fight was the inevitable climax to a smoldering feud between Ausley and O'Connell that stretched back at least several days and through a trail of inebriated nights together in downtown Cleveland speakeasies. It's possible that both versions are true: Ausley was no ascetic pacifist, and O'Connell, although an honorable World War I veteran and a graduate of Yale University, was known for relinquishing his normally charming disposition for a more ugly, foul-mouthed persona when in his cups. As his widow put it later, "Tom was my dear, big boy—his only fault was drink."

Up to this point, the Champion party resembled most of the other groups seated in Downing's that night: two noisy couples huddled over a table spread with bottles, glasses, and mix, wearing flashy clothes and too much jewelry (Mabel herself was wearing eight large diamond rings that night). But things changed fast after Ausley reacted to O'Connell's hot words. Ausley slapped O'Connell, and then O'Connell slugged him hard, knocking him to the floor. As Ausley got to his feet, Mabel jumped up and ran toward Ausley's topcoat, which was hanging on a wall hook. Springing to his side, she pulled out an enormous .38 caliber Colt revolver and shouted at her woozy husband, "Step aside, Daddy, and I'll fill him full of lead!" At these words, O'Connell, who had been lurching forward toward the couple, staggered back, slurring, "You bitch! You're not going to shoot!"

Tom O'Connell was wrong. Maybe it was the drink, maybe it was the excitement. Maybe it was even, as Mabel later claimed, that she feared for her life as the 5'10" O'Connell loomed over 5'3" Mabel. Or maybe it was just Ausley, who helpfully encouraged Mabel by screaming, "Shoot the bastard, Mabel!" Whatever it was, shoot Mabel did, missing with her first bullet but then stunning O'Connell with a slug that stopped him in his tracks. Moaning, "Oh boy, I'm shot! Don't shoot again!" he fell to the floor. But Mabel didn't stop. Walking up to the helpless O'Connell, she blasted him twice more at point-blank range, while her brave husband smashed the mortally wounded carnival promoter with a convenient chair. By now, the crowd in Downing's was in full panic mode, screaming and running for the exits as the patrons became aware of the lethal gunplay in the rear. Mabel and Ausley tried to flee out the door nearest to their table, only to find that it was a closet. Wheeling around, they ran toward the front door, where their Cadillac still sat at the curb. As they passed William Conklin, Mabel nonchalantly remarked, "Never mind the police, we're going now."

So was Thomas "Eddie" O'Connell, if not in the same direction. His liver, stomach, lungs, and virtually all of his other vital organs punctured, he lay bleeding heavily on the restaurant floor until Joseph Steffans, a compassionate taxi driver, took him to Huron Road Hospital. He was already in a fatal coma when he arrived there 15 minutes after the shooting, and the doctors just shook their heads. Meanwhile, Mabel and Ausley had failed to make their getaway. As Ausley struggled with his Cadillac's balky gearshift, Eyner Buhl, a Cleveland patrolman drawn from his East 17th beat by the sound of gunfire, jumped up on the running board, reached through the driver's window, and pulled the ignition key from in front of the startled Ausley. Searching for the suspected gun, the persistent Buhl eventually found the still-warm weapon in its hiding place underneath Mabel's dress and between her legs. Ausley was taken off to jail, and Mabel was rushed to Huron Road Hospital.

The idea was to have the dying O'Connell identify his shooter, but his comatose condition merely precipitated a comic scene.

Her husband helpfully encouraged her by screaming, "Shoot the bastard, Mabel!"

Walking up to the unconscious O'Connell, Mabel leaned down to his face and then turned to Sergeant Charles Snyder and said, "Didn't you hear him say I didn't shoot him?"

"No," replied the skeptical Snyder, "did you?"

"You bet I did, old dear," riposted Mabel. "He said I didn't shoot him." Minutes later, O'Connell died without saying a word, and Mabel was removed to face the music at the county jail.

The police-beat reporters of Cleveland's three daily newspapers leaped on Mabel Champion like famished panthers on fresh meat. The year 1920 had been a great one for tabloid-style Cleveland crime stories, highlighted by the screaming headlines of the McGannon murder trials and gangster "Jiggs" Losteiner's Waterloo at the "Battle of Bedford" shootout. Nor was 1921 a disappointment when it came to sensationalism, as it featured the long-sought convictions of both Judge McGannon and Eva Kaber. But 1922 had been a bust so far, a relative journalistic drought extended by the abrupt collapse of the ephemeral "Black Widow" investigation only two months before. Mabel was manna to starving journalists, and they gave the story all the push avid readers expected from the best practitioners of the *Front Page* journalism of the age.

It didn't even matter that Mabel, at least initially, wouldn't talk to them or, for that matter, to the Cleveland police. Sizing up her stony silence, reporters immediately dubbed her "the Sphinx" and embroidered their pulpy columns with breathless conjectures about her identity and fulsome descriptions of her appearance and personality. Spitting rhetorical questions like hot lead, a *Cleveland News* writer introduced Clevelanders to Mabel and Ausley Champion this way: "Who is the prepossessing young woman held at detective headquarters on the claim of eyewitnesses that she fired the three shots that slew [Thomas A. O'Connell] in a downtown restaurant in the theater district early Wednesday? Who is the young man, possessor of a handsomely appointed new Cadillac automobile bearing a Texas license, who was with the mystery woman when the fatal shots were fired and who claims an identity that is refuted from Kansas City by a man who declares he is the individual the man in Cleveland claims to be?"

Considering the confusion deliberately wrought by Mabel and Ausley, even managing to articulate these unanswered questions was a journalistic achievement. From the beginning, Mabel and Ausley lied about themselves, their past, and their relationship to each other. At first they denied they were married; then they insisted on it, after police found a marriage license dated 1917 in their room at the downtown Hotel Huron. Addressed by Ausley as "May," "Clara," and "Mabel," Mabel coyly refused to admit to any name for weeks after she was arrested for O'Connell's murder. All she would say was that she was innocent, she had no idea who had shot O'Connell, and that she didn't care what the police thought. As she laughingly told Captain George Matowitz, "Go ahead and charge me with murder. I don't care. I've got tuberculosis and I'll be dead in a little while, anyway." Ausley, likewise, spoke little and only to the purpose of confusing the cops, insisting at first that he was "Cliff Bennett," a shoe salesman from Kansas City, an imposture that disintegrated when the real Cliff Bennett of Kansas City got in touch with Cleveland police. When confronted with the details of his past police record, Ausley eventually confirmed his identity but admitted only that he "played cards for a living" before clamming up for good. All of which left reporters with little more to do than inflate the image of Mabel-as-Sphinx and meditate at length on her personal attractions, her enigmatic smiles, her stylish wardrobe, and her soft-spoken, if laconic, charm.

For all their hard work in the weeks after O'Connell's murder, the Cleveland police had little more to go on than the glamorous myths adumbrated by the newspapers. They managed to trace Mabel and Ausley back to Texas, where they had both been arrested on divers charges—the 27-year-old Ausley had served a two-year term in the Lone Star State's penitentiary for larceny before escaping—and then to Indianapolis, where Mabel was wanted for jumping bail on a larceny charge in the spring of 1922. But who they really were, where they came from, and what their actual relationship to each other was remained unknown to all. Indicted on a first-degree-murder charge by a grand jury (headed by, of all people, Raymond Moley, later famed as the kingpin of President Franklin D. Roosevelt's "Brain Trust"), Mabel was held without bail in the Cuyahoga County jail, while the luckier Ausley posted $5,000 bond on a charge of assault with attempt to kill, the result of his attentions to O'Connell with the restaurant chair. As he left Mabel at her cell door, he said, "Don't worry, I'll send you roses." And for once in his life, Ausley was as good as his word, sending elaborate nosegays of flowers and boxes of candy to Mabel every day.

Mabel worked hard to ingratiate herself with everyone as the three months before her trial plodded by. Pitching in to care for the sick girls in the county jail, she exuded kindly warmth and enticing femininity to all she encountered. Well, almost all; when confronted with O'Connell's grieving widow, she simply said, "Don't talk to me—I don't want to talk about it." But to all others she turned on the charm, beginning with Judge Selzer on the day after her arrest. Brought in for her arraignment, a *Press* reporter noted, "she walked up to the bench, smiled at the judge, and began chatting with him as if they were old friends." When he asked her why she kept a four-inch stiletto in her handbag, Mabel batted her eyes, smiled sweetly, and demurely purred, "Oh, I peel peaches with that." Kate Carter, sob-sister writer in residence at the *Press*, captured Mabel's carefully cultivated appeal in a profile of Mabel published on August 1:

A slip of a girl in a dark blue gingham dress, busily making a bed with the expertness of a hospital nurse. An imperturbable, smiling girl, with glossy black hair and an attractive face. Dressed with care, wearing chiffon stockings and gay satin slippers. Tucking gladiolas into a vase by her bedside, while "snappy" pictures of boats and bathing girls ornamented the walls. That may describe Mrs. Mabel Champion, "sphinx woman" . . . Mrs. Champion, who police say fired three shots into [O'Connell's] body from her husband's heavy revolver, was very polite, with an aroma of French perfume adding to the air of elusiveness which she possesses. "I really don't want to talk about it," she said, half-laughing as she picked up a box of expensive face powder. But I asked her how she passed the time in jail. "Nursing, mostly," she answered cheerfully. "Some of the girls have been ill. They seem to like to have me around. I read a little, but I don't write letters or sew anymore. I like best just sitting by myself and thinking."

Mabel's much-anticipated trial finally opened on October 23, 1922, after repeated delays caused by difficulties in securing eyewitnesses to the shooting. It was held before Judge Maurice Bernon, and Mabel was vigorously prosecuted on a first-degree murder charge by County Prosecutor Edward Stanton and Assistant Prosecutor James T. Cassidy. Mabel, attired in gowns custom-made for her trial, was defended by attorney Walter D. Meals before a courtroom packed daily with the "morbidly curious." History records that she was "clad in the latest creations of fashion in black that brought out all the attractions of her twenty-two years." The morbidly curious—mainly women and a surprising number of female teenagers—were not disappointed. Even before jury selection ended, Ausley Champion disappeared, jumping bail and leaving Mabel to fight for her life alone. Commenting on the abrupt cessation of the flood of flowers and candy to her cell, Mabel moistly lamented to reporters, "I guess I'm going to be alone. He certainly didn't do the right thing by me." Nor, as far as she was concerned, did Cuyahoga County prosecutor Edward Stanton, who proceeded to weave an airtight case around her. Practically everyone who had been in Downing's Restaurant on the fatal night took the stand, with various degrees of willingness—and offered their damning recollections of the fight between O'Connell and Ausley and how it had ended with the spectacle of Mabel blasting away with Ausley's .38 at point-blank range. Mabel's worst day came on Friday, October 27, when Joseph Shimendle took the stand. It was Shimendle who recollected Mabel's immortal assurance to Ausley ("Step aside, Daddy, and I'll fill him full of lead!"). Shimendle also unhelpfully contradicted the other eyewitnesses by remembering that Mabel had retrieved the revolver from inside her blouse, rather than from Ausley's topcoat. The state closed its case with a re-creation of the ludicrous scene at Huron Road Hospital and Mabel's farcical, if desperate, insistence that the expiring O'Connell had exonerated her. Summing up, Stanton put the state's charge against Mabel in stark, simple terms: "Cunning, clever Mabel shot O'Connell from the hip, from under her husband's coat. Mabel is from Texas, and in Texas they shoot from the hip."

Meals put up a terrific fight for his beleaguered client. His first stratagem in Mabel's defense was to blacken the character of the deceased, painting a sordid portrait of O'Connell as a brutish, drunken thug, small-time hoodlum, and "Paris Apache of the worst type." (O'Connell's actual criminal career amounted to a few arrests for assault.) Although Meals insisted that Mabel had not fired the fatal shots—he never did indicate who might have alternatively pulled the trigger—his argument was that O'Connell had brought about his own death, ingesting up to a gallon of booze that July night and digging "by his own hands the pit into which he fell." Rather than killing O'Connell, Meals pleaded, Mabel had been "playing the part of peacemaker" at Downing's Restaurant, and her only crime had been merely "protecting herself from the lunges of a drunken, infuriated villain." "Wherever he has gone," Meals thundered against the dead O'Connell, "his respect for womanhood will be increased."

As the first week of the trial came to a close, things weren't going well for Mabel. The increasing number of tears she shed in the courtroom and the annoyed faces she made at Stanton were a good index of just how badly her case was evolving. At least six eyewitnesses had her plugging O'Connell, and a clutch of police experts testified that although O'Connell had been shot at close range, it wasn't close enough to support Mabel's claim that he

---

Asked why she kept a four-inch stiletto in her handbag, Mabel demurely purred, "Oh, I peel peaches with that."

---

was physically attacking her. So Mabel, perhaps with the advice of Meals, made two changes in her defense. One was to soften her image further by playing on public sympathy for her lonely plight, while at the same time inventing a virtuous motive for her previous stonewalling about her identity and the events of the night of July 26. Speaking to a *Press* trial reporter, she unbosomed her idealistic impulses:

> I am fighting my battle alone for only one reason. Back in the west, in a small town far enough from the big cities to prevent them from gaining access to the news of the day, are an old man and an old woman. Both are gray. Both are upright and devout. It would break their hearts if they knew that a daughter of theirs was occupying a jail cell, awaiting the decision that may mean life or death. One is my father, the other my mother . . . It is true they could give me great assistance. But in obtaining that assistance I would give them a shock that might end fatally for one or both. So I have determined to keep this situation from them.

One hopes that Mabel's parents didn't read the next day's *Cleveland Press*, for it reported the other change in her strategy, which was to admit that she shot O'Connell. She hadn't meant to do it, of course, she tearfully testified, but the big drunken lug had attacked her, and what was a poor, frail helpless girl to do? She'd only retrieved the gun from Ausley's coat to scare O'Connell, and the first shot had come as they struggled for the gun. It had gone into the restaurant floor, and her second and third shots (she denied knowledge of a fourth) were "accidental," occurring without her being conscious of pulling the trigger. And whatever the lying testimony of the crowd at Huron Road Hospital, Mabel insisted, the dying O'Connell had exonerated her in front of several policemen and doctors.

The final arguments recapitulated the highlights of the two-week trial. Stanton argued that Mabel was a brazen, deliberate murderess and demanded death for her so that Cleveland might be safe from further episodes of drunken downtown violence: "Is this Cleveland? Or is it Paris, where Apaches of the underworld shoot men down in cold blood?" And Meals reiterated his portrait of Mabel as a helpless, simpering Southern belle, citing her "ladylike" behavior in jail and in the courtroom. Mocking Stanton's argument that she might have taken the gun out of her blouse instead of Ausley's coat, Meals jeered, "The prosecution would have you believe she drew this huge gun out of her bosom. If it had been a Springfield rifle, they would have had her drawing it out of her stocking."

The case went to the jury at 3:55 on Wednesday, November 1. After 28 hours of deliberation and eight ballots, the seven women and five men returned the next evening at 7:55 with a verdict of manslaughter. When Judge Bernon asked Mabel if she had anything to say, Mabel could only sob, "No sir, I don't believe so—except I don't believe—I'm—guilty." Immediately after that, Bernon sentenced Mabel to a 20-year term in Marysville Reformatory, the minimum term for manslaughter under a recently passed Ohio law. The jury's decision made Mabel the youngest woman in Cuyahoga County history to be convicted on a murder rap. But it could have been worse: six of the seven women on the jury had voted for first-degree murder on seven out of the eight ballots.

Bernon's opinion was that Mabel's jury had been "kind and merciful," considering the evidence against her. That wasn't Mabel's reaction, as she made clear in a lachrymose statement issued the day after her verdict: "I believed I have been unfairly treated. I am a stranger here without friends, and that makes it all the harder. I don't see how any court could have permitted a prosecutor to defame a woman's character like [Stanton and Cassidy] did mine."

If Mabel was displeased, the *Plain Dealer* was ecstatic about her conviction, as it came just a year after a jury verdict that let Marion McArdle, Eva Kaber's daughter and accomplice in the murder of Eva's husband, Dan, go scot-free in 1921. Trumpeting the Champion verdict as a first fruit of the recently enacted 19th Amendment, the editorialist crowed that Mabel's sentence "served notice that in Cuyahoga County it is no longer safe for a woman, even a young and exceptionally pretty woman, to kill a man at her own pleasure." Thanks to this kind of verdict, the editorialist continued, "neither murderously scheming wives nor gun-toting females can 'get away with it' in Cleveland." Meanwhile, the still absent Ausley was declared a fugitive from justice and forfeited his bond, while Mabel remained at the Cuyahoga County jail awaiting the outcome of her appeal.

Much to everyone's surprise, her appeal was initially successful. Ruling on April 2, 1923, the Court of Appeals ruled that Judge Bernon had committed "grave and prejudicial error" in not charging her jury to weigh carefully Mabel's self-defense plea. Mabel was ecstatic, not to mention unconvincingly pious at the news: "My prayers saved me. At the end of 20 years I would be wrinkled, gray-haired. There hasn't been a night I haven't cried as I said my prayers—the prayers my mother taught me when I was a little girl."

That was the last good news Mabel had. On September 29, 1923, word came from Los Angeles that Ausley Champion had been convicted of first-degree murder there. It seems that just three months after he fled Cleveland, Ausley had killed a man in a dice game in California. Despite the best efforts of his family—his mother perjured herself on the stand, and Mabel sold her remaining jewelry and fancy clothes to pay for his defense—Ausley went to the gallows on August 16, 1924. Mabel's explanation for her continuing fierce and unrequited loyalty was that whatever his faults ("How was I to know that he was a weakling and a drunk?"), Ausley was still her husband after all, and she had loved him since the long-ago day when he seduced her as a dewy-eyed adolescent Dallas Sunday-school student.

Mabel was already depressed enough when word came of Ausley's hanging. On January 16, 1924, the Ohio Supreme Court had upheld her original manslaughter verdict. For the benefit of reporters, Mabel, still at the county jail, waxed hysterical, raving that she couldn't survive her cruel and unfair ordeal. Blubbering to reporters, she once again put on her I'm-just-a-Texas-girlie-in-distress persona: "I cannot face this terror. I will go insane. I did what any woman would do. I shot Edward O'Connell because he insulted me. My husband was too drunk to defend me properly, so I did it for myself. Some help must come from somewhere. I am not bad. I am not a sphinx woman—which the dictionary says is a lioness with a woman's head. Why do they call me that?"

Despite her protestations, Mabel was sent to Marysville, after spending more than 20 months in the Cuyahoga County jail. Behind her fragile public image, however, lurked a colder, calculating Mabel already making plans to overcome her latest setbacks. She remarked to a fellow prisoner on route to Marysville, "A clever woman always finds a way. Twenty years? The judge may say 20 years—but Mabel won't be in Marysville 20 years from today."

How right the redoubtable Mabel was. Early on the morning of March 29, 1925, Mabel tucked a crudely fashioned dummy into her prison bed, picked up two suitcases, and walked out of Marysville Reformatory forever. Although she had been resident there only a year, it seems that she had quickly wormed her way into the confidence of her captors, winning special privileges as a "model prisoner" and gaining trusty status and access to the master keys. Dressed in civilian clothes stolen from night matron Laura Kissinger and carrying cash likewise purloined from that imprudently trusting woman, Mabel hailed a cab driven by hack man Guy Sewell and motored to Springfield, Ohio. There, after eating a "hearty meal" at the railroad diner, she boarded a train for Indianapolis . . . and disappeared off the face of the earth.

Despite a strenuous, prolonged, and nationwide manhunt, authorities never caught Mabel, although she was rumored to be headed toward Mexico and was spotted by hysterical witnesses in Detroit, Akron, Chicago, Toledo, and Shaker Heights. It was initially thought she was Cleveland bound to revenge herself on Prosecutor Stanton, and Cleveland police chief Jacob Graul warned his men to take no chances with the diminutive gunwoman, stating, "Mabel will shoot. She is a killer. She may try to shoot her way to freedom if cornered." But Mabel never showed her face in the Forest City again. Although it's improbable, given her lifestyle and age (which today would be over 100), this writer likes to think she's still out there, laughing her low Texas belly laugh at baffled lawmen who couldn't keep this sensational Jazz-Age baby tied down. †

"This is my last day!"

The Strange Death of Minnie Peters, 1906

All murders are not created equal. Circumstances of chance, style, and timing unpredictably determine that some homicides indelibly endure in the public memory while others are soon forgotten. One such inexplicable casualty of oblivion was the bizarre Peters horror of 1906—and that's a bloody shame. Although but a fortnight's sensation, its ghastly particulars comprised what still remains—after almost a century—Cleveland's best "locked room" murder mystery. It put one woman in the ground, one man in the police sweatbox, and numerous family friends and acquaintances under police suspicion and garish newspaper scrutiny. And not the least of its guilty pleasures was that it provoked a delightfully vituperative public hissy fit between respected Cuyahoga County coroner Louis E. Siegelstein and Cleveland police chief Fred Kohler.

Like most such tragedies, the Peters case was probably decades in the making—but the precipitating events with which we are concerned began exactly at 6 P.M. on Friday, November 16, 1906. That was the moment when Albert Peters, a fortyish and mustachioed man-of-all-work, returned after a hard day of toil to find his second-floor apartment at 3805 Payne Avenue locked. Having no key and unable to arouse his wife, Minnie, by his repeated knocking, Albert repaired to the grocery downstairs. There he found the building owner, grocer Henry Soeders, and some neighbors and said, "Something is wrong, and I can't get in." Accompanied by Soeders and next-door neighbor Michael McNierney, Albert led the group to his darkened three-room apartment upstairs and there, peering into the front-door keyhole, he spied the key on the inside. After discussing several options, Soeders persuaded Albert to jimmy open the pantry window (which opened onto the public hallway), and Albert crawled through it and went to the front door, which he opened to admit Soeders and McNierney. As the three men entered the front parlor, Soeders lit a candle and there in its flickering light they saw Minnie Peters lying on the floor.

She didn't look good. Lying on her left side, her hair partially concealing her face, the 45-year-old Minnie lay stone-cold dead in a large pool of congealed blood. There was blood spattered on almost everything in the room: the rug, the floor, the windows, pictures on the wall, and a mirror placed on a rocking chair close to the corpse. Even with her head partially obscured by gore and the knot of her long hair, it was obvious that Minnie's head had been beaten to a pulp with almost unbelievable ferocity. Her skirts and bathrobe were pulled up to her waist, exposing her underwear and stockings, and underneath her left side was found a large, heavy, and rather bloody machinist's hammer. Sinking to his knees by his wife's body and falling prostrate on her corpse, Albert Peters cried, "My God! My God! Didn't I tell you long ago not to kill yourself?" before lapsing into a paroxysm of broken German phrases and violent sobs. When his grief subsided, Henry Soeders sensibly said, "We must call the police."

When Cleveland police detectives Lieutenant Frank Smith, Captain Schmunk, and Detective Sergeant James Doran arrived at 3805 Payne they didn't discover much more than Albert had glimpsed during his first hideous look at the murder room. Minnie had obviously been dead for some time, and the detectives were puzzled by two details. One was the fact that all of the furniture was pushed up against the walls; the other was the wall mirror sitting on the rocking chair, with a saucer of varnish next to it. With little more to go on, they did the expected thing and took Albert Peters into custody for questioning. Seven hours later, after a vigorous interrogation during which he forcefully maintained his complete innocence, he was booked as a "suspicious person," pending further inquiry and more third-degree questioning.

Albert Peters's story was a plausible one, allowing for minor inconsistencies caused by his initial reluctance to be candid about the intimate details of his marriage to an indisputably troubled woman. Wed for about 15 years, Albert and Minnie had come to America in 1892, after leaving Minnie's two children by a previous marriage in a German orphanage. But whether in Germany or the United States, their union had not been a happy one, continually troubled as it was by Minnie's chronic physical and mental problems. Moving restlessly around the United States in quest of surroundings congenial to the unhappy, unhealthy Minnie, they had lived in dozens of places before returning to Cleveland in April 1906. Then, in only a short span of seven months, they lived at lodgings on Lorain Avenue, Vega Avenue, Rowley Avenue, Broadway Avenue, Pearl Court, and Willey Avenue, before finally landing at 3805 Payne at the end of October, just three weeks before. Not that any of the locations mattered much: Minnie Peters was a desperately unhappy woman wherever she went, as evidenced by her estrangement from most of her relatives and the unhappiness she inflicted on the long-suffering Albert. Albert later characterized their life together in these sad words: "My whole life was bound up in that woman and I did not consider any sacrifice too great for her . . . When my wife first became ill I thought she was going into tuberculosis and it was I that suggested to her that we go to California. Then she began to experience those strange spells, and thence forward I suffered as much as she did."

Further disclosures by Albert Peters, corroborated by friends and relatives, revealed that in the months preceding her death, Minnie Peters's sufferings had taken a particularly morbid and ominous turn. Brooding, bedridden, and often acting in a demented, raving manner, she became convinced that an unknown enemy was pursuing her to her death, and she began to talk constantly of suicide. Once, on the train coming back from California, she had begged Albert for his knife, saying she wanted to slash her wrists before her mysterious nemesis hurled her off the train. Shortly after that, she tried to slash her throat with Albert's razor and drink carbolic acid—or so Albert said. On Sunday, November 11, just five days before her death, she had proposed a suicide pact with Albert, saying, "I don't care for my life. I have nothing to live for but you, and if we could both go together I would be happy." That night Albert heard Minnie praying that God would take them both in their sleep. Two days later, at her insistence, they both made new wills, each leaving everything to the other in case of death. On Thursday, November 15, she wrote Albert a note that read, "This is my last day. They are going to take me to Newburgh [insane asylum]." Like all of Minnie's notes to her husband, it was signed, "Your unfortunate wife." And when he left her for the last time on Friday morning at about 6, she walked with him to the public stairway and said, "This is my last day. Kiss me good-bye. Good-bye, Papa." Her subsequent autopsy show no food in her stomach, and Albert stated that she had not eaten for at least three days.

That was enough for Cleveland police chief Fred Kohler. After hearing many credible witnesses testify to Albert's unfailing solicitude and care for his difficult wife, Kohler ordered Albert's release from jail on Saturday afternoon, November 17, and immediately issued a statement that Mrs. Peters had killed herself, "beating her skull into fragments with her husband's machinist's hammer." Elaborating further to a skeptical Mayor Tom Johnson, Kohler defended his unexpected call on the Peters case: "The woman was insane. She had repeatedly threatened to take her own life. She told her husband when he left that morning he would never again see her alive." When the still-dubious Johnson asked how the frail Minnie could have so stoutly and persistently wielded the heavy hammer, Kohler had a ready answer: "The frenzy of insanity. It

---

She became convinced that an unknown enemy was pursuing her to her death, and she began to talk constantly of suicide.

---

gives fictious [*sic*] strength. I have seen people who have nearly cut their own arms off in committing suicide who afterwards cut their throats."

Kohler's decision to release Albert Peters and his comments on the case ignited a firestorm of scorn in Cleveland. Jeering at his claims that Minnie had done away with herself, the *Cleveland News* sneered that Kohler was "working apparently on the Cleveland police theory that every murder case is a suicide unless the murderer surrenders himself." Cuyahoga County coroner Louis Siegelstein, who had just finished his examination of Minnie's corpse, was even more blunt: "Anyone who says this murder is a suicide is ridiculous . . . Any one of the six wounds was a fatal one. It is out of all possibility of belief that any human being could have inflicted those injuries on himself. It could not have been done by man, woman, or beast. That is not my opinion only. It is the opinion of the two other doctors who examined the body."

Siegelstein's statements were firmly supported by Assistant County Coroner J. T. Kepke, who asserted, "There is not a particle of doubt that the woman was brutally murdered." And Dr. C. L. Jaster of the Newburgh State Insane Asylum chimed in, stating that it was a "practical impossibility" for even a maniac to inflict such injuries upon herself.

Clevelanders quickly took sides in the dispute—and most of

them supported Coroner Siegelstein. HOW COULD A CORPSE TAKE ITS OWN LIFE? screamed the headline in the November 19 *Cleveland Press*. As Siegelstein noted, the evidence of his autopsy made a suicide verdict almost unthinkable. Using the round end of Albert Peters's machinist hammer, Minnie's assailant had inflicted 12 severe blows on her skull, any 6 of which were sufficient to cause unconsciousness or death. Two of the blows had been forceful enough to drive broken pieces of skull into her brain. Moreover, the disarray of the parlor, the centrifugal distribution of blood, and the condition of her clothes all pointed toward a homicidal assailant. And, as all who knew Minnie agreed that she was too weak to wield such a hammer, she could not have used it to kill herself. "To assert otherwise," concluded Siegelstein to a *Cleveland Leader* reporter, "is to violate good sense."

Fred Kohler didn't shy away from fights, and he waded with gusto into the public fray with Siegelstein. Denying that the hammer blows killed Minnie, Kohler insisted that she had instead choked to death on her own blood. Noting that all the windows and the only door of the Peters flat were locked from the inside and that no one saw anyone enter it on the murder day, Kohler scoffed at the idea of an unknown intruder. Since Albert Peters's alibi checked out—Dr. Corlett swore he had been at his Euclid Avenue house all day—Minnie's death could only have been a suicide. She had long been seriously depressed, she had told Albert that Friday was her "last day," and the details of the murder scene suggested that she had carried out her self-destruction with admirable precision. In fact, according to Kohler, Minnie's modus operandi for suicide followed a script familiar to police investigations of housewife suicides:

> Police records show similar incidents. The woman prepared for death—cleaned her house from parlor to kitchen—changed her clothing from the skin out—burned her papers—placed the mirror on a chair—then took a machinist's hammer and pounded herself—the blows increasing in force as her frenzy advanced . . . She placed that looking glass on the rocking chair

in such an angle that no one could see her reflection therein without standing up. This is a common practice for would-be suicides to stand before a mirror . . . the looking glasses being frequently shattered by the body striking them in the fall . . . It is not the function of Coroner Siegelstein to say how this woman came by her wounds . . . If I should declare that the woman was murdered, I would be hooted out of the office by the men under me.

Coroner Siegelstein riposted immediately. Asked why he still stuck to his suicide theory in view of Kohler's opposition, he replied: "I have only begun to stick. In the annals of surgical history there is no case of a person receiving wounds similar of those Mrs. Peters received and retaining consciousness long enough to strike the second blow."

Minnie Peters's funeral took place on Monday afternoon at the Flynn & Froelk morgue. It was attended by a crowd of "morbid persons, mostly women," and press accounts of the obsequies included the delicious rumor that a mysterious woman was seen "gloating" in triumph over the Minnie's open casket. As her coffin slid into the waiting hole at Monroe Street Cemetery, a weeping Albert was heard to mutter that it wouldn't be long before he was with her.

Anyone who thought Coroner Siegelstein's inquest would settle the acrid dispute over Minnie Peters's death must have been gravely disappointed. Opening on Monday, November 19, the inquest panel called several dozen witnesses—most of whom gave evidence supporting both the Kohler and Siegelstein hypotheses. Friends and relatives of Albert Peters testified to Minnie's chronic melancholia, irrational fears of a phantom stalker, and frequent threats of suicide. Their memories of the crazed woman were amplified by the text of a note—or rather the faint impression of a note on the top sheet of a paper tablet—found by Chief Kohler himself while searching the Peters flat two days after the murder. Verified as being in her handwriting, magnified to legibility, and translated from the German by Henry Soeders's daughter, Annie,

Minnie's last note seemed the final, anguished cry of a woman at the end of her psychological rope: "Schmidt, Girgen Soeders said nothing. To this I can swear. This was all that was wanted to set these people upon me. What is worse, you do not care for me. Dear friends, forgive me. If you can come as soon as possible. Your unfortunate wife."

Anyone who thought Coroner's inquest would settle the acrid dispute over Minnie Peters's death must have been gravely disappointed.

It took some time to sort out some ambiguities in the note. "Schmidt" was Max Schmidt, a friend of the family whom police initially suspected of being Minnie's lover. But after a prolonged, uncomfortable chat with him, Kohler's men concluded his interest in the dead woman was truly platonic. Minnie's fears about people being "set upon" her turned out to be her unfounded delusion that Henry Soeders, the landlord, was about to evict them. But the core of the note clearly demonstrated Minnie's fears of an impending doom and resonated with an urgent anxiety consistent with a suicidal mood. And the police insistence that no intruder could have entered the Peters flat was supported by Annie Soeders's testimony that she had been working in the building all day as a charwoman and had seen no one in the vicinity of the Peterses' door. With the key left on the inside of that locked door, it seemed impossible that anyone could have entered the apartment during the critical 12 hours of Albert Peters's absence.

Siegelstein was having none of it—and soon a small parade of surprise witnesses dramatically challenged Chief Kohler's suicide theory. In the first place, it turned out there was no proof that the Peters apartment had been locked from the inside when Albert and his witnesses returned there on Friday evening. Henry Soeders and the others had merely accepted Albert's claim that his door was locked. No one else had actually tried to open the door before Albert crawled through the pantry window to admit them, and no one present heard or saw him actually unlock the door. A reluctant Henry Soeders concluded his testimony with these ominous words: "I want to be understood plainly in this. I do not know who killed this woman, but if what I am about to say would hang [Albert Peters] I must say it . . . It is the gospel truth that Peters never unlocked that door. He swung it right open. There was no turning of a key and no sliding of a bolt."

The greatest challenge to Kohler's suicide scenario came from Conrad Voth, a journalist for a German Baptist periodical, *Der Sendbot*, whose office was directly across the street from Albert and Minnie's Payne Avenue apartment. First contacting Kohler on Sunday, November 18, Voth claimed he had seen a mysterious old man at the window of the Peters flat at about 12:30 P.M. on Friday. Appearing for a few seconds at the second window from the southeast corner of the apartment, the man had peered down at the street and then withdrawn. After talking to Voth, Kohler and his detectives dismissed Voth's sighting as a "phantom," but Coroner Siegelstein presented Voth as his star witness at the inquest's opening session. Firmly repeating his assertions, Voth described the man he had seen as about 5'8" tall, 50 to 60 years old, well dressed in a black cloak, wearing no hat, and sporting a short, well-trimmed beard. Voth said he would probably recognize the man if he saw him again and that he resembled a previous tenant of the Peters flat, an old man named "Grover." Kohler's men did what they could to disparage Voth's statements, claiming that he had failed to identify figures at the critical window in repeated tests staged by detectives and that his eyesight was poor. But Voth stuck doggedly to his story and succeeded in embarrassing his police detractors by correctly reading distant address numbers through the window of the morgue where the inquest was held. Whatever the scoffing of Kohler's finest, Voth's serious mien and precise testimony made a lasting impression, even if he did conclude with a gratuitous speculation on the deceased woman's private life: "I would not be surprised to learn any time that a man had been found, a man whom Mrs. Peters had known, and known intimately, though without the knowledge of her husband." Interestingly, Voth's invidious conjecture was echoed the following day by Jake Mintz, Cleveland's most famous private detective. Speaking to a *Cleveland News* reporter, Mintz theorized that Minnie had been murdered by a "moral degenerate," an unknown man who "had loved her better than her husband." Dismissing Albert as an innocent simpleton, Mintz argued that it was useless to question him further: "Do not ask Peters whom he suspects, for he is a man who would never suspect anyone of anything."

Additional support for the idea of an unknown intruder, possibly even Voth's bushy-faced stranger, came on Thursday, with the dramatic testimony of Isadore Rosenthal, a neighborhood schoolboy. He told the panel that he had been standing in the Grenloch & Gensert shoe store just below the Peters flat about 4 P.M. on Friday when he heard a sound "like a body falling" above. He had mentioned the noise to the store proprietor at the time, but the latter had been too busy to pay attention. The panel then went on to consider technical and inconclusive arguments as to whether the key in the front door could have been turned from the outside by someone using a pair of burglar's "nippers."

The inquest finally petered out on Thursday, November 22, with the question of how Minnie met her death unresolved. But Kohler and Siegelstein continued their public feud, each determined to have the last word. Even before all the testimony was in, Kohler stated unequivocally, "This incident is closed," and on Friday, November 23, the day after the inquest ended, he spluttered angrily: "The coroner jumped at conclusions, which he has since come to realize were wrong, and now he is exerting every effort to vindicate himself in his prejudged verdict. I'm just vexed. It's ridiculous, preposterous, asinine. He snaps his fingers at a trained police force, trained for just such action as the solving of death mysteries, and tells us to paddle our own canoe, that he'll paddle his."

As county coroner, however, Siegelstein was entitled to the last word, which came with his official inquest verdict on December 1:

"Minnie Peters came to her death from hemorrhage of the brain and a fractured skull, which were caused by said Minnie Peters having been struck a number of blows over the head with a blunt instrument by an unknown person."

And so ended, seemingly inconclusively, the Minnie Peters puzzle. Max Schmidt endured some additional, but fruitless, "sweating" as to whether his relations to the deceased were improper, and Albert eventually declared his conviction that Minnie couldn't have killed herself, saying: "She would have left a note clearing me . . . she told me many times that she would be murdered, but always promised me faithfully that she would not harm herself." Albert, who had been fired by Dr. Corlett on account of the unpleasant publicity, soon found another job and new lodgings free from disquieting bloodstains. And curious Clevelanders turned to other sensations of the day, like Mayor Johnson's protracted war for three-cent streetcar fares and ongoing public concern about industrial trusts.

But before you dismiss Cleveland police chief Fred Kohler as an utter moron, consider this: He may have been right about Minnie killing herself. Her previous behavior was consistent with such an end, and the odd circumstances of the death room—especially the mirror on the chair—closely followed the scripts for female suicides familiar to contemporary policemen. And, believe it or not, there is some evidence that Minnie Peters actually could have killed herself with her husband's hammer. Chief Kohler came in for some knowing sneers and smirks six months later, when Frank E. Woodworth of Painesville, perhaps inspired by newspaper publicity, tried to kill himself with a heavy hammer. Woodworth, despite being a heavy, muscular fellow, failed in the attempt, neither fracturing his skull nor even losing consciousness. When baited by newsman as to why the strong Woodworth failed where the weak Minnie had allegedly succeeded, Kohler replied, "Woodworth didn't have Mrs. Peters's nerve." But several other cases, relatively unpublicized, impressively bolster Kohler's hypothesis. Four years before the Peters case, on March 6, 1902, Henry L. Dauernheim, a wealthy, 50-year-old paper merchant from St. Louis, had killed himself by beating in his skull with a heavy sledgehammer. Just 19 months after Minnie Peters's death, Rachel Goldfadoon of 2663 East 25th Street tried to kill herself with a hatchet; she did not succeed but managed to inflict seven ugly wounds on her skull. And in March 1911 businessman William Staum of Syracuse, New York, beat himself to death with a hammer in circumstances eerily reminiscent of the Peters case. Found lying in a pool of blood, the despondent Staum had locked his door and hit himself 8 to 10 times with a heavy hammer, penetrating his brain with several blows. The official coroner's verdict on Staum's death was suicide. The Minnie Peters case remains unsolved. †

Assassin from Nowhere

Christina Lipscomb's Terrible Secret, 1908

Sensational murder cases with toxic racial aspects seem to be a 20th-century American specialty. Our grandparents witnessed the lengthy tribulations of the Scottsboro boys, and those middle-aged or older recall the lynchings and homicides of the Civil Rights era. More recent years, of course, have brought the O. J. Simpson trials with their never-ending reverberations and animosities. But for sheer unpleasantness and gratuitous racial discord, it would be hard to beat several other episodes of the last decade: the Stuart case in Boston, the Smith tragedy in South Carolina, and the Tawana Brawley circus in New York. Charles Stuart, you may recall, set off a frenzied racial manhunt when he shot his pregnant wife, Carol, to death and then told police that a mysterious black man had gunned her down while the couple was sitting in their car.

Susan Smith, somewhat more notoriously, triggered a similar, if briefer, dragnet in South Carolina when she drowned her two sons and blamed the deaths on—you guessed it—a mysterious black killer who came out of nowhere. Not to mention the infamous Tawana Brawley, whose malicious fiction that she was assaulted and abused by white lawmen ruined both her own life and those of the accused.

Cleveland, too, has had its share of racially charged crimes during this century, from the sex- and gunfire-flecked career of John Leonard Whitfield to the bloody carnage of the 1968 Glenville shootout. But what most Clevelanders don't know is that the Forest City pioneered the bogus racial manhunt almost a century ago, back when Cleveland boasted relatively few African Americans on whom to blame its not infrequent homicides. It is for that reason alone that the Lipscomb murder is worth remembering, not to mention the added attraction of Christina Lipscomb, one of the most determined and dazzling women who ever behaved badly in the Western Reserve.

The Lipscomb affair erupted on the dark winter night of Wednesday, February 26, 1908. A report came into the Cleveland police's 12th Precinct station on the far West Side that there was a badly wounded man at Schwab's saloon. The flying squad of detectives who arrived at the West 105th Street saloon at 8 P.M. found John Lipscomb, 38, covered with blood and sinking fast from three serious gun wounds. One bullet had drilled a hole through his hips, another had perforated the left side of his throat, and the third had smashed through his jawbone and almost severed his tongue. Taken to St. John's Hospital in an ambulance, Lipscomb went into emergency surgery while Cleveland police detectives scrambled to solve Cleveland's latest and most puzzling street crime.

It took a while for their investigation to get on solid ground. Christina Lipscomb, the victim's 33-year-old wife, had been with him when he was shot and had talked briefly with the police at Schwab's tavern. But the comely Christina turned up missing at the hospital, so veteran detectives James Doran and John T. Shibley went over to the Lipscomb home at 2613 East 65th Street. Unable to rouse anyone there, Doran kicked the door down and entered. He didn't find Christina inside, but he and Shibley picked her up several hours later in company with Roland ("Roly") French, a boarder who lived with the Lipscombs. After preliminary questioning, Christina and Roly were taken to the hospital bed of John Lipscomb at 2 A.M. The lawmen present there could not disguise their chagrin when the wounded man, unable to speak because of his almost-severed tongue, scrawled on a slate held up to him, "My wife didn't do it. French didn't do it. It was a white man disguised with a mask."

But was it? Christina's story, at last unfolded with copious tears and sighs, didn't exactly agree with her husband's. The preliminary details of their stories were consistent. John and Christina had left the home of her sister, Mrs. George Treat, in West Park at about 7:30 P.M. Walking east on Lorain Avenue near West 112th, they had decided to pick up the eastbound streetcar a little further east, so as to avoid an extra nickel fare. Lorain Avenue at that time was a semi-rural thoroughfare with a streetcar line down the middle, and there were no houses within 200 feet of the road. Three hundred feet behind the Lipscombs ambled a party of three men on their way to church: D. R. McGinty, Dan McGinty, and Dan's uncle, Thomas Nolan. Five hundred feet ahead trudged James Havlin, a lineman for the Cuyahoga Telephone Company. It was a calm, cold night, and the ground was covered with several inches of snow.

It happened just after 7:40. Christina's version was that John had just dropped behind her a step to allow her to pass an impeding telephone pole. As he did so, she heard him say, "What's the matter?" Turning around, she saw a black man press a revolver against her husband and shoot him three times. As she screamed, "My husband is shot; my poor husband is shot!" John fell to the muddy street, the black man fled northward through a snow-covered empty lot, and the other Lorain Avenue pedestrians began to run toward the wounded man in the street. The last thing Christina remembered was fainting beside her husband.

That was Christina's story, which she stuck to through many

skeptical police interrogations. But while John's version, painfully extracted at length from the gravely wounded man, agreed in most details with Christina's, he insisted that his assailant was a white man and that he would "know him in a thousand" if he ever saw him again. The gunman, John disclosed, was about 5'9" and 175 pounds and wore an overcoat and cap. Convinced that he was going to recover, John refused to give the police any further details, vowing repeatedly that he would seek his own private vengeance when he got out of the hospital. Just in case, though, John begged the doctors to let him know if he was going to die, so he could have an opportunity to change his story.

The police were admittedly baffled by the contradiction between the couple's stories. They didn't much care for the statements of the supporting eyewitnesses, either. Tom Nolan had been the one closest to the shooter. He said he was "sure he was a Negro, for I got a good look at him." Nolan's companion, Dan McGinty, supported his vision of a lone gunman running from the scene but was unsure of the man's race. But James Havlin, the telephone lineman walking ahead of the Lipscombs, contradicted everyone, insisting that he had seen pistol flashes coming from two directions. This implied there were two gunmen, possibly one white and one black, for the police to identify and apprehend. Muddying the tangled narrative further, Havlin informed the police that when he arrived at the crime scene, Christina told him a story different from the one she gave the police: "There were two men. They jumped out at the same time. They didn't say anything but began shooting. I think one was a colored man."

Chief Fred Kohler and his detectives were very unhappy with the progress of the Lipscomb case in the days that followed the shooting. Lingering near death in his hospital bed, John Lipscomb would sometimes indicate his readiness to make a final statement, only to lapse back into stony silence when he thought he was getting better again. On the chance he might eventually make up his mind, Kohler put a round-the-clock squad of detectives in his hospital room and concentrated on his only genuine, if somewhat uncooperative, witness: Christina Lipscomb.

Fred Kohler may not have known the French expression *cherchez la femme*, but he had handled enough murder cases to know that the Lipscomb mystery reeked of domestic strife. The sleuthing of his detectives soon revealed, despite the contrary insistence of John and Christina, that the Lipscomb marriage had been a discordant one. Christina had often complained to her friends and relatives that John was a pathologically jealous man who treated her badly. The particular object of his suspicion was the Lipscomb boarder, Roly French, and it was with undisguised satisfaction that the investigating police discovered that Christina and Roly had lived together in Chatham, Ontario, the previous summer. And while Roly had an ironclad alibi for the night of February 26—he was drinking in a Woodland Avenue saloon at the time of the shooting—the Christina-John-Roly triangle was enough to suggest a potential murder motive. Police scrutiny of Christina intensified after her sister-in-law, Mrs. George Lipscomb, disclosed that John had told her only three days before the shooting that his wife had said to him, "I'll kill you or get someone else to do it."

But if Christina was the shooter, why couldn't anyone, especially her wounded husband, identify her as the gunwoman? And where was the revolver, for which a 20-man squad of detectives searched vainly for hours in the sloppy winter mud of Lorain Avenue? With both Christina and John stonewalling them, all the police could do was wait for John to decide that he was really dying and to issue cryptic, if suggestive, statements to the press. "We are satisfied of the identify of the man who shot," police inspector Rowe announced on February 29. "He was not a robber." Chief Kohler went further in speaking to reporters that afternoon, saying, "I think it is a family affair. We are on the track of the truth. We may make an arrest within a few days." Twenty-four hours later, Kohler changed his mind, stating, "We know who did the shooting but as Lipscomb will not aid us, preferring to obtain satisfaction himself, there will probably be no arrests."

The break Kohler's men were hoping for came on Wednesday, March 18. Told by his doctors that he was about to die, John Lipscomb motioned St. John's Hospital physician Dr. J. M. O'Malley to his side. Speaking with great pain and difficulty, he managed to blurt out, "My wife did it." Two detectives and a stenographer were brought into the room, and John Lipscomb repeated his statement for the record. Early the next morning, he died after a three-week struggle with the fatal bullet, which had migrated from his throat to his lungs.

The police waited a little longer for the jaws of their trap to shut. As the inquest into John's death opened on Friday morning, March 20, Assistant County Prosecutor M. P. Mooney had Detective Shibley bring Christina in for an intensive "sweating" session immediately after John's interment in Calvary Cemetery. Mooney got right to the point: "Mrs. Lipscomb, your husband is now dead. Tell the truth. You and your husband quarreled that night. He pulled a revolver, you grabbed it, and shot him. Now if this is true, I don't believe any jury will convict you of any crime."

Still ignorant of her husband's deathbed statement, Christina merely repeated her dubious version of the shooting and said again and again, "I did not kill him. I did not kill him. I did not kill him."

The stage was set for Dr. O'Malley's dramatic disclosure at the Monday-morning inquest session, and as soon as he finished his testimony about John's last words, Christina was taken into custody and rigorously interrogated. It was the standard police "sweating" practiced by Kohler's men at the time: a dozen detectives shouting at the suspect, no food, no water, no breaks, and absolutely no lawyers allowed as they pestered the defiant Christina for hour after hour. She held up well at first, just laughing at Kohler when he said, "Did you shoot him?" But shortly before midnight, Tuesday, March 24, Christina began to break. Going over her story for the 21st time that day, she stumbled on a detail. Minutes later, she collapsed, sobbing out her guilt and signing a confession written out by the jail stenographer. Her confession, which included the obligatory disclaimer ("It is made without promises of any kind being made, and [it] is voluntary and not under threats"), confirmed what police had suspected from the beginning. The Lipscombs had begun quarreling as soon as they left the Treat house in West

Park, Christina admitted. They were arguing over Roly French's attentions to Christina, and the dispute climaxed with John striking Christina as they walked down Lorain: "I will tell you the truth now. My husband was cruel, unreasonable, and jealous from the day of our marriage. I lived in fear of him. He was jealous of every man I knew. My husband drew a revolver when we quarreled. I struggled for possession of it. It went off and the bullet struck his throat. Maddened at the charges he made against me I fired again, and the bullet lodged in his jaw. A third time I pulled the trigger and wounded him in the hip."

Concluding her statement, the exhausted widow cried, "Do what you see fit: I saw him die and he is writhing before me now!"

Within 24 hours Christina had recovered her aplomb. Shortly after her arraignment before Judge William McGannon (who 12 years later would face charges of his own, stemming from an evening murder on a Cleveland street), she angrily repudiated her confession, claiming that it had been coerced from her by threats of prison and false promises that she would not be prosecuted. Just after being indicted by the grand jury on a second-degree-murder charge on Wednesday, March 24, 1908, Christina detailed the police duress that had produced her confession. Claiming that she was "sick and half-crazy," she dwelt on the pitiful image of a helpless woman beset by bullying detectives: "I was arrested at 3 P.M. Monday and from then until 12 o'clock at night I was kept going over and over that awful affair till faint and overcome, I dropped asleep on a couch at the police station. Then they all asked questions. I told them again and again what I knew. It grew late and I was so tired. Then they told me they had proof that my husband mistreated me, and that self-defense was natural."

Claiming that her "confession" was a police-dictated tissue of lies, Christina now returned with renewed fervor to her original a-black-man-from-nowhere fantasy.

Christina's stance played well in Cleveland newspapers, which gave ample publicity to her coercion claims (POLICE MADE ME CONFESS, screamed the March 24 *Cleveland Press* headline) and featured flattering sketches of the slim, black-clad widow in their pages. Both the police and the prosecutor's office were incensed at Christina's about-face, and Chief Fred Kohler spoke for Cleveland's outraged authorities the day after Christina disavowed her confession. "It's the usual sympathy plea of the man or woman who is caught," he fumed. "She is one of the shrewdest, coolest persons who ever went through the police cross-examination in Cleveland."

Christina's intensely anticipated trial probably didn't turn out the way either she or the police expected. The trial opened in Judge Simpson Ford's courtroom on Monday, May 4, and her jury was quickly selected with only one candidate dismissed. Prosecutor Mooney presented the state's expected case, arguing that Christina and John had been fighting over Roly French's attentions to her when John pulled out a gun. While they struggled for it, the gun went off, wounding John, and then Christina, fearful he would get up, shot him two more times while he was lying on the street. As Mooney presented his case, the demure, black-clad widow shook her head several times and audibly murmured, "No, no, it is not true!" several times.

Defense attorney Edmund Hitchens countered with Christina's original version of the night of February 26, claiming that a mysterious black man had cold-bloodedly fired three shots into John Lipscomb. Hitchens bolstered his mystery-gunman theory with allegations that a man, seen by two children in the house next door to George Treat's West Park home, had stalked John and Christina from the moment they left there. But Christina's improbable story, with or without the stalker embroidery, was just filler. It soon became clear that Hitchens had staked his case on keeping Christina's March 24 confession out of the trial record. With its insistence that the police had tricked her into confessing by a combination of threats and promises, Hitchens's dogged cross-examination extracted damaging admissions from Inspector Rowe about his interrogation of Mrs. Lipscomb. Admitting that he had played the classic "good cop" foil to his menacing colleagues, Rowe repeated what he had told Christina just before she signed her confession: "Now just tell me all about it and you will be free and happy by tomorrow noon. Just say that you shot him. I know that you did what was right and I give you credit for it. Any jury in the country will say that you were justified. I know how the detectives have hounded you at the bedside of your husband. I know just how they are and I feel sorry for you."

As the next day's *Plain Dealer* put it, "On the stand, those who conducted the examination admitted they had pretended to be her friends eager to aid her." The same day the prosecution received another serious setback when Judge Ford ruled Dr. O'Malley's testimony about John's deathbed statement inadmissible. Ford had little choice in the matter; as Dr. O'Malley conscientiously testified on Monday, the dying, delirious John Lipscomb had not only accused his wife of shooting him but also his doctors, his brother, and the detectives in his hospital room.

Shortly after the afternoon session ended on May 5, the prosecution recovered some ground when Judge Ford reluctantly allowed Christina's confession into the record over the strong objections of attorney Hitchens. "I do not hold that this is a bona fide confession," ruled Ford. "I will let the jury decide whether it was obtained from her by coercion or not. They may wholly disregard it, if they see fit."

But the expected struggle over the validity of Christina's confession never took place. When the next trial session opened at 9 A.M. on Wednesday, May 6, Judge Ford announced that the confession would be entered into the record. Immediately afterwards, Prosecutor Mooney rose from his seat and asked that Christina's murder indictment be nulled. Blandly admitting that the state possessed no real evidence except for the disputed confession, Mooney asserted that he had pushed the case to trial only because of Christina's unwarranted slurs on the methods of the Cleveland police and the prosecutor's office. Now that the confession had been admitted as valid evidence, the trial's purpose had been served. Justifying the unexpected outcome, Mooney said:

That confession shows that she acted in self-defense. We see no other course before us than to move that she be discharged.

The killing seems plainly justifiable . . . From the first we have considered it impossible to make a case against her. The trial was for the sole purpose of bringing the facts before the public and showing that the police department and prosecutor's office did not obtain the confession by undue force and persecution of the woman . . . The case was brought to preserve the integrity of the prosecutor's office, and of the police department. Had [Christina's] charges not been made, the case would have been nulled when the trial opened . . . Had the black mark the defendant's counsel tried to give not been wiped out, police and prosecutors would have been placed under a handicap in future cases that they would have been unable to overcome.

Still dressed in grieving black, Christina Lipscomb walked out of Judge Ford's courtroom a free woman. Before disappearing into obscurity, she would only say, "I am unable to say anything. I have been sick in mind and body ever since this horrible occurrence. I am happy to be free again."

Christina Lipscomb was never prosecuted for making false statements to the police, much less for her inflammatory lies about a mysterious black gunman. It says much for the racial climate of the age that neither the newspapers nor the Cleveland police authorities even commented on her criminal, racist libel. No one but Christina was completely satisfied with the official verdict on John Lipscomb's death, especially since no one remembered him ever carrying a gun or threatening his wife. Whether Christina Lipscomb was guilty of murder remains an open question, but it is certain that she set a nasty racial precedent resounding down to the present day and, no doubt, beyond. And the Lipscomb case remains something to remember the next time someone pontificates—as in the Sheppard case—on the superior sanctity of "eyewitness" testimony. †

The Phantom Flapper Killer

The Mystery of Margaret Heldman, 1928

Although she was quiet and kept to herself, everyone noticed the girl on the outbound Canton–Waynesburg bus that cold December night. It wasn't just her striking outfit: a blue chinchilla coat cut in a masculine style, a close-fitting black felt turban hat with a brilliant pin, flesh-colored hose, oxford shoes, and gloved hands. It wasn't just her looks either: she seemed about 22 years old, about 5'4" and 120 pounds, had light brown hair, and was described by all who saw her as a "beauty." But what drew all eyes to her was the extreme pallor of her face, her brooding intensity, and the way she kept nervously putting each hand in the opposite sleeve of her coat. Here was a girl, everyone said to themselves, with something on her mind.

George Patterson, the bus driver, noticed her, too, as did W. E.

McCombs, the proprietor of the Rite-of-Way Inn in the village of Waco, where the bus let her off, just several miles and about 10 minutes from Canton. Both Patterson and McCombs had seen the same woman the night before: she had gotten off at the Waco stop at 8:10, immediately taken the return bus back to Canton—and showed up again on the 9:10 bus, only to once more depart on the return bus to Canton. Both men thought she was a "spotter" for the bus company checking up on their work. This night, December 6, 1928, the young woman stepped off the bus and asked McCombs if he would turn on his light to signal the return bus to Canton; she expected to be back in several minutes and didn't want to miss it. She then turned around, shoved her hands in her sleeves, started walking up the hill toward a group of houses, and disappeared from view.

But she didn't disappear from Waco. About 100 yards away, just over the crest of the hill, she turned into the driveway of Vernard Fearn. Fearn, a 35-year-old coal merchant and mine operator, lived there in a brand-new house he had built for his wife, Mary, and their nine-year-old daughter, Kathryn. Mary was making dinner in the kitchen when she heard the young woman rap at the front door. She opened it, and the woman said, "Is Mr. Fearn at home?"

Mary replied, "Yes, won't you come in?"

"No thank you," said the pale female, "I'll only be a moment. I'll stay right here."

Mary went and told Vernard there was someone at the door for him and returned to the kitchen.

As soon as Vernard opened the front door, the young woman pulled out a .380 Colt revolver and quickly, calmly, and wordlessly pumped five steel-jacketed bullets into him. Three slugs smashed into the front of his chest, another entered his side as he spun around, and a fifth bullet went into his back as he fell to the porch. A sixth bullet grazed his neck, and then the young woman fired two more slugs into the screen door frame, as if to say, "Take that, too." She then turned around, stepped off the porch, and began walking back down the hill to the Rite-of-Way Inn. She got there just before the return bus to Canton arrived and was on it when it left ten minutes later after refueling. About ten minutes to seven, she got off the bus at the McKinley Hotel in downtown Canton and disappeared into a crowd of Christmas shoppers. The "Phantom Flapper Killer" sensation had begun.

The Stark County police had no idea as to the identity of the mysterious, vanished killer. The search for the shooter, immediately dubbed the "Phantom Flapper" by newspaper writers, focused on the meager clues provided by those who had seen the attractive, quiet gun-girl during her bus trips to Waco on December 6 and the previous night. But other than her physical appearance and demeanor, they had nothing to go on in this seemingly inexplicable murder. Within hours, it was rumored in the newspapers that the "Phantom Flapper" killing would never be solved.

Mary Fearn wasn't much help to Stark County sheriff Edward Gibson and his investigative team. Although she and her daughter Kathryn had gotten a good look at the gun-girl as she finished firing, the newspapers reported that both of them said she wasn't anyone they had seen before, although Mary allowed that there was something "familiar" about the assassin. Drawn to the porch by the sound of the gun, Mary had tried to help her husband as he staggered, bleeding heavily, to the kitchen. Cradling the dying man in her arms, she said, "Who did this to you?"

"I don't know. I . . . never . . . saw . . . her . . . before," groaned Vernard before expiring a few moments later. Mary also remembered that she had heard Vernard say to his killer as he was falling, "Why are you doing this? What did I ever do to you?"

Inevitably, the focus of the investigation turned to Vernard Fearn's private life. With no apparent motive, such as robbery or a feud with a known enemy, Sheriff Gibson's men concluded that Fearn's killing had to have been an act of private vengeance, triggered by unknown aspects of his lifestyle. And although Mary Fearn and Vernard's friends fervently described him as a paragon of uxorious behavior and manly virtues, Stark County lawmen soon began to think otherwise. A local boy, Vernard was remembered pleasantly by Canton-area folk as a promising semi-pro baseball player, a brave veteran of World War I, and a hard worker and entrepreneur who paid his debts and was active in community affairs. But the Vernard Fearn who worked so hard also played pretty hard, Gibson's men discovered, and they began to search among the many area dance halls that he had passionately frequented in the months before his death and interview their female habitués. They didn't come up with a definite suspect immediately, but they did find that Fearn had often flirted heavily with female strangers at the all-night dances and marathon contests he had attended. Moreover, he had asked some of these women out on "dates," although the police couldn't unearth any proof that he had kept any of them. Six days went by without any apparent progress on the case, although Sheriff Gibson and Stark County prosecutor Henry Harter Jr. kept promising that they were on the verge of arresting a suspect. Wild theories began to circulate to fill the vacuum created by the absence of substantial clues. One story was that Fearn had merely been lured to his front porch by the attractive chinchilla-clad stranger while another, unknown man had ambushed him, shooting from a hidden spot on the front lawn. Another idea was that the phantom gun-girl was a professional "hit man" from Canton's underworld, the downtown "Jungle," whence she had been recruited for the job by unknown persons. Still another theory had her acting as the outraged champion of a younger sister—presumably a soiled dove whose soiling had been the work of Vernard Fearn—while a still-wilder rumor had it that Vernard had been assassinated by a man disguised as a woman. Meanwhile, Sheriff Gibson and Prosecutor Harter fed the rumor mill by taking flying trips to small towns in Ohio and Pennsylvania to run down tips on supposed sightings of the gun-girl.

Actually, Gibson and his men had quite a bit of information about the killer, if not her actual identity. With nothing amiss in Vernard Fearn's business dealings, it was obvious, whatever Mary Fearn said about her husband's saintliness, that his killer had acted out of strong personal motives. Moreover, it was clear that she hadn't cared about getting caught after she pulled the trigger eight times. She had made no fewer than three trips to Fearn's house, taking two bus trips to Waco on December 5, only to find that he was not at home that night. She had made her final journey on December 6, still wearing the same clothes she had worn the night before. It was also obvious that she was not a person of means, as the police had never known a killer who would take the bus in lieu of an available automobile. So, when not taking side trips to check out fugitive clues, Gibson and Harder kept hammering away at Mary Fearn, hoping that she would eventually reveal the sordid wrinkle in Vernard's life that had led to his violent death. In the meantime, public interest—and greed—was stoked by the announcement that the Stark County commissioners were offering a $1,000 reward for the apprehension of the phantom flapper. Within days, wary policemen and alert citizens were harassing every good-looking woman wearing a chinchilla coat or a black felt turban. On December 12, three young men in New Philadelphia were charged with assault and battery against a young woman whom they tried to capture for the reward money.

Unexpectedly, the "Phantom Flapper" mystery ended with the same surprising and sudden violence with which it began. On Thursday, December 13, at 6 P.M.—exactly one week to the hour after Fearn was murdered—a car screeched to a halt in front of Sheriff Gibson's office in downtown Canton and began honking frantically. Gibson ran out to find Wilbur Heldman, 27, a furnace salesman, sitting in his car. In the passenger seat next to him was Margaret Heldman, the "Phantom Flapper Killer," bleeding and near death from a bullet through her heart. Jumping on the running board, Gibson directed Wilbur to Canton's Mercy Hospital, where Margaret Heldman died at 7:30 P.M. Before expiring, she tried to speak, but she could not, and she never really regained consciousness.

The story Wilbur Heldman told lawmen and reporters seemed to put an end to the week-long mystery. It was a sad tale. Like Vernard Fearn, Wilbur was a product of the Canton area and had worked there selling furnaces for some years before he met Margaret in August 1927. Fresh out of DuBois, Pennsylvania, the impressionable Margaret Horner, just graduated from high school, was working as a ribbon clerk at a Canton department store when she was smitten by the older, seemingly worldly Wilbur, and they were married only three weeks later after a whirlwind courtship. Their mutual infatuation, alas, did not last, and their subsequent months of married life were marked by frequent quarrels, separations, in-law squabbles, and fleeting reconciliations. By Wilbur's account, at least, Margaret was a cold, morose person and a psychopathic liar, and even his best efforts failed to satisfy his unhappy, restless wife. A child, Emmett Heldman, born in September 1928, failed to cement their precarious union, and in November of that year they moved to Lorain. Wilbur's initial story to the police was that they had gone there to make a fresh start—but Margaret's in-laws and Wilbur's acquaintances said it was so Wilbur could establish a 30-day residency in Lorain as a legal prelude to divorcing Margaret. At the same time they moved to Lorain, they placed their infant son, whom Wilbur claimed was neglected by his mother, in foster care in Canton.

How much Wilbur Heldman knew about his wife and when he knew it would become the crux of the ensuing investigation and the nub of unanswered questions that resound to this day. Wilbur told police that his first inkling that there was something going on between Margaret and Vernard Fearn had come in early November. Casually perusing some letters that she had written to her mother and sisters, Wilbur discovered that Margaret was telling them that Wilbur was about to divorce her because of a man named Fearn. Margaret went on in these letters to disclose that she had met Fearn at a dance and that she had later agreed to go for a "ride and x x x" with the married coal merchant. That was enough for Wilbur: he confronted Margaret with the evidence of her adultery and insisted that they relocate to Lorain and start all over again.

Margaret had left Wilbur on Monday, December 2, telling him that she was going to visit her sister, Mrs. Laura Pierce, in Canton. When she returned home on Friday, the day after Fearn was shot, Wilbur asked her how her trip had been, and she replied, "Just fine." Wilbur's suspicions, however, became aroused over the weekend. While reading the *Cleveland News*, he became aware that Vernard Fearn—not exactly an unknown name in Wilbur's house—had been shot with an unusual weapon, a .380 Colt that, police said, was a difficult gun for which to find cartridges. As it happened, Wilbur possessed just such a rare gun, and he looked up from his paper and said to Margaret, "You know, I believe you killed this man Fearn."

Within days, wary policemen and alert citizens were harassing every good-looking woman wearing a chinchilla coat or a black felt turban.

"Don't be foolish," replied Margaret calmly, "why would I want to do a thing like that?" Wilbur—or so he told the cops—let the matter drop.

After all, it didn't seem probable that mousy little Margaret could have done such a thing, even though the clothes of the sought-for gun girl—the blue chinchilla coat and black felt hat with pin—matched Margaret's only complete outfit of clothes perfectly.

Three days went by. Wilbur tried to ignore his growing suspicions, but he couldn't put them off anymore after finding a crumpled note in some trash he was about to burn in the furnace. Dated December 2, the day she left to "visit her sister" in Canton, it read:

I am leaving out of your life forever and I truly am sorry for all the trouble I have caused you, and rather than try to go through the rest of my life under a lie I am taking this means to tell you the truth. I can't face you and tell you this, so I am leaving this to explain the thing you don't know. He has made my life a hell on earth. He came to my house . . . he threatened to expose me if I didn't do as he wanted me to . . . I can't stand the worry any longer and to be away from my baby. So I do hope you can forgive me and give our baby a good home. Love him even if you don't me for I do surely love you. [Signed] Margaret. Please do not tell my mother.

That was enough, even for slow-on-the-uptake Wilbur. Confronting Margaret, he said, "Get your coat on, we're going to see Sheriff Gibson. If you've done this, you'll have to pay for it." According to Wilbur, Margaret didn't even try to deny her guilt. She simply stalled for time, begging Wilbur to wait until the morning. But Wilbur, for once, was firm, and they left for Canton late on the afternoon of December 13.

It must have been a tense two-hour drive to Canton. While Wilbur drove, he later told police, Margaret haltingly confessed the terrible sequence of events that had brought her to this fateful journey. She had met Vernard Fearn at a dance hall, she said, sometime before she married Wilbur. As Wilbur didn't dance, the lonely Margaret soon found opportunities—perhaps during her periodic estrangements from Wilbur—to dance with Fearn at the all-night hops that went on until Sunday morning in Canton. Sometime in 1927 Fearn picked her up in his coal truck while she was hitchhiking home from the Canton library. Instead of taking her home, however, he drove her to a remote spot in the country and raped her. She was too ashamed to tell her new husband about her outrage, and in the months that followed, Fearn forced his physical attentions upon her repeatedly, threatening to tell Wilbur and to ruin her public reputation if she resisted his vile desires. She had taken all she could take by the fall of 1928, and she decided to kill Fearn with Wilbur's gun, which was kept in the house and which she knew well how to use. She had made two futile trips to Waco on the night of December 5 and returned the next night to find and kill Fearn. Although she had expected to be caught immediately—hence the discarded "suicide" note to Wilbur—she had managed to make it back to Canton safely and then had taken a bus to Akron, where she spent the night at the Bond Hotel before returning to Wilbur on Friday morning.

Just before they entered the outskirts of Canton, near Mallet Creek and the Red Raven gas station, Margaret turned to her husband and said, "What do you think they'll do to me? You don't think they'll be brutal to me?"

"Well," replied the maddened Wilbur, "if you don't get the electric chair, I'll miss my guess."

There was a moment of silence, and then Margaret said, "Be sure to take good care of baby."

Wilbur riposted, "Better than you ever did," and then, as the "Welcome to Canton" sign on Route 57 came into sight, he sighed, "Thank God. It won't be long now." A moment later, without a word, Margaret reached into her blouse, hauled out Wilbur's .380 Colt, and shot herself in the chest. The bullet entered her lungs, penetrated the apex of her heart, smashed through her back, and embedded itself in the metal frame of the front-seat upholstery. Screaming, "Margaret, don't die!" and sideswiping other cars in his haste, Wilbur sped to Sheriff Gibson's office and thence to Mercy Hospital.

That seemed to wrap it up, at least to the satisfaction of Wilbur, Sheriff Gibson, and the avid newspapermen thronging the Canton area. But just as abruptly as the case was resolved, it began to dissolve anew. Margaret Heldman's mother and sisters were outraged at Sheriff Gibson's ready acceptance of Wilbur Heldman's story, and they demanded—and got—a second autopsy of Margaret's body, conducted by physicians in DuBois, Pennsylvania, where she was taken for burial the following week. Although that postmortem confirmed the conclusion of Stark County coroner T. C. McQuate that Margaret had died from a single bullet in the heart, Margaret's relatives refused to believe Wilbur's version of their last day together. Margaret would never have committed suicide, they insisted, and her so-called "suicide note," like her November letters confessing adultery to her family, had either been forged or written under Wilbur's dictation and duress.

Public opinion, which had initially rallied around Wilbur, began to sour toward him in the days that followed Margaret's dramatic demise. Much of the rationale for Margaret's shooting of Fearn depended on an uncritical acceptance of what Wilbur—with no corroborating witnesses—claimed that Margaret had alleg-

edly told him on their last ride together. But there were conflicts
in Wilbur's varying stories as to how Margaret had procured the
cartridges for his gun and just how much he had previously known
about her affair with Fearn. The letters written to her sisters and
mother implied that she had committed voluntary adultery with
the straying coal merchant. But at the same time, the dates on the
letters, their postmarks, and internal evidence suggested that Wilbur had enjoyed full knowledge of their contents well before they
were posted and that he might have even forced her to write them.
The Stark County authorities and the public wondered what kind
of man would: 1) insist on taking his wife to the police before getting her a lawyer or even checking her story out; and 2) continue
the journey to Sheriff Gibson's office—instead of the hospital—
after Margaret had critically wounded herself. Within a week of
her death the Stark County police—together with much of the
public—were beginning to believe that Wilbur Heldman was at
the very least an insensitive, inhuman creep, if not a lying murderer who had pulled the trigger on Margaret himself. Two days
after her death, Wilbur was arrested by Sheriff Gibson and held as
a witness for the judicial hearing into the deaths of Vernard Fearn
and Margaret Heldman.

   That hearing, which opened before Justice of the Peace Don-
ald Smyth on December 31, further sullied the reputations of the
two dead principals. Despite their previous public statements, it
turned out that both Sheriff Gibson and Mary Fearn had suspected
Margaret Heldman was the phantom flapper pretty much from the
start. So had Margaret's family, and the hitherto unknown appearance of Margaret's father in Canton during the post-murder week
suggested that there had been some clandestine communication
and negotiation between Margaret's family, the authorities, and
Mary Fearn. Such suspected behind-the-scenes collusion would
also account for the fact that Sheriff Gibson had apparently been
waiting for the Heldmans when Wilbur's car pulled up at his office. At the hearing the exposure of Margaret's letters frankly confessing her adultery to her kin further undermined the rationale
for Wilbur Heldman's story about an avenged rape. The hearing

ended with his being booked on a charge of "moral murder" and bound over to the next session of the grand jury. Wilbur Heldman, Stark County Prosecutor Harder charged, had either shot his wife himself during their last car ride or had deliberately frightened her—with his brutal talk of the electric chair awaiting her—into pulling the trigger herself. Wilbur's behavior, Harder continued, was all the more callous, as no jury in Ohio would have convicted Margaret Heldman after hearing the story she never got to tell anyone except Wilbur.

No one believed at the time of his arrest that Wilbur could be convicted on the existing evidence—and they were right. As the *Cleveland News* forthrightly put it, the murder hearing before Smyth established only that Heldman had been "mighty frank about his domestic affairs," not that he had killed Margaret or forced her to kill herself.

Moreover, Prosecutor Harder never produced a pair of witnesses who, he claimed in late December, would disprove Wilbur's claim that Margaret had shot herself at the location he identified on Route 57. And so the weeks went by, the story disappeared from the newspapers, and finally, on April 11, 1929, after he had spent four months in jail, the Stark County grand jury refused to vote a true bill on Wilbur Heldman, and he walked out of court a free man.

It is a maddening fact that no one will ever know the whole story behind the murder of Vernard Fearn. The evidence of Margaret's November notes and the grudging later admissions of Wilbur Heldman and Mary Fearn support the conclusion that Margaret and Fearn slipped freely into an adulterous relationship sometime in 1927. Whether he initially raped her or subsequently forced his attentions on her is unprovable, but his truck was frequently seen parked outside Margaret's home while Wilbur was away during the next 16 months. How much her husband knew about this affair is also unknown, although both he and Mary Fearn knew or suspected a lot more than they initially told police in the wake of Vernard's murder. But exactly what caused Margaret to kill Fearn is a secret that died with her. Did she fabricate or fantasize some or all of the terrible story she allegedly told her husband about Vernard's predatory behavior? Did she kill Vernard because he forced her to continue their relationship—or because he wanted to break it off? Did Wilbur Heldman make her write those self-incriminating letters to her family? Did he force her to write her final "suicide" note, or did he forge it himself? Did she really murder herself as the car passed the Red Raven gas station on Route 57? Or did Wilbur either shoot her himself—his continual lack of knowledge concerning the whereabouts of his gun remains a puzzlement—or, did he, as lawmen charged, deliberately terrorize her into doing the deed herself? All we can really be sure of is that Margaret Heldman, the "Phantom Flapper Killer," took all of these secrets to her grave with her. Let us bid farewell to this unhappy, mysterious woman with the verses of a poem which was found in her handbag after her death:

A house to clean and a man to scold
And a warm little sleeping babe to hold.
What does a woman want but this,
A house and a man and a child to kiss?
A cake to bake and a floor to sweep
And a tired little child to sing to sleep.
And a man to welcome when work is past—
These are the things whose lure will last!
A vote and a job? Oh, I suppose
That there are women who yearn for those.
Who'd rather be footloose, gay and free
But—a house and a child and a man for me.
For a house I'll choose this house to keep
To scrub and dust and paint and sweep;
For the child our own Elizabeth Ann:
And silent: awkward for you the man!

A Most Unquiet Grave

The Sarah Victor Scandal, 1868

> When arsenic was alleged to have been found in my brother's stomach, no person could possibly have been more astonished than I was.
>
> — Sarah Maria Victor

No matter what one believes about the William Parquet murder mystery, this much is certain: after 138 years the known facts and puzzling ambiguities of his dreadful death still provoke shudders in even the most seasoned connoisseur of Cleveland crime. Did Sarah Maria Victor methodically poison her own brother with arsenic after first forging his will, his power of attorney, and two insurance policies on his young life? Did she nurse him tenderly in his sickbed during his weeklong death struggle, seeing to his every comfort and striving with all the resources at her command to keep him from the grasp of the Grim Reaper? Or was that deathbed vigil a contrived charade to facilitate and mask further administrations of fatal white powder to her helpless, trusting sibling? Was Sarah Victor really the cold-blooded and calculating murderess whom the Cleveland newspapers joyfully vilified and 12 Cuyahoga County jurors voted to send to a hangman's scaffold? Or was she—as her own memoirs and her many friends insisted—simply the most traduced, betrayed, and unlucky female ever to be brought unjustly before the bar of Forest City justice? Therein hangs one of the juiciest tales of Cleveland Gilded Age depravity . . .

As she was an habitual, even congenital, liar, it is difficult to chronicle the early years and antecedents of Sarah Victor with exactitude. Born in Pickway, Ohio, she was the sixth of nine children born to a Frenchman named Parquet and his first, American-born wife. Sarah persistently cultivated the impression that her father was a man of means when she was born on May 5, 1827, yet there is little except her dubious assertion to support this notion. Sometime in the early 1830s, Sarah's mother came to Cleveland with her children—husbandless and with little more than the clothes on their backs. Sarah's story, retailed almost three-score years later, was that her father had become insane when his endorsement of a friend's bad loan forced him into utter bankruptcy. Whatever the reason, Parquet was often absent from home during Sarah's childhood. The most likely explanation from the available evidence is that he was simply a hardened, improvident sot. Mid-century Clevelanders would remember him as a quaint, somewhat comical figure, who sold apples on the street with his children, a jack-of-all-trades whom little boys mocked with shouts of "Old Pockets," their disrespectful corruption of his surname. Said to be violent toward his family when in drink, he had a crazed temper reputedly equaled on such not-infrequent occasions by the pugnacious demeanor of his wife. In any case, "Old Pockets" could not keep his family from penury. In the late 1830s his daughter Sarah was "taken" by a family named Wemple in Collamer, a small rural village in what is now East Cleveland. Such informal adoptions were quite common at that time, and there is evidence that some of Sarah's siblings were also adopted by childless couples who felt sorry for the perpetually indigent and quarrelsome Parquet family.

Many such extralegal adoptions worked out; Sarah Parquet's did not. Completely uneducated when she came to the Wemples, she was soon withdrawn from the local public school after her schoolmates teased her for her ignorance and adoptive status. But Sarah was nothing if not intelligent, and after a term at a private school, she returned to confront her erstwhile tormentors with unrivaled academic superiority. As she entered adolescence in the late 1830s, however, things took an irreversible downward domestic turn. Sarah's subsequent story was that her relations with the Wemples deteriorated when she was unjustly blamed for petty thefts committed by their adopted son and because she abandoned their Presbyterian affiliation to worship at the local Disciples church. The story told later by others—and repeated publicly in newspapers—was that Sarah became incorrigibly defiant and disobedient. The gossip in Collamer was that she refused to do any housework, stayed out until all hours, and was often discovered with members of the opposite sex in unsanctioned circumstances. By the early 1840s, the Wemples had given up on her. Sarah eventually returned to the domestic irregularities of her father's household. In her absence, Sarah's mother had died, but "Old Pockets" had hastily acquired a new spouse, a widow named Austin, who gave him three more children and died forthwith. The two children most important to our narrative were William, born in 1839, and Libbie, born in 1842.

Dependent on her own resources at a young age, Sarah tried domestic service in the households of several of Cleveland's most respectable families, including those of Seth Abbey and Dr. Horace Ackley. (Members of the Cleveland renowned Rowfant Club on Prospect Avenue might well be shocked to learn that their home, Dr. Ackey's former residence, was once the workplace of Sarah Victor.) Somehow, things just never worked out. Sarah's version of her various fallings-out with employers consisted of a litany of excuses, all hinging on innocent misunderstandings, domestic accidents, and unforeseen emergencies. But persistent rumor had it that a résumé of bad behavior and missing personal property followed young Sarah Parquet as she flitted from household to household in Cleveland during the early 1840s. Finally, in 1842, the town became too hot for her, and she "lit out for the territory" to make a new life.

The territory (rural Wisconsin) was new enough, but the patterns of Sarah's old life followed her there. Married in 1843 at the age of 15 to a young farmer named Charles Smith, Sarah found herself the mother of three children by 1850. Alas, domestic felicity eluded her. According to the lachrymose account in her ghost-written autobiography, Charles Smith was a no-good, alcoholic, philandering scoundrel and lazy bum. Despite her finer instincts, however—or perhaps because of them—Sarah stayed with him, notwithstanding his numerous extramarital affairs and even after he brought a prostitute into their home as a "boarder."

Things hit rock bottom for Sarah Parquet Smith about 1850. By that time she had returned to Cleveland and was desperately trying to make ends meet by running a rooming house on Ohio Street. According to Sarah's later story, Charlie did nothing to support her and the children, although Cleveland journalists would eventually make uncharitable references to a certain "Buckeye Insurance Co.," a fraudulent concern with which he was closely associated in his Cleveland years. Finally, by about 1854, Sarah had endured enough. After a fight in which Charlie threatened her with a pistol, she fled their hovel, divorced him, and sought anonymity by changing her dwelling and her name. Her new surname, "Victor" (never legally assumed), was taken from the brand name of a patent stove she purchased, although unkind journalists would later suggest that she chose it as a token of her triumph over Charles Smith.

Little is known of Sarah's next decade and a half except one fact and a plethora of lurid rumors. The fact is that starting in 1859 she became the kept mistress of one Christopher Columbus Carleton, an insurance broker who pursued his vocation with his son-in-law James in the firm of Carleton & Lee. Carleton's wife had died in

1858; Sarah, by her own admission, was financially destitute. It was probably just a matter of time before the worldly Carleton slipped into an irregular relationship with the attractive divorcee who looked far younger than her 32 years. Within several years Carleton gave Sarah a life tenure in his two-story, medium-sized white frame house at 18 Webster Street. There is ample evidence that they lived together for the next decade in what a future prosecuting attorney would characterize as "concubinage."

As for the rumors, well, *nothing* was too awful to say about Sarah Victor once she had been publicly pilloried as the poisoner of her own brother. Ill report of her ranged from the infamous to the just plain weird. Vilified as a prostitute and brothel keeper in the public prints after her murder indictment, it was asserted that she had run a notorious house of ill fame in Fremont, Ohio, before transferring her trade in female flesh and debauched misery to Cleveland. Or, as the *Cleveland Leader,* Sarah's most censorious critic, put it in florid dudgeon:

> About this time she was kept as a mistress by a certain man [Christopher Carleton], but is thought to have been public property to a considerable extent. She did not confine herself, either, to prostituting her own virtue, but was the means of robbing many a hearthstone of its most cherished gem. Never, till the great day of accounts will it be known how many homes she has blighted, how many hearts she has caused to be broken, how many wives she has ruined, how many maidens she has led astray. She seems to have made a business of securing victims to the hellish passions of wicked men. Many a heart rending story could be told of her accomplishments in this direction. But the mind revolts from such unnamed crimes.

Not content with such undocumented imputations of her vileness, the Cleveland newspapers also competed with each other in cataloging Sarah's alleged oddities during the decade before her extreme notoriety. It was said that she wore green goggles and a Shaker bonnet for several years, in a vain effort to disguise her identity, presumably from the bibulous Charles Smith and the minions of the law. It was asserted that she assiduously practiced her poison craft on her neighbors' cats, dogs, and chickens so regularly that the wary soon learned to keep domestic pets away from the vicinity of 18 Webster Street. It was rumored that she had murdered

---

She seems to have made a business of securing victims to the hellish passions of wicked men.

---

her father and her son Charles—*and shed not a tear in public for them!* None of the rumors was ever proven at her murder trail or later, except for the admitted fact that Sarah had lived "in sin" with Christopher Columbus Carleton for ten years.

Sarah herself was keenly aware of how badly the stain of her acknowledged unchasteness colored public perceptions of her. In her autobiography she would ruefully admit that she had erred most imprudently in transferring her affections from the abusive Smith to the evasive Carleton: "I did not, until it was too late, realize that I was shunning the rock only to fall in the whirlpool, or *vice versa.*" As for the green goggles and bonnet, they were probably assumed to temporarily hide the serious burns that Mrs. Victor received in a house fire caused by her son Charlie, who was playing with matches.

By 1865 Sarah Victor was doing pretty well, considering her 38 years of hard knocks. Although Carleton refused to make good on his ancient promise to marry her, their relations were constant and convivial, and he delivered on his promise of a life interest in the house on Webster Street. Sarah was a member in good standing of the Trinity Episcopal Church on Scovill Avenue and much involved in its charitable activities. Working as a skilled seamstress over the years, Sarah had acquired a small store of capital and had begun to speculate modestly in real estate, buying and selling small lots. She had enough funds to afford the domestic services of two women, Annie Miller and Anna Morehouse, and there was also the rent contributed by her younger half-sister, Elizabeth (Libbie) Gray.

Libbie was 15 years younger than Sarah and had already compiled an unfortunate domestic history. She had been unhappily married several times, most recently to a "Dr." Gray, who had become notorious for vending a patent medicine known as "Golden Pain Searcher" on the streets of Cleveland. Working in a millinery shop, Libbie, together with her young son, lived on and off with Mrs. Victor in imperfect amicability for most of the mid-1860s. It was clear to everyone who knew the two sisters that they didn't get along; it was equally clear that Sarah dominated everyone in the house and ruled their lives with an iron hand and unforgiving discipline. Then, about the end of 1865, William Parquet came to live at 18 Webster Street.

William, Sarah's half-brother by her father's second wife, was 26. He was five feet, five inches tall with a light complexion, dark hair, and gray eyes. Although illiterate, he was considered of average intelligence by those who knew him, and his health was generally good, as evidenced by his three years of military service during the Civil War, which included involvement in most of the battles of General Grant's 1864 Virginia campaign. Sarah would later claim that she was close to William while he was in the army and would cite the many letters she wrote to him at that time. Naturally, however, she was not able to prove exactly when she wrote her alleged letters (to an illiterate!). The epistles in reply from the unlettered William to his beloved sister Sarah were suspiciously undated and improbably well-written missives from a completely unlettered man. There were, however, two other alleged documents that William was kind enough to send his sister during that long, cruel war: a power of attorney (giving her complete financial control of his assets) and his will (leaving everything to Sarah Maria Victor). But more of that later . . .

William came home from his three-year stint in the 12th U.S. Infantry in the fall of 1865. Although his discharge was quite honorable, Sarah said he came to her house completely broke, having nothing more to show for his long military service than a letter of praise from his commanding officer. Well, not *just* that: William also returned with a distinct case of syphilis, for which Sarah soon referred him to a Cleveland physician, Dr. Levi Sapp, for the usual heroic mercury treatment.

About this time, Sarah also took out an insurance policy for $2,300 on William's life. Sarah would later claim that it was William's idea and that he had insisted it be done while he was in the army, when violent death seemed imminent every day and all of his fellow soldiers were doing the same. The blunt fact, however, is that the application for the insurance was dated September 5, 1865—five months after the end of the war. Moreover, it was clear in retrospect that William, ever illiterate, did not fill out or sign the application himself. Cynical souls will delight in the disclosure that the insurance policy, No. 218,555 with the Connecticut Life Insurance Company, was taken out through insurance broker Christopher Columbus Carleton. The premium was $51.50, with $29 paid in cash by Mrs. Victor and the remainder loaned on a note incurred by the same Sarah M. Victor. Neither Carleton nor his partner, Lee, could remember even seeing William Parquet about the insurance, remembering only that Sarah seemed to have complete charge of the matter. Dr. S. R. Beckwith, who examined William on behalf of the Connecticut Life Insurance Company, pronounced him a good risk, despite his bout with venereal disease, and the insurance policy went into effect in the fall of 1865.

William stayed at Sarah's house until the spring of 1866. His life there could not have been too dramatic, as Sarah did not allow him to have visitors at the house, and she insisted on accompanying him on those rare occasions he ventured out. He then took a job as a hostler at a tavern run by E. M. Fenner in Euclid Township. And on March 16, 1866, he made application to the firm of Carleton and Lee for $1,500 in accidental death insurance. Mrs. Victor would initially claim, at William's inquest, that she knew nothing about the accidental death policy. She later changed her story at the trial, recalling vividly that William had insisted on the policy, as he was fearful of working around Mr. Fenner's horses. Once again, someone other than William Parquet signed his name to the policy, and Mrs. Victor, once again, paid the premium. No one seems to have thought it odd that an ex-soldier who had spent four years around horses was now afraid to be in their presence.

Two months later, William had an accident in Fenner's barn, falling into a hayrack and painfully injuring his side. He was treated by Dr. Sapp, and everyone believed (and ultimately testified in court) that he made a full recovery from the injury. Everyone, that is, except Mrs. Victor, who insisted only after his death that William had been much troubled by his injuries during the last nine months of his life. Whatever the truth, it is a matter of record that William returned to his usual work at Fenner's within several weeks of his injury, and none of his fellow workers nor his employer noticed any decline in his health.

In January 1867 William quit his job at Fenner's and again took up residence at Sarah's house on Webster Street. The likely reason was an unrequited romantic attachment that he had formed to Ann Fenner, one of his employer's daughters. Sarah would later insist that William was driven away by Ann's parents, who wanted someone with better prospects in life than an illiterate handyman for their daughter's intended. But there was never any evidence that Ann returned William's affections, and she herself testified to the contrary at Sarah's trial. It is true that William died and was buried wearing a ring locket with her picture in it—but he had stealthily acquired the picture from one of Ann's sisters.

William's last public appearance was on December 23, 1866. Attending a Christmas party at the Fenner house, he was seen there by Carrie Libenthal and Martha Burns, both of whom would recall that he seemed in good spirits, danced up a storm, and was "real lively."

Just when William Parquet began to sicken unto death will never be known. His sister Sarah would always claim that his decline began on the evening of Saturday, January 26, when he slipped off the front steps of her house and hurt himself. Sarah's thought was that he had aggravated his old hayrack injury. She immediately put him to bed with a mustard poultice and a dose of ginger tea. William was better the next morning, Sarah would recall, but still rather low. Yet not low enough, apparently, for Sarah to call in a doctor, or low enough for anyone else in the house to even notice that William was not himself.

There was no ambiguity about the next phase of William's illness. Sometime during the night of Monday, January 28, he became ill in his bedroom. Wracked by stomach pains and paroxysms of vomiting and uttering painful groans, he became so ill that Sarah took him into her own bedroom. William was no better on Tuesday, shrieking in agony, retching uncontrollably, complaining of stomach pains, and crying ceaselessly for water and alcohol. Either that day or the next—no one could ever remember which—Sarah called in Dr. Sapp. Although somewhat puzzled by his patient's symptoms, Sapp made a tentative diagnosis of dysentery and prescribed the usual regimen of aconite and bryonia. He specifically cautioned against giving William any alcohol and asked that he be called again if William's condition worsened. Before he left, Mrs. Victor expressed her belief that William was going to die. Nonsense, retorted Dr. Sapp, there was no reason to think Sarah's brother was in any danger of death. But Sarah told Dr. Sapp that William had already told her that he thought he was going to die. There was no doubt in her mind he was right: she told Dr. Sapp that she had already seen one sister and one of her own children die *right after they had experienced similar premonitions of death.*

William Parquet never left his sister's bedroom alive. Over the following week, he continued to suffer terrible stomach pains, continual vomiting, persistent thirst, and strained and bloody stools. Throughout his prolonged agony, Sarah was at his side, giving him most of his medicine and nourishment and maintaining a practically ceaseless bedside vigil that was the admiration of all who witnessed her apparent sisterly devotion. Some of William's many visitors during his seven-day agony were puzzled—especially in retrospect—that Sarah frequently administered various kinds of alcohol and heavy doses of chloroform to her suffering patient. But Sarah would brook no interference or advice with her nursing.

Everyone, especially her sister Libbie, knew better than to contradict the imperious Sarah. Nothing was done to or for William without her say-so.

For six days, William Parquet lingered in pain, never getting much better or much worse. On Sunday night, February 2, there was a noticeable decline in his condition. Just after Sarah gave him some whiskey, William went into a screaming fit and someone volunteered to go for Dr. Sapp. "No," said Sarah, reiterating her comment that William was going to die anyway and adding that Dr. Sapp didn't want to be bothered in the middle of the night. In any case, Dr. Sapp showed up the next morning and, after examining his patient, pronounced him in no danger of death.

Dr. Sapp was in for a big surprise. Shortly after 5 A.M. the next morning, William roused himself from his near-coma and said to Sarah, "Goodbye, Sister." A short time later, he muttered, "I'm going home" loud enough to be heard by several of those in the sickroom. At 6 A.M. he expired, and Dr. Sapp was called in.

Dr. Sapp, a competent homeopathic physician, was, to say the least, greatly puzzled by William's death. His observations had not led him to expect anything like this outcome. He immediately asked Sarah to let him perform an autopsy to determine the cause of death. Sarah adamantly refused, even after Libbie and various neighbors and friends added their support to Dr. Sapp's entreaty. It was William's last request, she tearfully told Dr. Sapp, that she not allow the doctors to cut up his dead body. According to Sarah, William had been traumatized as a young boy by Cleveland medical students, who had gruesomely paraded a "resurrected" corpse through the streets and forced the impressionable William to watch their grotesque procession. It was simply out of the question, insisted Sarah, especially as she knew that medical students often stole parts of autopsied corpses as grotesque trophies for their private revels.

Eventually, Sarah tentatively agreed to allow just Dr. Sapp and Dr. Beckwith to examine William's corpse, but it is a fact that no autopsy was performed before William was buried in the family plot at Woodland Cemetery on February 6, 1867. Later—much

later—Sarah would change her story and insist that she had forbade the postmortem because she feared exposure of William's
"private disease" through some physical evidence that he had suffered from syphilis. But Dr. Sapp testified that there was no such
evidence on William's body, and Sarah, in her 1887 autobiography,
ultimately denied ever mentioning William's venereal disease to
Sapp or anyone else.

   William Parquet's body was not to rest in peace. Several hours
after the funeral, Sarah, apparently concerned that the doctors
might still insist on an autopsy, returned to Woodland Cemetery.
There she mentioned her concern to cemetery foreman Patrick
Barry and asked him to bury a box containing the bones of two of
her children on top of William's casket. This was done, and the dirt
was shoveled back over the grave. Sarah remained apprehensive
that someone would disturb her brother's grave and returned there
periodically to mark it with twigs, so that she would know if anyone had tampered with it. And she told her servant, Anna Miller,
that she was going to have someone watch the grave to prevent any
disturbance. (At the same time, Sarah saw to it that William would
at least be able to see whoever might come for his body: his casket
had a glass window inserted in the top, just over his face.)

   William Parquet's death was a matter of considerable speculation to all who knew him—and his sister Sarah had a different
answer for just about everyone who asked her about it. Under
"Cause of Death" in the Woodland Cemetery register, she wrote,
"Inflammation [infection] of the Lungs." Several weeks after William's death, at the time she filed for payment of the $1,500 acci-
dental death policy, she told James Lee that he had died from the
effects of his hayrack accident at Fenner's. She told her servant
Anna Morehouse that William had died from the effects of the
"private disease" he had contracted while in the army. She told her
neighbor, Hannah Newell of 21 Webster Street, that William had
died of an "inflammation of the stomach" caused by his hayrack
accident. She told her neighbor Miss Ida Weile of 16 Webster
Street that William had died of heart disease. And she told Dr.
Sapp that she thought William's death was caused by his eating a

frozen turnover or pie that he had consumed on the Monday night he was taken sick . . . but more of that later.

Sarah's statements to her relatives and neighbors about William's insurance and personal property were of like diversity. She told Libbie that William had left no insurance but had bequeathed

---

Visitors were puzzled that Sarah frequently administered various kinds of alcohol and heavy doses of chloroform to her suffering patient.

---

all of his real and personal property solely to her, including several property lots and his watch. After Libbie prodded her further, Sarah eventually produced a handwritten will to that effect, allegedly sent to her by William while he was in the army—but which she would not allow Libbie to read. Sarah told her friend Eliza Welch after William died that he had left no insurance whatsoever. She told E. M. Fenner (at the time she successfully dunned him for some of William's back pay) that William's insurance policies had lapsed before his death. Sarah told Anna Morehouse that she had tried to obtain the army bounty due William but had been unsuccessful—which was a lie. She also asked Anna to tell everyone that she had not gotten any insurance from William's estate. And Sarah told her neighbor Jared Newell that she had received no insurance at all.

Sarah Victor suffered no such confusion in securing the insurance money. Several weeks after William's death she showed up at the offices of Carleton & Lee to file papers for payment of both William's life and accident policies. James Lee told her plainly that there was no question of filing for the accident policy, as William's death had clearly not been accidental. Sarah tried to insist that William had died from the after-effects of his hayrack fall but did not pursue the matter emphatically, perhaps fearing that an autopsy might ensue if she persisted. In due time, a check for $2,300, issued by Carleton & Lee, was promptly cashed and turned back to the firm for piecemeal disbursement as required by Mrs. Victor. During the following year, Lee and Carleton paid out various sums to her; there was only about $500 left when she was arrested in February 1868. Sarah also filed for, and collected, William's back pay from E. M. Fenner and the remainder due from his army bounty, neither of which she shared with Libbie or anyone else.

Somehow, some way, various disquieting rumors about William Parquet's death began festering throughout Cleveland in the months that followed his demise. Maybe it was the multiple, conflicting stories told by Sarah to her friends, relatives, and neighbors. Maybe it had something to do, as Sarah believed, with her sister Libbie's anger about not getting any of William's estate. Maybe it was Sarah's continual apprehension about someone digging up her brother's body, a fear that seemed suspicious to those curious about the manner of William's demise. Maybe it was even, as Sarah claimed in her autobiography, a bizarre plot by her neighbor Jared Newell to blackmail her and to divert attention away from Newell's own murderous past.

By the late fall of 1867 there was a general rumor that William might have been poisoned. Indeed, Sarah herself eventually brought the matter up with E. M. Fenner, sweetly inquiring whether someone in his family just might have poisoned William to keep him away from Fenner's daughter Ann. Not surprisingly, Fenner was shocked and offended by the question, but when he demanded to know where Sarah had heard such a story, she confessed she couldn't quite remember the name of the woman who had told her such a horrid tale.

Matters took a more ominous and concrete form when Sarah's sister Libbie became involved. Still living at 18 Webster Street, Libbie was incensed at Sarah's getting everything; she didn't believe that William had left no insurance. When she found out about the property lots, the army bounty, and the personal effects, she began making inquiries. Eventually, a merchant on Erie Street tipped her off about the insurance. She went to the offices of Carleton &

Lee on December 17 or 18, 1867. Mr. Lee candidly admitted to her that her sister had received the $2,300 insurance payment, and Libbie forthwith paid a call on probate judge Daniel Tilden. Tilden was aroused enough by her suspicions to send her to Cuyahoga County sheriff Felix Nicola, who began making discreet inquiries of his own. His investigation culminated in a journey to Woodland Cemetery on January 28, 1868, and the exhumation there of William Parquet's body in the presence of Deputy Sheriff George Ridgeway, Dr. Proctor Thayer, Professor J. L. Cassels, and a cemetery work crew.

Meanwhile, Sarah was busy. She had become aware of the suspicions swirling about her and during the last weeks before William's exhumation labored mightily to prepare the minds of her friends and neighbors for what might come. About the time William was being hauled out of the earth, she recalled to Annie Miller that William had become ill after he ate a frozen turnover brought into the house by Libbie. Sarah also confided that the turnover might have been originally shoplifted by William that evening at a local grocery, the point of her confidence to Annie Miller seeming to be that the turnover had not been of *her* making or provision and that it was Libbie who brought it into the house. At this time Sarah also mentioned William's "private disease" as the reason she had opposed an autopsy and told Annie further that she herself had once suffered from syphilis, shamefully inflicted upon her, she implied, by her no-good, long-gone husband. Sometime during those same few weeks before the arrest, she told the same insinuating story about the turnover to Sheriff Nicola.

Sarah had gone to see Nicola because she was concerned about the ugly rumors that were circulating; she asked Nicola to stop Libbie from telling libelous stories about her. She also tried to enlist Dr. Sapp as an intermediary, hinting in a letter to him that Libbie and others were attempting to blackmail her for things she hadn't done. Dr. Sapp refused to become involved, as did Cleveland's U.S. postal authorities when Sarah asked them to assist her in tracing what she said was a threatening letter.

The storm finally broke over Sarah Victor's head on Febru-

ary 5, 1868. After receiving a report from Chemical Professor
J. L. Cassels on his analysis of William Parquet's internal organs,
Cuyahoga County coroner J. C. Schenck swore out an inquest
panel composed of citizens H. H. Little, Moses Hill, S. H. Fox,
William Bowler, N. A. Gray, and Charles Whitaker. After a visit
to Woodland Cemetery to view William's body, they returned to
Sheriff Nicola's office and began taking testimony from the first
witness called, Sarah Maria Victor.

Sarah would later maintain that she was caught completely by
surprise when Deputy Sheriff Ridgeway called on her and asked
her to come downtown with him that afternoon. But come she
did, without protest, and at 3:30 P.M. she took the stand and told
her version of her brother's death in a flood of tears. Producing
his alleged will and power of attorney, she stated that he had died
from injuries sustained in his hayrack mishap and that his final
illness had seemingly been triggered by eating a piece of pie or
turnover. She admitted giving William brandy, whiskey, wine,
milk, lemonade, gruel, coffee, and tea during her weeklong sickbed vigil. She insisted she did not know that Dr. Sapp had forbade
the consumption of any alcohol. She also denied giving William
any chloroform during his final illness. She admitted that she kept
arsenic in the house to kill rats, storing it under a rug in her sister
Libbie's bedroom As soon as Sarah finished her testimony, she was
arrested by Sheriff Nicola on a charge of murder and removed to
the county jail.

Why Sarah had been so quickly charged became clear with the
next day's testimony. Dr. Sapp, the first witness, testified about the
symptoms of William's death struggle and his shock at the unexpected death of his patient. He recounted Sarah's fervent opposition to an autopsy, recalled Sarah's morbid emphasis on William's
alleged premonitions of death, and mentioned his surprise at dis-
covering that William had been given frequent alcoholic drinks
contrary to his expressed orders. He also produced the letter he
had received from Sarah three weeks before, seeking his aid against
Libbie's supposed machinations against her. The undated missive

made it clear that Sarah was more than willing to play the character assassination game herself:

I thought I had better let you know doctor, the son of the man that we were speaking about [probably Jared Newell, Sarah's neighbor, whom she claimed was mixed up in the plot to blackmail her] saw me at your office, and will probably tell her [Libbie] they saw me there and she may not call on you. If she don't wont [*sic*] you call on her as soon as you can, I will pay you for your trouble. You might say I heard what she had reported and called on you and said if there are any doubts or suspicions that anything was wrong on my part that all should be investigated for the satisfaction of respectable people but not for such low creatures as those who wrote those low letters. Tell her please that as she has circulated bad things that I had done, that to prove me guilty she must prove herself innocent and truthful and by so doing she must bring those that has known her from a child and through life and that I must do the same; tell her friends of a few weeks won't answer, for it is a serious case and if you take it in hand it must be a thorough thing. Then ask her what reference she can give, ask her what places she lived in before she came here, and what names she can give you to write to, and what was her name when she lived there, and what church was she a member of, the clergyman's name, the occupation of her husband and such other questions as you think of, and if she don't answer satisfactorily and freely, tell her you are not quite satisfied, and that she must bring forward all those that have made themselves interested. Doctor, you can do and say more than I and I leave it all to you as my friend and physician. [Signed] S. M. Victor

Dr. Proctor Thayer testified next. The widely respected Cleveland physician and frequent expert witness in criminal trials described William's exhumation and stressed the corpse's unusually good state of preservation, a condition often correlated with the presence of arsenic in the body. Indeed, William's corpse had been so well preserved, Thayer marveled, that the lungs were still inflatable and Deputy Sheriff George Ridgeway had immediately recognized the deceased, whom he had known casually. Thayer told further of how he had taken tissue samples from William's vital organs, placed them in sealed vessels, and given them to Professor John L. Cassels.

Cassels now took the stand, and it was his testimony, more than that of any other witness or any item of circumstantial evidence, that propelled Sarah Victor toward a hangman's noose. Cassels was one of the founders of the Cleveland Medical College, a widely respected scientist, and a frequent expert witness whose word carried great weight with jurists and juries. He testified that he had run five different tests over the course of a week for the presence of arsenic in the stomach, liver, kidney, and heart of William Parquet. He had found none in the kidney, spleen, or heart, and only a small trace in the liver. But he had found two or three grains in the stomach and suspected that several more grains had been lost in the testing process. Cassels told the inquest panel that the deceased could only have lived from five to seven days after ingesting such a quantity of arsenic, and that the absence of significant amounts of arsenic in organs other than the stomach indicated that a large dose of arsenic had been ingested shortly before death, most likely within the final 24 hours. Noting that the symptoms of arsenical poisoning were "pain and heat in the region of the stomach, thirst, sometimes vomiting, sometimes diarrhea, green and bloody stools . . . dysentery, great prostration, death preceded sometimes by convulsions"—all symptoms exhibited by the deceased—Cassels concluded, "there is no doubt in my mind that the person died from the effects of arsenic."

Other witnesses followed Cassels, but it was clear what the verdict would be when he had finished his testimony. If William Parquet had died of a fatal dose of arsenic administered within the last 24 hours of his life, there was only one logical suspect. At the end of the second day's testimony, the inquest panel deliberated for just ten minutes before issuing its verdict that "William Parquet came to his death from the effects of arsenical poison administered, as we believe, by Mrs. Sarah Maria Victor." Unable to make bail, Sarah remained ensconced in one of the more genteel suites of the county jail, with her meals sent in from the nearby Richards & Company restaurant.

Sarah soon secured the counsel of one of Cleveland's leading defense attorneys, Marshal S. Castle, well-known to crime connoisseurs for his ferocious, if unsuccessful, 1865 defense of Dr. John Hughes, the poetaster murderer of Tamsen Parsons. Although assisted by local legal lights R. P. Ranney, C. W. Palmer, and James M. Coffinberry, Castle handled virtually all of the trial burden. In her 1887 autobiography, Sarah bitterly attacked Castle's handling of her case, from the moment he waived her preliminary examination before Justice of the Peace G. A. Kolbe on February 10. She also claimed that Castle took on her case only because he wanted the fee, and that he forced her to sign over to him all of her remaining assets. In addition, she declared (19 years after the fact) that Castle was "almost constantly under the effects of liquor" during her two-week trial. Whatever the truth of her unlikely accusations, it was the perception of most trial observers that Castle had an unruly, irrational client who constantly badgered him with her own legal tactics, most of which were concerned with the counterproductive character assassination of prosecution witnesses.

Sarah's trial on a first-degree-murder charge opened before Common Pleas Judge Horace Foote on Wednesday, June 10, 1868. She sat at the defense table, attired in black, listless and silent except when prompting M. S. Castle to harry her enemies with innuendo. The 36 men in the venire were quickly whittled down to an acceptable jury of 12 men, all of them from the western side of Cuyahoga County. Those few excluded were challenged on the usual grounds of having already formed an opinion as to Sarah's guilt or innocence or because they opposed capital punishment. And then, after a break for lunch, prosecutor J. M. Jones opened for the state with a lucid, uncomplicated charge that Sarah had murdered her brother for his insurance money. Citing the evidence of Thayer and Cassels that William had died of arsenic administered within

24 hours of his death, Jones outlined Sarah's ceaseless attendance at his sickbed and the strong improbability that anyone else could have had the opportunity to administer the fatal dose. Declining to make an opening defense statement, Castle merely offered the usual caution to the jury that his client deserved the presumption of innocence. Then the first of 39 witnesses was called.

Thayer and Cassels repeated their inquest testimony, dwelling in detail on the large amount of arsenic in William Parquet's stomach and the absence of any organic disease. Thayer particularly stressed the fact that chloroform could be used to mask the symptoms of arsenic poisoning. Then prosecutor Jones began to weave the web of circumstantial evidence tying Sarah to the arsenic with a parade of witnesses to her conduct in William's sickroom. Servant Annie Miller swore under oath that Sarah insisted on doing all of the cooking for William herself and that she had administered most of his medicine and liquids while he was bedridden. She recalled Sarah's suggestive remarks about the famous turnover just a week before her arrest and noted that Sarah had concluded that conversation by giving Annie a present of two chains and a bracelet—something the stingy Sarah had never done before. At this point, prosecutor Jones abruptly halted Annie's testimony, objecting that Sarah was telegraphing signs to the witness on how to answer his questions. M. S. Castle vehemently denied the charge, but it may have influenced the jury, as they had already heard Annie emphasize how domineering Sarah was in her domestic circle.

The testimony of various witnesses about William Parquet's alleged will and power of attorney was muddled and inconclusive, particularly as to the handwriting and the validity of the witnessing signatures. But it was clear, even after some of the testimony was excluded, that the illiterate William could not have written or signed either of the documents. Which meant that Sarah Victor was at least likely to be a forger, if not necessarily a cold-blooded poisoner. And the testimony of other witnesses as to Sarah's administration of her brother's assets before his death further cemented her image as a scheming, grasping conniver. Several Cuyahoga County officials offered detailed accounts of how Sarah had transferred much of William's real estate into her own hands even while he was alive. They were followed by a parade of Sarah's neighbors, all of whom testified as to her iron control of the sickroom and her passionate aversion to an autopsy.

Sarah's already bleak prospects took a decisive turn for the worse on the fourth trial day, June 13, with the appearance of her half-sister Libbie Gray on the stand. Demolishing Sarah's after-the-fact story about the mysterious turnover, she recalled that it was of Sarah's making and re-created the context of William's Monday-night snack in damning detail:

> [He] complained of being hungry and went to the cupboard and ate a piece of pie; I asked him for a piece and he told me to go and get a piece for myself. I said nothing to Annie Miller about eating that pie. After he told me to go and get a piece he offered me a piece; I said if I can't have the whole I don't want any.

Libbie, who made a good impression on the jury and spectators, further tightened the looming noose around her sister's neck by recalling that Sarah had administered multiple doses of chloroform to William throughout his illness and ordered others to dose him with the same, despite Dr. Sapp's orders to the contrary. Libbie also remembered Sarah giving William a small quantity of a white powder, probably morphine, on the end of a knife blade. She denied spreading rumors about her brother being poisoned and insisted that she had never discussed the matter publicly until it was all over the newspapers in February.

Marshal Castle didn't help his client with his nasty cross-examination of Libbie Gray. Rather than confuting any of the damning details of her testimony, he chose instead to blacken her character by demanding to know whether she had been married to a succession of men, including a Mr. Bayless, a Mr. Robinson, a Mr. Gibson, and a Mr. Karther. His tactic, clearly prompted by whispered conferences with Sarah, backfired miserably, exciting sympathy for Libbie, who, at Judge Foote's sympathetic prompting, declined to answer Castle's insinuating interrogatories. A little while later, Castle tried the same tactic on Anna Morehouse as she left the stand, audibly baiting her with the taunt, "You haven't seen your husband since you were here, have you?"

"No," said the imperturbable Morehouse, "I haven't and I don't want to and it is a pity there ain't more women that do as I do!"

Four days later, after a forced recess because of Mrs. Victor's deteriorating health, prosecutor Jones avenged Libbie Gray's ordeal with his brutal cross-examination of Christopher Columbus Carleton. Carleton's testimony about both the insurance and the details of William's sickroom was redundant, but Jones had decided to use him to destroy Sarah's character for the edification of the jury. After establishing that Sarah had paid virtually no rent on her Webster Street house for 10 years, Jones asked Carleton outright whether Sarah had not, in point of fact, been his "kept mistress" for the last 10 years. Judge Foote immediately cautioned Carleton that he need not incriminate himself by answering, and Carleton remained silent. Not dismayed, Jones hammered back, demanding to know whether Carleton had paid Sarah "a stipulated price per week for her concubinage" during her decade's residence at 18 Webster Street. Carleton again refused to answer, but the damage had been done: Jones had established that Sarah was a kept woman with no other apparent means of support than the petty earnings from her needlework. The implication was clear that her precarious financial security might well have made the possibility of William Parquet's insurance a tempting opportunity.

All this was but a prelude to the main event, Sarah's direct testimony on Thursday morning. The courtroom was packed, with many women present, as Sarah, dressed entirely in funereal black and sporting a black veil, was helped to the witness chair. She testified well into the afternoon, repeating much of her inquest testimony and adding new details. She remembered much more about the famous turnover, asserting that she had begged William not to eat it because it was "frozen," and it might make him sick. She denied spreading conflicting stories about his cause of death, insisting that she had always thought he died from the effects of his hayrack fall in Fenner's barn. She admitted giving Billy a little whiskey once during his last illness but denied dosing him with divers kinds of alcohol or even knowing that Dr. Sapp had prohibited the same. And she denied repeatedly dosing William with chloroform during his sickbed ordeal, admitting that she had only done it once or twice and then thrown it out the window.

Sarah suddenly rose to her feet,
began gesticulating in a wild manner,
and commenced a delirious rant
against her adversaries

Late that afternoon, prosecutor Jones caught Sarah in a carefully laid trap. They were discussing Sarah's sly query to E. M. Fenner as to whether some of his family had poisoned William to keep him away from Ann Fenner. Sarah repeated her story that the notion had been suggested to her by an unidentified woman but admitted that the woman had not actually used the word "poison." Jones pounced: Why, if that was the case, had Sarah used the word "poison" in her subsequent colloquy with Fenner? Sarah tried to evade a direct answer but eventually muttered that she had only "inferred" poison from the woman's conversation. A similar embarrassment ensued when Sarah disputed Anna Morehouse's story about her having had syphilis. Sarah vehemently denied having such a conversation but refused to reply when asked if she had ever, in fact, had syphilis.

A few minutes later, after the last witnesses had testified, M. S. Castle informed Judge Foote that the defense had concluded its presentation. As he finished, Sarah suddenly rose to her feet, began gesticulating in a wild manner, and commenced a delirious rant against her adversaries, especially Libbie Gray. It was apparent to everyone that Sarah still thought she was in her jail cell as she raved on in the crowded courtroom:

She [Libbie] has gone by my window four times—why will she do so? She makes me feel so badly—are they going to sell my life for her friendship? What am I here for? Four months in jail? I did not think she would let me stay here so long—ain't this too bad. Mrs. Hatch [Sarah's jail attendant], she will repent it. I know she will. I never want to see her till she comes here and tells me she is sorry—then I'll forgive her. She don't know how bad she makes me feel. I do believe she will come forward before the trial comes on and say that I am innocent. She throws her head, poor girl, girl! The Lord forgive her. I've suffered, I've suffered. Tis hard, ain't it, Mrs. Hatch? Now I'll go and lay down and think no more about it. I don't want to see her, poor girl. Poor boy—I wonder if she's gone to put flowers on his grave today—the papers say they are going. I must live a little longer. Give me medicine. Give me strength. The most glorious day of my life will be when I go into the Court House. I will see Mr. Jones and tell him all about it. After this is over I don't care to live any longer, after I have proved myself innocent. That miserable Newell. He wanted the land. I wouldn't sell it to him. He is the cause of all this—that miserable man. Why won't they tell me the whole truth? Did I ever think I should come to this? Why does she go to the City Hotel to board—to put poison in my food? Poor boy. She knew she hadn't a dollar in this world. I got that land for him that he might have a way to save his money.

Mr. Castle said they would kill me. Poor girl—why don't she come to see me? She knows. That miserable man, that miserable Newell. I've suffered so much in my life.

Seemingly oblivious to where she was and what she was doing, Sarah mumbled on in this fashion for some time, as her attorneys and Dr. Beckwith tried to calm and quiet her. Removed to a settee, she finally subsided after Beckwith gave her some wine and a powerful sedative; she was taken back to jail. By 6 P.M. she was reported to be herself again, and the next day's *Plain Dealer* expressed the skepticism of many who thought Sarah was laying the groundwork for the old insanity dodge: "Those who have known her for years state that she has often had these fits when excited, and they need cause no alarm for her safety."

Sarah returned to court on Friday and, after the appearance of the 39th and last witness, Homer B. DeWolfe began the closing arguments for the state. The case, he said, was a simple structure of five propositions: 1) William Parquet had died of arsenic poisoning; 2) Sarah had a strong economic motive for administering the poison; 3) Sarah had both the means and opportunity to administer the arsenic; 4) the case against Sarah was based on the general principles of circumstantial evidence; and 5) all circumstantial evidence in the case pointed without exception to Sarah Maria Victor. DeWolfe then reviewed the symptoms of arsenic poisoning for the jury and recapitulated the testimony of witnesses about William's sufferings. He stressed Sarah's need for money and dwelt upon her successful machinations to obtain William's personal property, his bounty money, and his insurance—her claims to which were supported by an improperly witnessed and highly suspicious will. He noted that Sarah had admitted having arsenic in the house and that she, by the testimony of many witnesses, was in William's sickroom almost constantly. And DeWolfe particularly stressed Sarah's refusal to allow an autopsy on her dead brother as evidence of her guilt.

DeWolfe devoted much of his final peroration to the question of circumstantial evidence. Aware of the popular prejudice against it, DeWolfe remarked:

In cases of suspected poisoning, the evidence must of necessity be circumstantial, for no one who poisons another ever calls a jury of twelve men to witness the act. Poison is peculiarly a woman's weapon, and especially the weapon of abandoned women.

DeWolfe ended his powerful presentation with a plethora of citations from legal authorities to the effect that circumstantial evidence was as strong in some cases as direct evidence.

C. W. Palmer's opening argument for the defense acutely zeroed in on the most glaring weakness in the state's case. Palmer stressed that there was only the testimony of one man—Professor Cassels—to support the claim that William Parquet had died of arsenic poisoning. William might well, Palmer insisted, have died of some internal inflammation, as his sorrowing sister Sarah believed in good faith. Cassels was an expert—and experts had been known to be wrong. And Cassels's belief that the fatal dose had been administered only 24 hours before death was inconsistent with the testimony of many witnesses that William's symptoms had been the same throughout his weeklong illness. Ergo, if Sarah had been giving William all that chloroform to mask the effects of her arsenic—as claimed by the state—why had she bothered with it, since she didn't give the fatal dose until almost a week had passed? Summarizing his objections to the seemingly damning evidence, Palmer pleaded that all of the circumstances pointing to Sarah's guilt were equally supportive of her innocence.

M. S. Castle began his final argument on Saturday afternoon, June 20, by reviewing his own authorities on the strength and meaning of circumstantial evidence. But he didn't get very far before adjournment. The trial was further delayed until Monday afternoon by Sarah's continuing psychological deterioration. But after Castle finished on Monday, prosecutor Jones rose to his feet and unleashed the flood of his scalding commonsense logic on Palmer and Castle's alleged sophistries. Jones noted that their "pretense" that William had died from "some kind of inflammation" was a common ploy in poisoning cases like this one. Indeed, he scornfully declared, the state had thoroughly proved that William had died of arsenic poisoning and "if it had not been proved, the crime might as well be struck off the statutes." The defense, to be sure, had disparaged the accuracy of Professor Cassels's chemical tests—but why had they not produced even one expert witness to challenge his evidence? Only Sarah Victor had profited financially from the death of her brother, and there was ample evidence that she had labored mightily and stealthily to that end. Her story about keeping arsenic under the rug of her sister Libbie's bedroom to kill rats was an obvious attempt to throw suspicion on Libbie, especially as Sarah had kept a cat for six years. And the various stories Sarah had told about the famous frozen turnover—or was it a pie?—were transparently clumsy attempts to prepare an alibi.

Jones resumed his attack on Sarah on Tuesday morning, but he didn't get very far. Sarah had become more and more agitated as he continued his argument, and she had another outburst when Jones mentioned her attempts to throw suspicion on the Fenner family and others with her 11th-hour talk of poison. Raising up her head, which had been buried in her handkerchief for much of the trial, Sarah looked at Jones and shouted, "Don't tell them any more that ain't true—don't, I beg of you!" She was immediately given another sedative by a sheriff's deputy and soon calmed down. But as Jones ended his argument by noting that there was not a single living witness to confirm Sarah's statements about what had happened in the sickroom, Sarah suddenly raised her right hand and said to Jones, "Yes, there's a God! There's a God who knows!" C. W. Palmer managed to hush her up, and Jones concluded his argument, pleading with the jury not to be blinded by "mawkish sentimentality." Actually, Jones had already shrewdly allowed for that possibility, tempering his demand for a death verdict with a suggestion to the jury that "if they found anything in her conduct or life to warrant it, they might commend her to the clemency of the Governor for commutation of sentence."

Judge Foote's charge to the jury was a careful one, stressing the laws covering circumstantial evidence and the necessity to allow only such evidence as seemed true "beyond a reasonable doubt." It is possible, however, that Judge Foote subtly tipped his hand in his final comment to the jury, solemnly warning those 12 West Side men: "A reasonable doubt of Mrs. Victor's guilt acquits her; but it would be at the peril of your own souls to acquit her if you believed the crime to be proved, and had not reasonable doubt." The jury went out at 12:15 P.M. on Tuesday, June 23, 1868.

Apparently, Sarah's jury elected not to imperil their souls overmuch, as they returned with a verdict of "guilty of murder in the first degree" after little more than four hours of deliberation. After foreman Charles H. Babcock read the verdict, Castle had the jury polled and they all firmly repeated, "Guilty." Sarah, weak and pale, sat slumped in her chair with her head buried in her arms. She showed no reaction whatsoever until she returned to the jail, where she fainted and lapsed into a stupor. The next morning, lawyers for the Connecticut Mutual Life Insurance Company filed suit to recover the $2,300 they had paid Sarah on the policy covering William Parquet.

Sarah's physical and mental condition continued to decline during the 10 days between the verdict and her sentencing. By the time she appeared before Judge Foote again on July 3, she had lost more than half of her original 130-pound weight and appeared to be a distracted, mumbling wreck of her once imperious self. Carried by deputies to a table, she sat before Judge Foote, playing with a fan and an orange with a string around it and staring vacantly at nothing. Occasionally, she could be heard muttering, "I don't want to hear Mr. Jones talk so hard against me any more." By the time Jones asked Foote to pronounce sentence, Sarah had launched into the verses of "There Is Rest for the Weary," audibly singing:

In the Christian's home in glory,
There remains a land of rest.

Sarah showed no reaction to the sentence, except for a slight startled jerk of her body as Judge Foote uttered the words "To be hung by the neck until dead." It was later reported in the newspapers that he added the traditional sweetener, "And may God have mercy on your soul"—but some present would later insist that he pointedly omitted the phrase.

Sarah's scheduled execution date was August 20, 1868, but it is probable that few thought she would ever mount a scaffold in downtown Cleveland. It was believed that no woman had ever been executed in Ohio, and a growing chorus of voices pleaded that Sarah's life be spared because of her insane condition and her physical frailty. Some still thought she was faking it, and their point of view was expressed by the *Cleveland Leader* the morning after she was sentenced, its correspondent editorializing: "It may seem to some a little hard that a woman in such condition should be thus sentenced, but the court and prosecution had medical advice to the effect that all her insanity is assumed." Within ten days, however, the *Leader* had altered its opinion to align with its traditional opposition to capital punishment. Sardonically jeering at those who wanted Mrs. Victor's life spared merely because of her physical condition, the *Leader* wondered:

> We now learn that Mrs. Victor is acting in the most disgusting manner. She does not seem disposed to die game. From a woman of a hundred and thirty pounds she has run down to about sixty, and is so weak that the sheriff had to carry her into the court room, and she could not stand up to receive sentence. At this rate unless execution is hurried, there will not be weight enough in her body to hang . . . If it is shameful to sentence sixty pounds of flesh to the gallows, how is it helped by making it a hundred and thirty? Does the shame decrease as the flesh increases?

The *Leader* further noted that Mrs. Victor was *not* the first woman to be hanged in Ohio: some years before a black woman had been hanged for killing a fellow convict in Columbus, and no "mawkish sentimentality" had been mustered to prevent *her* execution.

Sheriff Felix Nicola, no mawkish sentimentalist himself, became convinced within a few days after Judge Foote's sentence that his prisoner was insane, and he wrote a letter to Ohio governor Rutherford B. Hayes to that effect. Nicola's opinion was backed by the medical advice of Drs. Beckwith, Schneider, Verdi, and Peck. This was exactly what Hayes, probably unaware of the previous Columbus hanging, wanted to hear, not wishing to be the first Ohio governor to permit the hanging of a female. And so, on July 15, Hayes postponed Sarah's sentence until November 20, 1868, and ordered Nicola to take her to the Northern Ohio Insane Asylum in Newburg until her reason was restored. Although Sarah gained most of her weight back during the three months she spent there, she was judged to be still insane in October and Governor Hayes commuted her sentence to life imprisonment. She was bundled off to the Women's Ward of the Ohio Penitentiary in Columbus. One of the conditions of her commutation was that she be held in solitary confinement for the rest of her life.

Seven years went by. Sarah's physical health soon recovered its wonted robustness, and by 1875 it was apparent that her reason, if ever truly absent, was fully restored. Living in a cell especially constructed for her, she almost never left its walls, received few visitors, and devoted herself to making quilts and clothing for various orphanages throughout Ohio. Perhaps as a token of her revived mental health, Sarah also began legal efforts in 1875 to get herself out of prison. These bore first fruits in 1877, when Judge Bingham of the Franklin County Common Pleas Court, after 18 months of consideration, shocked Ohio jurists on June 28, 1877, with a ruling that Sarah Victor be returned to Cuyahoga County to be hanged. Bingham's tortured legal reasoning was that, as Sarah had never legally consented to the commutation of her death sentence, it was still in effect; her legal status was that of an escaped prisoner still under sentence. No one expected Bingham's drastic ruling to stand, and Sarah remained in prison until it was duly struck down by the Ohio Supreme Court. But the case was a good index of Sarah's desperation to get out of prison and did much to remotivate both her partisans and enemies in the crusade to spring her from prison.

More years went by. Ohio governors came and went, Ohio Penitentiary wardens arrived and departed—and Sarah Victor stayed in her private cell, sewing and appealing, appealing and sewing as the years went by. Eventually, the mandate of solitary confinement was relaxed, and Sarah was permitted to give newspaper interviews, in which she excoriated her enemies and proclaimed her complete innocence. Finally, on Christmas Day 1886 Governor Joseph B. Foraker granted her a pardon after she had served 18 years of her life sentence. Just after she walked through the gates of the Penitentiary, she told a *Plain Dealer* reporter:

Yes, I am free at last; free from further punishment of a crime I never committed. I have a number of friends in Cleveland, who never believed me guilty of the crime, and with whom I shall make my home in the future . . . I shall face the world as an innocent person wrongfully punished should do; but it may be some little time before I am able to comprehend the great change in my life that has been so suddenly and unexpectedly brought about. I have lived all these years in the hope that justice would at last be done and though it has been long delayed, I will try to begin life where I left it twenty years ago.

Perhaps not surprisingly, Sarah Victor soon realized she could not resume her wonted Cleveland life. Although she had amassed a small sum from her fine needlework during all those years in prison, all of her Cleveland property was gone. Judge Foote, Marshal Castle, and C. W. Palmer were now dead. Christopher Columbus Carleton, although still to be found in the Forest City, was distinctly averse to rekindling their erstwhile ties when apprised of her impending return. "I know nothing whatever of Mrs. Victor," he told a *Plain Dealer* scribe, "don't know where to direct you to, and in fact I haven't thought anything about it." Soon conscious of her isolation and continuing notoriety, Sarah elected to stay in Columbus, where she had found a home with Mrs. James Taylor and been befriended by several females active in the Women's Christian Temperance Union. Eventually, she made her home in Corry, Pennsylvania, with the family of Dr. Gray, her sister Libbie's exhusband and sometime purveyor of the "Golden Pain Searcher."

Of Sarah Victor's further fate we know little, except that the Connecticut Mutual Insurance Company never got its $2,300 back from her and that in 1890 she successfully disputed the legal suit of one Henry Bowen, who claimed that she still owed him $118 for medical treatment while she was in jail awaiting trial in the spring of 1868. Sheriff Nicola was called as a witness in Bowen's suit, and he testified that only Dr. Beckwith had attended Sarah in jail and that Bowen was known to him only as a horse doctor and seller of lightning rods. The case was dismissed, and Sarah Victor returned to the obscurity that had blessed her before February 1868.

Sarah did leave one further testimonial to posterity, a lengthy, tearful autobiography ghostwritten by one Harriet L. Adams and published the year after Sarah got out of prison. Adams, it seems, had been approached by representatives of the WCTU to help Sarah, and her aid took the form of translating Sarah's anguished, self-serving, and melodramatic recollections into publishable form. Ungracefully entitled *The Life Story of Sarah M. Victor for Sixty Years: Convicted of Murdering Her Brother, Sentenced to Be Hung, Had Sentence Commuted, Passed Nineteen Years in Prison, Yet Is Innocent, Told by Herself*, Adams's tome was a 431-page rant filled with self-pity and unsubstantiated character assassination. Claiming she was innocent of any guilt in her brother's death, Sarah held that the charges against her had been contrived by her neighbor Jared Newell. It seems that Newell—who was now conveniently dead—had been connected with the 1853 murder of a Cleveland prostitute named Christiana Sigsby. Newell suspected, Mrs. Victor now stated, that she knew of his involvement in the Sigsby murder and capitalized on Libbie's known resentment about her brother's will to falsely incriminate Sarah and deflect attention from his own guilty past. Moreover, she now claimed that William Parquet had likely been a suicide; indeed, Sarah now recalled several occasions on which she had prevented him from taking his life. The revisionist tales now told by Sarah were preposterous, as were her attempts to refute the testimony of the dozens of prosecution witnesses at her trial. Replete with affidavits of her good character from those who had known her in prison and her new chums in the WCTU., *The Life Story of Sarah M. Victor* remains an obscure but amusing classic of cloying, mendacious self-pity.

So, did Sarah Victor really kill her brother for the insurance money? All of the evidence against her, as in the case of Sam Sheppard, was circumstantial. Some distinguished jurists had doubts about convicting her on that basis at the time, and the strictly circumstantial nature of the case was a factor in her eventual pardon.

Indeed, in a similar case 50 years later—the Kaber arsenic *cum* murder-for-hire affair in Lakewood—virtually identical criminal counts of arsenic poisoning were withdrawn by the prosecution as being too weak to prove in court. And for all of its 39 witnesses, the state could not produce one who could say that he or she had seen Sarah give her brother arsenic in his sickroom during the week of his last illness. But, as in the case of Sam Sheppard, what *other* conclusion could a rational human being draw from the circumstances? There was no other person with an apparent motive for William's death—unless Sarah's weird story about Jared Newell was true. (The Christiana Sigsby murder was never solved, and there is nothing to connect Newell to it except Sarah's unsupported accusation.) It was apparent that Sarah lied about everything connected with her brother's death—unless one is willing to believe that *all* of the witnesses against her, including the respected Drs. Sapp and Beckwith, perjured themselves. Moreover, Sarah *acted* like a guilty person from start to finish, from the moment she informed Dr. Sapp of her premonitions of William's death, through her hysterical opposition to an autopsy, and on to her clumsy attempts to conceal her inheritance and manufacture alibis about pies. And her own version of the events, like Sam Sheppard's fable about the "bushy-haired intruder," was simply unbelievable from start to finish. Virtually nothing in the skein of events that led to William Parquet's death could be explained without assuming that Sarah had plotted to poison him with arsenic from the start.

It is perhaps fitting that no one knows where Sarah Victor sleeps today, untroubled by the accusers who pursued her in life. William Parquet also rests undisturbed in an unmarked grave in Woodland Cemetery, presumably with the bones of Sarah Victor's two children still in a box on top of his casket. Perhaps, too, that window in the top of his casket is yet intact, affording a convenient view should his errant sister decide to look in on him just one more time. †

Three Distaff Poisoners

Elsie Bass, 1917; Anna Kempf, 1928;
and Dorothy Kaplan, 1956

Poison is primarily a woman's weapon. Although some of the most notorious poisoners in the history of the world have been men—William Palmer, Graham Young, Thomas Neill Cream, and Dr. Crippen come to mind—even a casual perusal of accounts of such crimes offers compelling evidence that killing by poison is disproportionately attractive to women. The advantages of poison as a method of human disposal for women are obvious. Poisoning is generally furtive, an ideal quality for someone confronting an adversary of superior muscular strength or social power. No messy hand-to-hand combat, knowledge of firearms, or knife-fighting technique is required. Poison is easily acquired, hidden, and disguised: many lethal poisons have nonhomicidal uses and are part of the fabric of everyday life, as any amateur gardener or pest control professional can attest. It can be stealthily administered and difficult to detect—as many a delayed exhumation has shown.

A wide range of motives inspires the female use of poison. Some women use it simply as a tool for elimination, while others employ it for radical behavior modification. Still others use it to end not only the lives of those entangled in their personal miseries, but their own as well. The following are three case studies of female Cleveland poisoners whose stories illustrate the wide range of motives and results possible when ladies turn to Borgian methods.

"I Wouldn't Even Kill a Rat"
Elsie Bass, 1917

Elsie Bass was angry. Three days in a row she had gone to the back porch of her house at 2045 West 32nd Street to get the daily bottle of milk delivered there—and each time she had found it gone. Today, Thursday, November 15, 1917, she was determined to do something about it. At first she thought it was the milk company's fault, but her milkman assured her he had delivered it and suggested that perhaps it was being stolen by mischievous boys. That made sense to Elsie. She told her husband John as he left that morning that she was determined to catch the milk thieves that very day.

Elsie Bass wasn't kidding. The first hint that she had taken decisive action came Thursday night at the home of John Perko, age 9, of 2025 West 32nd Street, just a few doors away from the Basses' back porch. John, a student at St. Mary's School, became violently sick shortly after he arrived home late Thursday afternoon. Vomiting, feverish, and tormented with an unappeasable thirst, John begged for water throughout the night. Shortly before 9 the next morning he died, just before the family doctor arrived.

Things were not going very well either at the homes of John's best friends, George Foley, 9, of 2100 West 32nd and Joe Pozsgai, 8, of 2051 West 32nd. Like John, both George and Joe became violently ill shortly after they got home from school on Thursday afternoon. John and Joe wouldn't tell their mothers what was wrong, but George's mother eventually wormed the truth out of her reluctant son. He told her that he had gotten sick shortly after stealing a bottle of milk off neighbor Elsie Bass's porch. He, John, and Joe had drunk it there at about 4 P.M. on Thursday, and George had vomited immediately after they ran from the porch and hopped over a fence. Mrs. Foley didn't know quite what to think about that, but she instinctively continued to dose George with the large quantities of salt water that apparently saved his life.

Mrs. Foley thought much more about it the next day when her older son reported the death of John Perko. After talking with Mrs. Perko and Mrs. Pozsgai, Mrs. Foley consulted family physician Charles H. Hay. Hay contacted District Physician T. G. Duncan, who notified Cuyahoga County coroner P. J. Byrne. An hour later Cleveland Police detective Charles H. Snyder knocked on Elsie Bass's door.

Elsie refused to admit anything at first, only repeating, "I didn't do anything to the milk." But when Snyder finally told her John Perko was dead, she screamed, "I didn't mean to kill anyone! I'll tell you all about it!" Several hours later, after an interrogation by Snyder, Lieutenant Edward Donahue, and Detective Henry Kiehl, Elsie signed a full confession and was booked for first-degree murder.

Elsie's account of the poisoning varied little in its various retellings, although she sometimes denied knowing the potency of her preferred substance. An immigrant girl from Hungary in 1911, Elsie had endured a hard life both there and subsequently as a Cleveland charwoman before marrying Jack Bass in 1913. She didn't like being taken advantage of—which is why she reached into her cupboard for some rat poison when she figured out what was happening to her milk. That Thursday afternoon, she retrieved the milk bottle as soon as it was delivered and brought it into her kitchen. There, she poured out a cup of the milk, mixed it with a healthy dose of some old rat poison she had previously acquired at a Clark Avenue drugstore, and poured the mixture back in the bottle. She resealed it, set it back on her porch, and awaited events, concealed behind an adjacent window.

Elsie didn't have to wait long. This was the fourth trip to the Bass porch in as many days for John, George, and Joe. They laughed as they opened the bottle and took turns at swigging it down. George took the first drink, Joe followed, and John finished it off. Investigators later theorized that most of the arsenic poison had settled to the bottom of the bottle, which is why John Perko was the one to die from its effects. All three boys were terribly sick by the time they got home.

It is likely that no one in Judge Willis Vickery's Common Pleas courtroom believed Elsie Bass would be convicted on her first-degree-murder charge. The all-male juries of the era were notoriously reluctant to convict females on capital counts, especially one as attractive as Mrs. Bass proved to be when her trial opened on January 29, 1918. The state's prosecution was led by County Prosecutor J. J. Babka and Stephen Young, while attorneys Lewis Greenfield and George S. Myers defended Mrs. Bass. The facts were not in dispute, although the defense tried to diminish the effect of her confession by charging that the Cleveland police had used "loud and threatening" language during her interrogation. After medical professionals testified as to the facts of John Perko's death, Elsie took the stand to repeat her assertion that she had not meant to kill anyone. As the rapt spectators scanned her pretty face, she plaintively insisted, "I did not know that it was poison that would kill anybody. I thought it would make their stomachs sick and they would not come back again."

Less persuasively, perhaps, Elsie also denied having any recollection of her detailed, signed confession. After Judge Vickery instructed the jury that a second-degree-murder conviction was not an option, the conclusion of the Bass case became predictable. After less than three hours of deliberation, her jury returned a verdict of manslaughter at 5:20 P.M. on January 31. On February 7 an angry Judge Vickery, sourly noting the many letters he had received from Cleveland mothers seeking clemency for Elsie, sentenced her to an indeterminate term in the Marysville Reformatory. "To allow this woman to escape punishment," thundered Vickery, "would be to let down the bars for women to poison children." But during the next ten days Vickery either changed his mind or decided to make glad the hearts of potential Cleveland child poisoners. For on February 18 Vickery nulled Elsie's prison sentence and put her on probation. Her last words for the public as she left the courtroom were appropriately grateful, even if they did not exactly strike a note of profound remorse:

> Oh, I'm so glad. They're not going to send me away. It has always seemed like a horrible dream to me. I would rather have died than to have been sent away. I can scarcely believe the awful thing really happened. I'm going to live right, now, always.

"What Could a Woman Do?"
Anna Kempf's Desperate Deed, 1928

As Mrs. Julia Babel, Anna Kempf's mother, later put it, Anna looked "queer" when she came home shortly after eight on the night of Wednesday, October 3, 1928. Home was Mrs. Babel's house at 2803 Bridge Avenue, and along with divers boarders, it sheltered Anna and her three children: Julia, 7; Margaret, 6; and Mary, 3. And it wasn't just Anna's expression that was different—surpassing even the inner turmoil normally evident in her face, which reflected the travails of a hardworking 28-year-old mother with an estranged husband and three dependent children. Anna had brought home some decorative wax flowers, an unusual, frivolous, and even foolish gesture in a household where every penny counted.

Another oddity was the pint of chocolate ice cream Anna opened when she got to the kitchen. Ice cream was a special treat in the cash-strapped Kempf family, and even the children sensed that their mother was in some kind of rare mood. But they all waited patiently while Anna mixed up the ice cream in another room and spooned it into two bowls, one for her mother and the other for

herself and the children. The ice cream was just as good as everyone thought it would be, and little Mary even got seconds. Then
Anna did another unusual thing, which was to leave them all and
go for a "walk" in the neighborhood.

When Anna returned almost two hours later, one of Mrs. Babel's roomers was just loading the children and Julia into his car.
Shortly after Anna's departure, Mary had become violently sick,
soon followed by her two sisters. When their frightened grandmother called the doctor, he told Mrs. Babel to get them to City
Hospital (now Metro) as soon as possible. They were just leaving
in the roomer's car when Anna showed up and became violently ill
herself. Minutes later they were rushed to the waiting physicians
at the hospital.

As she lay in pain on a cot there, Anna gasped out her dreadful
confession to Cleveland police lieutenant John Luttner, who happened to be on duty at the hospital that night. Anna told him the
details of how she had stopped at the grocery at 2528 Lorain on her
way home from work and asked clerk Lucy O'Rhynare for some
rat poison. Her first choice proved too expensive, so after some
dickering, Anna settled on a cheaper, powdered version. Then she
went to a nearby drugstore, bought the wax flowers and the chocolate ice cream, and brought them home to her mother and children.
There, out of their sight, she carefully mixed the poison and most
of the ice cream together, reserving an uncontaminated bowl for
her mother. After they finished eating it, she left the house because,
she told Luttner, she "didn't want to see them suffer and die."
When she finished her confession, Luttner brought in Lieutenant
Charles Timm, and she repeated her confession for a stenographer
and signed it. When Timm asked her, "Didn't you realize the children might die of poison?" she replied, "I intended they should."
Her purpose, she confessed to Timm, was to kill herself and her
children, sparing only her mother.

Anna Kempf wasn't much of a success as a suicide and murderer. Owing to their stronger constitutions, both she and her two
older daughters survived her dose of rat poison. But when little
Mary Kempf died the next morning, Anna was placed under ar-

rest. A month later a Cuyahoga County grand jury indicted her for first-degree murder. Just before she came to trial in December, however, additional charges of second-degree murder and manslaughter were added, at the suggestion of Chief Criminal Court judge Walter McMahon. Given the past squeamishness of Cuyahoga County juries when it came to convicting females on first-degree-murder counts, McMahon has taking no chances that Anna would walk away scot-free from her heinous deed.

By the time Anna went on trial a month later, however, public opinion had surprisingly shifted strongly in her favor. Thanks to voluminous sob-sister coverage in Cleveland newspapers, especially the *Cleveland News,* most adult Clevelanders were familiar with the sad details of Anna's unhappy life by the time she sat in the criminal dock. With visiting judge George A. Starn of Wooster presiding and James Connell and Andrew Kovachy defending, it was clear that prosecutors Maurice Meyer and Jack Persky would be fighting an uphill battle against public sympathy for Anna Kempf's life.

And what a depressing life it was—as her lawyers Connell and Kovachy mournfully showed in their examination of witnesses to her doleful biography. Born in Hungary at the turn of the century, young Anna had been indentured out at the age of seven to a farm overseer who paid her nominal wages to her exploitative guardian. Anna had eventually escaped her serfdom by emigrating to America, but her lot here was hardly an improvement. In 1919 she married Joe Kovacs, a former Hungarian policeman. But when Joe found he couldn't get a job as a policeman in Cleveland, he refused to take any other job, and Anna was forced to go to work to support herself and their children, Julia and Margaret. Anna finally divorced Kovacs in 1923. The next year she married Jacob Kempf, and they moved to what seemed like better prospects in Parma. Several years later, however, Jacob quit working too and after repeated estrangements left Anna for good in June of 1928. By that time Anna had a third child to support, and Jacob was remiss in his support payments. Anna was living at her mother's house on Bridge Avenue and working nine-hour shifts six nights a week for the Industrial Fiber Company, a rayon manufacturer. Anna told sympathetic journalists that she paid her mother her entire weekly wages of $12 for her family's room and board. By the fall of 1928, after Anna refused to help her mother propagate an eccentric religion concocted by Mrs. Babel herself, Julia told Anna to start paying her $15 or face eviction. At the end of her financial rope, Anna spent months trekking to every private and public welfare organization in Cuyahoga County, begging them all for some financial assistance. She even tried to give her children away to an orphanage, but everyone she talked to spurned her pleas for help. When she found out she was about to lose her job, she decided to kill herself and take the kids with her.

The challenge facing the prosecution became clear on December 3, the first day of the trial proceedings, when prospective juror Ralph Nellis was rejected because he had formed an opinion about Anna's guilt or innocence. As court clerk Frank Malley handed Nellis his $6 fee for jury duty, Nellis loudly said in court, "Have this cashed for me and give the money to Mrs. Kempf to buy Christmas presents for the other two girls."

Anna herself was most persuasive on the stand. Speaking through an interpreter in her native Hungarian, she reiterated the details of her excruciating life and convincingly articulated the desolation that had pushed her to attempted murder:

> I had gone everywhere for help and the grave seemed the only place left for me to go with my children if I wanted to be happy with them. What could a woman do? I went from office to office in the courthouse; talked to police; everywhere for months and months I look for help. And who is to help me? Nobody! Is it bad to leave such a life?

After her recitation of horrors, Anna's plea of temporary insanity must have seemed pretty persuasive to the seven men and five women on the jury, especially after Anna's mother calmly testified about her own religious "visions" and admitted that she had threatened to evict her own daughter and grandchildren over a matter of $3 a week. No doubt the jury was further impressed by Mrs. Babel's statement that she had enjoyed a precognitive warning of Mary Kempf's impending death. The court-appointed psychiatrists (then called "alienists"), Drs. H. H. Drysdale and John Tierney, further damaged the state's case with their muddled analysis of Anna's mental condition at the time of the murder. Tierney argued that Anna's disinclination to poison her mother argued against a state of temporary insanity. But Drysdale, who probably gave expert medical testimony at more Cleveland trials than anyone except Dr. Sam Gerber, then confused the jury with his report that Anna's state at the time of the poisonings had been sane but "ruffled," "panicky," and "agitated beyond normalcy."

Prosecutor Maurice Meyer partially threw in the towel even before the case went to the jury. On December 7, he informed the Court that the state would not demand Mrs. Kempf's life, even if she were convicted of first-degree murder. Meyer needn't have bothered: after futile deliberations through the following day, the jury reported itself hopelessly deadlocked; Judge Starn dismissed them. The devastating effect of Drysdale's and Tierney's testimony became clear when it was subsequently reported that the baffled jury had requested a dictionary from Judge Starn. It seems they were confused by what the doctors meant when they used terms like "normal," "panicky," and "ruffled."

Undaunted, Prosecutors Meyer and Persky opened their second prosecution of Anna Kempf two days later, on December 10, 1928. It quickly mutated into her third prosecution when visiting judge Roscoe G. Hornbeck of London, Ohio, had to dissolve her second jury when one of the jurors came down with influenza. By this time it was, as presiding criminal court judge McMahon put it, "evident that no jury will convict or perhaps agree in a murder trial for Mrs. Kempf." McMahon suggested a plea bargain to a manslaughter charge, but Anna initially refused, saying:

> If taking the life of my daughter was murder, then let God hold me to account. No one can ever get me to admit that what I did was wrong in the eyes of man or the law. I'll go on trial a dozen

times before I could admit myself guilty of murder. It wasn't murder.

The following Monday, after some time to think it over and following her first visit to her daughters Julia and Margaret at the St. Joseph Orphanage on Woodland, Anna surrendered and pleaded guilty to the manslaughter charge. Judge Hornbeck immediately sentenced Anna to probation with palpable relief, remarking, "No jury would have found this mother guilty . . . There is no question but that she was temporarily insane when she gave the poison to her children but she is normal now." And, like others exposed to the details of Anna's life, Judge Hornbeck took the opportunity to criticize the social service organizations that had so signally failed to help Anna Kempf in her hour of desperate need. After Anna was released from jail she and her children disappeared into the obscurity whence they had come before the terrible events of October 3. In 1956, at the time of her mother Julia's death, Anna was reported to be married again and living in California.

"I Just Wanted to Slow Them Down a Little..."
Dorothy Kaplan Delivers the Milk, 1956

Things should have been just peachy for Mr. and Mrs. Louis Elgart as the winter of 1956 waned toward spring. Louis was the proprietor of a men's clothing store, Elgart's Men's and Boys' Store at 4266 Fulton Road, and both he and his wife Ruth had worked hard to make it a success. But there was much more than business success to the attractive and talented University Heights couple. Louis, a cousin of nationally known big band leader Les Elgart, fronted a performing Cleveland band of his own, and Ruth was a pianist of the first rank. Studying with jazz legend Teddy Wilson, she had also performed with the Tommy Dorsey Orchestra and singer Frankie Laine, not to mention writing the Glenville High

School fight song. Louis and Ruth were personable and cultured and often entertained other musicians and friends in their second-floor apartment at 14144 Cedar Road through many a night of music and conversation. And yet, as February 1956 arrived, they were deeply unhappy.

Things had started going wrong from the day they moved into that Cedar Road apartment in November 1954. Sure, the suburban neighborhood was all that it should be, and the apartment was just what they wanted. But their downstairs neighbor, Mrs. Dorothy Kaplan, was driving them crazy. She had been a thorn in their side from the day they moved in, and their relations with her just got worse and worse. Complaining about the "noise" of Ruth's piano playing, Dorothy, who lived in the flat beneath, often banged not only on her ceiling but even their walls from outside their apartment. When she wasn't doing that, she was arguing with her truck-driving husband, Thomas, creating a constant tumult of shouts, screams, and unbridled profanity. Then came the deluge of harassing telephone calls, with no one at the other end when they were picked up. It had gotten so bad by the end of 1955 that Ruth had begun circulating petitions throughout the building as part of a campaign to persuade the landlord to evict the Kaplans, but he refused to take any measures against them.

Things went further downhill in early February 1956. Several times after using the apartment building's laundry facilities, Louis and Ruth discovered that their washed garments were saturated with what appeared to be "grease." When the washer repairman informed them that it was brown shoe polish, Louis and Ruth learned from the building custodian that Mrs. Kaplan's regular rotation in the laundry schedule came just before theirs. Clearly, their living situation was deteriorating rapidly, and they began thinking about finding another place to live.

They were still thinking about it when events took a more drastic turn on the morning of February 16. Louis, as usual, drank a large glass of milk. He remembered thinking that it tasted kind of odd, but he attributed this peculiarity to some ice crystals. And he didn't give it much more thought, even after he became violently ill with stomach pains at his store a few hours later. He managed to drive himself to City Hospital, but after he was examined there the staff doctors told him it was just "muscle spasms."

Louis thought more about it two days later when he felt something peculiar in his first mouthful of milk. He stopped drinking it and decided to let the bottle of milk evaporate on a window sill. It did—and the next day Louis Elgart discovered definite shards of broken glass in the residue at the bottom of the bottle. He immediately called his milk supplier, the Dean Dairy Company at 3211 Mayfield Road.

After making their own tests, the concerned staff at Dean's Dairy immediately turned the case over to Cleveland Heights health inspector Dominic Tomaro. He personally tested the next bottle of milk delivered to the Elgarts' milk chute and discovered no fewer than 186 pieces of glass in it, not to mention a considerable amount of glass powder too fine to be picked up with tweezers. After an interview with the Elgarts disclosed their longstanding feud with Dorothy Kaplan, Tomaro had a chat with the police.

Captain Harry A. Gaffney of the University Heights Police Department was not an impetuous man. He waited until three more glass-contaminated bottles were delivered to the Elgarts' milk chute before setting his trap. Early on the afternoon of March 1, he sent Detective Thomas Jarvis into the Elgarts' apartment building. Jarvis, who was equipped with a newfangled "walkie-talkie" two-way radio, secreted himself in a custodian's closet with a discreet view of the Elgarts' milk chute, and Gaffney settled down to wait in the seat of his police car outside the building.

They didn't have to wait long. As expected, Mrs. Kaplan arrived at the milk chute shortly after the Dean's dairyman delivered a marked bottle and took it to her apartment. Minutes later she returned and was arrested by Gaffney and Jarvis as she put the freshly contaminated bottle back in the chute. Back in her kitchen, they discovered the hammer she had used to break up the glass from a small prescription bottle. She immediately confessed, saying, "I didn't want to hurt them. I just wanted to slow them down a little. They made too much noise up there."

Although Dorothy Kaplan was immediately charged with attempted poisoning, a serious felony that could merit a 2-to-15-year prison sentence, she almost as quickly posted her $1,000 bond and was released to await the consideration of the grand jury. A horrified Louis Elgart was moved to comment:

> I'm not going to return to that apartment until something is done about that woman. I stayed with relatives last night and my wife Ruth stayed away from the suite, too. Honestly, I think the police made a mistake in letting her out on bond.

Dorothy Kaplan was bound over to the grand jury on March 13, and it was already clear that her defense would stress her mental condition. During the 90-minute hearing conducted by Mayor Earl W. Aurelius, her defense attorneys Michael J. Picciano and Robert I. Koplow repeatedly drew attention to details suggestive of a plea of mental illness. These included 1) the phenobarbitol pills found in Dorothy's kitchen and purse; 2) her medical treatment for high blood pressure during the previous two years; and 3) the statements made by arresting officers Gaffney and Jarvis that she "looked sick" when taken into custody. Dorothy aided their strategy with a petulant statement that she had only poisoned the milk to make the Elgarts "sick" so she could "get some sleep for a couple of days."

The wheels of justice ground slowly in the Elgart poisoning case, probably to the satisfaction of no one but Dorothy Kaplan. After more than a year of legal delays, Dorothy Kaplan finally pleaded guilty to the poisoning charge on May 27, 1957. Judge Earl Hoover then had her jailed, pending a probation report. Three weeks later, Hoover sentenced her to two years' probation, on condition that she continue her ongoing psychiatric treatment. A tearful and grateful Kaplan commented as she left the courtroom, "I surely have learned my lesson." †

Seduced and Abandoned

Jennie Droz, a Girl of the Cleveland Streets, 1871

It is commonplace that we know little about the sexuality of our ancestors. There will never be a history, for example, of the sex lives of late-19th-century Clevelanders. If hardly ascetic, 19th-century Victorians—English or American—were reticent about their sexual behavior and habits and unlikely to chronicle them in print. Because most 1870s Clevelanders were representative Victorians, much of what little we know about Forest City sexual proclivities of that decade comes from the criminal record. And most of that documentation comes from the era's celebrated murder trials, for it was usually only the egregious rupture of civic norms implicit in homicidal acts that exposed ugly, or at least indelicate, sexual realties to public view.

The Galentine-Jones murder case of 1870 was one such revealing episode. Superficially, of course, it was the edifying tale of a wronged man enforcing the "unwritten law," for such was the claim made by dentist Jay Galentine after he shot down Dr. William Jones for the crime of "raping" Jay's wife, Mary. The trial, to the pious titillation of Clevelanders, exposed the indelicate truth that Mary had whiled away her husband's prolonged absences by allowing Dr. Jones access to her person as many as five times a day. (For more details of this entertaining scandal, see "Cold Lead for Breakfast" in *They Died Crawling*, 1995.)

It's a safe bet that no one living now has heard of the Jennie Droz affair. That's a shame, because it is at least as illustrative of the gamy sexual realities of the era as the Galentine-Jones burlesque. True, it lacks that aspect of comic absurdity that informed the latter scandal from beginning to end. But its sordid details bring to light matters never discussed in more "proper" histories of Cleveland: prostitution, venereal disease, the sexual victimization of female servants, and the plight of the "fallen woman." Not to mention the fact that it offers an entertaining tale with a satisfying and surprising ending.

We could begin the Jennie Droz story in a number of places. One would be 1850, when Jennie Droz was born in Mecklenburg, Germany. The daughter of Ferdinand Droz, a jeweler and sometime foreign passenger agent, she came with her family to Cleveland in 1851, one of the many German immigrants who flooded into the city after the failed 1848 Revolution. Another place would be Jennie's childhood home at Pearl and Detroit Streets on Cleveland's West Side, where she grew up during the 1850s. (The West Side is also where Drs. Galentine and Jones resided at the time of their unfortunate 1870 interchange.) There the Droz family flourished: Ferdinand; his wife; his sons, Louis and Philip; and his daughters, Jennie and Lucy. As testimony of their status as new Americans, Philip and Louis were employed by the Cleveland Fire Department in 1869.

That year is probably the best place to pick up the Jennie Droz tale, for here commenced her undoing. Like many teenagers before and since, Jennie chafed at the rules and discipline of her respectable bourgeois West Side home. Her discontent flared up in the summer of 1869, when at the age of 18 she came under the sympathetic influence of a Mrs. Rachel Duffy, the wife of a bartender at Blanchard's saloon on Detroit Street. Ferdinand Droz would later publicly blame Mrs. Duffy for luring his daughter into secular temptations, but Jennie herself denied at her trial that she needed assistance in being led astray. Whatever their relationship, it is a fact that Jennie stole away from her parents' home one summer night in 1869, possibly with the material assistance of Mrs. Duffy. Several weeks later, in August, Jennie's outraged parents discovered she was working as a maid at the Cliff House, a splendid luxury hotel on the eastern banks of the Rocky River. Because she was 18, there was nothing her anguished parents could do but worry that young Jennie might succumb to worldly and impure snares in such a place.

Worldly and impure snares were not long in presenting themselves. Capitalist Daniel P. Rhodes and other Cleveland investors had opened the Rocky River Railroad "dummy line" two years earlier, in 1867, and they opened the Cliff House in January 1869 to provide a diverting destination for moneyed Clevelanders weary of city scenes. The Cliff House was initially managed by Lucien Phillips, but before the end of its first year its affairs were turned over to brothers Edward and Julius Fisk. By January 1870 Julius was fully in charge of its operations. Thus and so smoothly was the scene set for Jennie's ruination.

As is so oft the case, more is known about the killer of Major Julius Fisk than about the victim himself. He must have been, as his contemporaries would have said, a "man of parts." Born in 1828, he enlisted in Company S of the 2nd Kansas Cavalry Regiment in 1862 and was wounded at Cane Hill, Arkansas, on November 28, 1862. Mustered out of the same regiment with the rank of major on April 18, 1865, he turned up five years later in partnership with his brother at the Cliff House. Described by his friends as affable, courteous, extraordinarily generous, and possessing an iron constitution, the Major seems to have been a moderately handsome man, albeit a bit on the fleshy side. He was above medium height and sported dark Burnside whiskers. It's probably fair to say, too, that the 42-year-old Julius was something of a ladies' man, judging from his behavior toward Jennie Droz.

Jennie's downfall proceeded apace from the moment Julius arrived at the Cliff House. Julius quickly took note of the comely dining-room girl, and a week later he invited Jennie to his room. He behaved himself properly on that occasion, but his demeanor soon changed. Some days later he began to woo her in earnest, telling her she was too good to be working as a hotel maid, that she deserved fine clothes, that she ought to be his mistress. He also took to lurking in corridors and staircases, touching and grabbing the girl as she toiled through her menial chores. Jennie refused his initial proposition, and then, after telling her he would go to Kansas and then send for her, he tried to be intimate with her. She angrily repulsed him but quickly found Julius Fisk was a hard man to circumvent. Luring her again into his Cliff House quarters on some pretext one night, he offered her a glass of wine. Either it was drugged or Jennie had no tolerance for alcohol, for she passed out and Fisk thereupon "accomplished his purpose." Jennie predictably wept when she recovered her senses, but the affable Julius assured her all would be well.

Contrary to Julius's bland assurances, Jennie's life quickly deteriorated. Edward Fisk's wife, Adeline, had noticed the growing intimacy between her brother-in-law and the dining-room girl—and she didn't like it. The Cliff House was already developing a reputation as a dissolute and lewd hotel, and Adeline decided to arrest its moral decline. On March 2 she summarily fired Jennie Droz. Very shortly afterward, Jennie discovered that she was pregnant and that she was showing unmistakable symptoms of "a loathsome disease."

Indeed, Jennie had contracted a virulent case of syphilis from the hearty major. There weren't very effective treatments for the disease in 1870, and Fisk didn't try very hard to help her. Jennie apparently first consulted a physician herself (who of all people turned out to be Dr. William Jones, soon to be shot down by Dr. Galentine). His treatment failing, she begged Fisk to help her in her diseased, pregnant, and penniless state. She probably threatened him with exposure, too, doubtless the wrong tack to take with the steely Civil War veteran. Upon hearing her threats, Fisk coldly warned her that if she uttered a word against him, he would denounce her as a "woman of the town," and she would be put

---

The Cliff House was already developing a reputation as a dissolute and lewd hotel

---

in jail. He also procured some mail-order patent remedies for her worsening infection, none of which helped alleviate her symptoms or mental distress.

Late in August or early September of 1870, an unwelcome Jennie showed up at the Cliff House again. Her mother had died earlier in the year, her death hastened by sorrow over Jennie's disgrace, and Jennie was too ashamed to return to her father's home. Living with various relatives or in cheap hotels and boarding houses, she tried to make a living by sewing and, eventually, as a prostitute on the streets of Cleveland. But by late August both her pregnancy and her disease had taken their toll, and she now threw herself on the tender mercies of her seducer.

What happened after that is murky. Major Fisk, still wishing to conceal his relations with her, put Jennie up in a nearby barn for eight or nine days. There she gave birth to a baby, but whether it was stillborn or strangled by Major Fisk she never knew. What she did know was that Major Fisk soon ejected her from Cliff House with warnings not to return.

Jennie resumed her life as a prostitute on the Cleveland streets. Often too sick to work at anything else, she took in sewing when she felt well enough and wrote several heartbreaking letters of appeal to Major Fisk. He apparently remained deaf to her appeals. And so it continued for several months more, as Jennie got sicker, more indigent, and desperate.

The bottom fell out on Thursday, February 16, 1871. Jennie was down to her last two dollars, and her landlord had attached her trunk in lieu of back rent. Multiple appeals to the major had proved fruitless, but Jennie decided she would give him one more chance. Walking from her current quarters at the Cleveland Hotel at Ontario and Prospect, Jennie went to Michael and Thomas Powers's gun store on Superior Hill (now the site of the Western Reserve Building). She entered the store about 11:30 A.M. and said she wanted a gun, and Thomas showed her a $7.50 revolver. She couldn't afford that, so he brought out a $2.50 pistol. Even that was beyond her slender means, but after consulting with Michael, Thomas allowed her to depart with the pistol after she gave him $2 and a ring as security on the 50 cents owed. (Gunsmith Thomas Powers became the father of two Catholic priests, one of them the legendary John Mary Powers, the charismatic pastor of St. Ann Church in Cleveland Heights. For more details on the remarkable Powers family, see *Angels on the Heights: A History of St. Ann's Parish, 1915–1990*, 1990.)

That evening Jennie walked over to Erastus Briggs's livery stable on Detroit Street. She said she wanted to rent a horse and buggy for several hours and that she would pay Briggs the hire on her return. She then drove the horse and buggy out the Detroit Street toll road, telling tollgate keeper Edmond Ruhill that she would pay him on her return trip.

Jennie arrived at the Cliff House about 8:30 P.M. Fisk soon became aware of her presence, and they chatted amiably in front of several witnesses, including maid Margaret Twohig and hostler William Albon. Their conversation continued in a desultory fashion until sometime after 9 P.M., when Jennie mentioned there were two lively girls over at William Patchen's hotel, across the Rocky River. She asked Julius if he would send William Albon to bring them over to the Cliff House.

Jennie's pretext worked like a charm on the susceptible Fisk, always agreeable to the company of attractive young women. Albon left the hotel about 9:30 P.M., and Jennie immediately began her real business, which was to beg Fisk one last time for emotional and financial support. Their interview took place in the hotel's reception room, a comfortable 10-by-12-foot area, and lasted almost an hour. Again and again, Jennie reiterated her desperate poverty and the ravages of venereal disease, all too visible on her face. But Major Fisk remained a cad to the end. It was not in his nature to help the woman he wronged, and he summarized his feelings even as he and Jennie heard the sounds of Albon's buggy returning, shouting, "I'll be damned if I help you at all."

That was all Jennie Droz needed to hear. All of the miseries of the past 13 months were now heartlessly punctuated with the finality of Fisk's callous retort. As Jennie later put it, "If he had said one kind word, I could not have shot him." That not being the case, she removed the single-shot revolver from her purse and fired once.

They were both standing as the gun went off. The bullet hit Julius just about an inch or so above the right ear. The lead ball penetrated three or four inches, inflicting mortal damage and flattening itself before coming to rest at the base of the brain. Without further ado, Jennie replaced her pistol in her purse and calmly walked out to the piazza. William Albon was there, having just returned from his futile errand at the Rocky River Hotel. "William," she said, "I have shot him. Will you drive me to town and give me up to the police?"

"Shot who?" he replied.

Jennie merely repeated, "I shot him" several times and then jumped in her buggy and drove off.

Major Fisk was still alive at about 10:40 P.M. when William Albon found him in the reception room. He was sitting in a chair, with a dog on his knee and blood coming out of his mouth. He was breathing hard and unable to speak. Dr. William Carter was sent for, but it was too late by the time he arrived about 45 minutes later. After he certified that Julius Fisk was dead, Albon was sent into the city to notify the police and Cuyahoga County coroner J. C. Schenck.

Meanwhile, Jennie calmly drove back the way she had come.

Passing through the tollgate, she told keeper Ruhill that she was unable to pay him and continued on her way. Arriving at Briggs's stable at 11:40 P.M., she simply sat in the buggy until the stable clerk came out to see what was the matter. She was apparently in a state of shock, simply muttering over and over, "I wonder if the major

---

"If he had said one kind word,
I could not have shot him."

---

is dead. I wonder if the major is dead."

Assisted out of the buggy by the puzzled clerk, she sat down in the waiting room, saying, "I feel so queer." She repeatedly asked the clerk to check and see if there was still a bullet in her pistol. There was not, and when she explained that she only had a penny left, the clerk took the gun as security for the buggy hire.

Jennie walked back to her room at the Cleveland Hotel. About an hour later, when Cleveland police sergeant E. B. Gaffet and patrolmen H. A. Cordes and Thomas Thompson tracked her down there, Jennie was lying fully dressed on her bed, with the door unlocked and a lamp burning. Rising as the officers came into the room, she immediately agreed to go with them to the Central Police Station; she told them that her pistol was at Briggs's livery. She refused to answer most of their direct questions but volunteered some information, which Cordes later recalled at her trial:

> She said she went out there to see if Fisk would not do something for her and give her some money. He would not, and she shot him in the head. She said Fisk had seduced her and given her a loathsome disease. Said she should not be glad to have him die, that she loved him. Said she had received letters from Fisk saying that if she did not shut up he would put her in the workhouse.

Astonishing everyone by her calm demeanor, Jennie Droz was taken off and locked up in a jail at the Central Police Station. When she was arrested she had but one cent and two receipted doctor bills in her purse.

Criminal justice procedures in 1870 were not quite what they are now. Almost as soon as Jennie was ensconced in her cell, a *Cleveland Leader* reporter was allowed to interview her for that day's edition. Repeating what she had told her arresting officers, she added more details about her seduction and shabby treatment. She was more reticent at the murder inquest the next morning. Convened in the very murder room itself by Coroner Schenck at 10 A.M., the proceedings included appearances by Margaret Twohig and William Albon, Dr. Carter, and Herman Patchen. The only interesting item to emerge from their testimony was Patchen's disclosure that he had found a seven-shot, loaded pistol in the pants Fisk was wearing when he was killed. Then Jennie took the stand, accompanied by her defense attorneys, Samuel E. Adams and Robert Davison. Still calm and collected, she gave her testimony in a quiet voice, wiping away a furtive tear several times. Forthcoming on her tenure at the Cliff House, she refused to answer a number of questions about the actual shooting. When the testimony concluded, Coroner Schenck quickly ruled that Fisk had died from a pistol ball at the hands of Jennie Droz.

Taken back to her cell, Jennie more freely unbosomed herself to another *Cleveland Leader* reporter. Enlarging on her wrongs, she denied that she had led an immoral life before she met Fisk. Though she admitted she had been a prostitute for the past four or five months, she pleaded penury as her excuse, claiming she didn't know there was a retreat for "fallen women" in Cleveland: "I know nothing but my sin and I had no way to live but to make it deeper." She admitted shooting Fisk but allowed that it was "awful," as she had loved Mr. Fisk. She said she had hoped she had only wounded him and that "he would live to be a better man." The *Leader* correspondent amply repaid Jennie for her interview, writing that although there were two sides to the story:

Everything connected with the fearful tragedy gives an appearance of candor to the prisoner's statement. It hardly seems possible, if she were ruined, that she would have singled out for her vengeance any one except the person who had wrought her disgrace.

The day after the inquest, Jennie was arraigned in the Cleveland police court. Her attorneys waiving an examination, she was incarcerated in the Cuyahoga County Jail, then located on Frankfort and Seneca Streets (West 3rd Street). The following day, at 3 P.M., funeral rites for Major Fisk were held at the Cliff House. The services were conducted by the Reverend James Erwin of the Franklin Street Methodist Church, who told the grieving mourners that Fisk's unexpected end demonstrated the shortness of life and the need to be prepared for death at any time. It was noted that Dr. Carter had done a splendid job in repairing the violence to Fisk's person. As an admiring reporter wrote,

> Aside from the slightly livid appearance of the skin, and large purple spots about the shoulders where blood seemed to have settled, one might have believed that Major Fisk was but sleeping.

The wheels of justice commenced their regular, if not always predictable, grind. On Friday, May 12, 1871, Jennie was indicted by a Cuyahoga County common pleas court on a charge of manslaughter. The newspapers reported that she "manifested much joy" at news of this, as well she might. Considering the methodical way she had gone about acquiring a weapon, arranging transportation, and contriving to be alone with Fisk, it seems the all-male jury had likely stretched the bounds of chivalry to accommodate Jennie Droz.

When she came before Judge Foote to hear the indictment, she appeared much as she had at the time of Fisk's slaying: a small woman with large black eyes, short black hair, and even features, although the effects of syphilis had taken their toll on her once fine complexion. She was dressed entirely in black, complete with a black-beribboned black hat and a black cross at her throat. Her face was covered with a black veil. When asked how she pled, she whispered, "Not guilty," and her trial was scheduled for June 5. A bail bond of $3,000 was immediately arranged and accepted, and Jennie returned to her father's home to await justice.

One hopes that her sojourn there was more pleasant than her stint in county jail. There, she claimed, she was chronically subject to dreams in which Major Fisk would appear before her or she would waken on her cell bed with pistol shots ringing in her ears. However nightmarish her nights, however, her days were enlivened by frequent visits from her friends and the sympathetic society of fellow prisoner Kate Tracy, confined there on a grand larceny conviction.

It was rumored at the time of Jennie's indictment that the manslaughter count had been chosen over more grave charges in hopes Jennie would plead guilty to this lesser charge. If so, her prosecutors were disappointed, because she stuck to her stance of innocence even as the date for her trial was continually postponed for one reason or another. By the time she actually went on trial, in late May of 1872, the charge had been readjusted to murder in the second degree. When her case was called on May 29, she was ready to be prosecuted in Judge Paine's court by H. B. DeWolf and Samuel Eddy. Jennie, still dressed in her all-black outfit, was represented by Samuel E. Adams and M. S. Castle.

DeWolf's opening statement made it clear he would simply let the facts speak for themselves. He detailed Jennie's careful arrangements for the murder, methodically citing the many circumstances of motive, means, and opportunity. Samuel Adams, on the other hand, made it clear he would rely on the jury's emotional sympathies. Deftly, he painted the portrait of a trusting, then ruined, virgin, who had so foolishly "reposed confidence in his honor and promises of marriage." Then followed the catalog of her woes: her dismissal, her pregnancy, her "loathsome disease," and her desperate poverty. Skillfully, Adams reiterated Fisk's refusals to aid the wretched Jennie and led the jurors up to the winter of 1870–71 and the climactic day of February 16, when, he intimated, Jennie decided to kill *herself*, not Fisk:

> She was then in a boarding house without a dollar, her trunk had been seized by the landlord, and at that time her disease had assumed a most aggravating character. It was almost a moment of life or death to her. At that eventual moment she applied to Fisk and asked him to make some provision for her. He promised to do so but did not, and her last hope was dissipated. If she bought the pistol it will be proved that she bought it for purposes of self-destruction. She had become wearied of life. We expect to show that this girl, if she shot that man, did not buy that pistol for that purpose, and she shot him at a moment when her reason was overthrown.

Given the emotional appeal of Adams's presentation and the sordid character of the murder victim, it is likely that the trial might as well have ended there. But it continued, as witness after witness recounted the shocking details of Jennie's relations with Fisk and the events of February 16. Coroner Schenck, Erastus Briggs, Thomas Powers, Edmond Ruhill, William Albon, Margaret Twohig, and several newspaper reporters took the stand before Dr. N. M. Jones testified late that afternoon. A physician and brother of the murdered Dr. William Jones, he had also treated Jennie for the secondary stages of syphilis. His testimony was particularly crucial, as there had been persistent rumors that physicians had concluded Jennie suffered from no venereal disease at all.

Shortly afterward, the state rested, only to make way for defense witnesses Drs. W. J. Scott, H. F. Biggar, E. Sterling, N. Schneider, and P. Thayer. Their subject was the secondary stages of syphilis, in particular its psychological effects. They were united in proclaiming that the disease in that stage often produced "not only depression of spirits but often affects the brain and prompts to suicide or impulsive acts belonging to the emotional insanity class."

The stage was now set for the star witness, and Jennie did not disappoint her enthralled audience. (Readers of the *Cleveland Herald* may have been disappointed: it refused to print the more earthy details of Jennie's testimony, piously noting that the "disgusting details of her testimony were eagerly listened to by the prurient crowd of spectators.") Testifying for two days, she detailed the lurid circumstances of Fisk's seduction, his subsequent spurning, the onset of her disease, and the gothic scenes in the Cliff House barn.

During cross-examination Prosecutor DeWolf attempted several times to suggest she had been less than a pure maiden when she met Fisk, but she disarmed his imputations with firm but demure denials. DeWolf also successfully attempted to introduce her letters to Fisk into the trial record, but the letters only supported the defense portrait of the accused as an innocent, trusting, if feckless ingenue. Full of girlish endearments ("Mr. Fisk, don't be mad at me will you, for I will do most anything for you," "I send you a hundred kisses and my love," "I hope that you didn't sleep with no girl yet") and pathetic pleas for money, they simply reinforced Jennie's image as Fisk's artless victim. More seriously, during rebuttal, DeWolf put Rocky River Railroad superintendent George G. Mulhern and the Cliff House bartender on the stand in an attempt to besmirch Jennie's character. Mulhern related a conversation in which Jennie boasted of sleeping with a young man named Charlie Knapp, and Dolan testified that she had expressed a sexual preference for one of his fellow employees. Judge Paine promptly struck Mulhern's testimony from the record, and the opposing attorneys made their final arguments.

We have no copy of the closing arguments. That's a pity, because Adams, Eddy, DeWolf, and Castle were among the finest attorneys of the day, all of them celebrated for their rhetorical powers. But we do have Judge Paine's charge to the jury. In it he properly stressed the meaning of "malice" pertinent to the second-degree-murder charge and the importance of judging Jennie's intention when she went to Cliff House with a loaded pistol. Although Paine did not tip his hand, he was careful to caution, in light of the defense's medical evidence, that the jury not be fooled into permitting a "license of crime" by accepting a "counterfeit insanity." The case went to the jury late in the afternoon on June 4, 1871.

Twenty-five hours later, the jurors reported to Judge Paine that they were hopelessly deadlocked. Despite many ballots, they had never come close, and Judge Paine immediately discharged them. It was said that the final ballot stood ten to two for acquittal; another report stated the voting at nine to three. The courtroom emptied, and Jennie Droz returned to her father's home to await another murder trial.

It never came. Jennie Droz was never reindicted for the murder of Julius Fisk and never stood trial again. One surmises that Prosecutor DeWolf and his cohorts saw the writing on the wall and decided to let the matter rest. And that writing was the "unwritten law"—for women. Although not articulated as often and publicly as the one for men (i.e., it's okay to shoot your wife's lover if you catch him in the act), a perusal of 19th-century murder trials suggests that a corollary rule operated for women. And the rule was that if a virtuous woman was treated badly enough—and certainly seduced, abandoned, *and* poxed Jennie qualified—then it was understandable, albeit regrettable, if the woman took her fatal revenge.

The rule worked for Jennie Droz in 1872, and it worked again for Mrs. Anna George in 1899, when the latter was accused of murdering President McKinley's brother-in-law George Saxton in Canton. Say what you will about the sexism implicit in all-male juries, you have to admit that justice was surely done in the case of poor Jennie Droz. †

"Straighten Them Out"

The Horrific Deeds of Mary Barger, 1953

Physicians are required to have licenses. Automobile drivers have licenses. Even dog owners must have licenses. Parents, on the other hand, do not. Given that absurd reality, it's a reasonable notion that Helen and Celia Barger should never have been born. It's a terrible thing to say, or even think—but consider just how unwanted and unlucky those two children were.

Their father, John G. Barger, one of 10 children, grew up in rural Ohio. Enlisting in the Army Air Force in 1941, he served through World War II. Afterwards, he decided to stay with the Air Force, eventually achieving the rank of technical sergeant. Sent to Korea when the war broke out in 1950, he spent 18 months there and endured 144 combat missions before being routed back to the States. He also acquired a wife, Sally, which is where the Barger story really begins.

Many military service marriages don't work out, and the Barger union was no exception. Married to John in 1944, Sally gave birth to their first daughter, Helen, in 1945 and a second daughter, Celia, in 1947. Despite their offspring, though, the marriage didn't thrive, and by 1949—-just two years after Celia's birth—conjugal relations had deteriorated to the point where John had to put the girls into St. Peter's Orphanage in Memphis, Tennessee. The details of the marital breakup are sketchy, but the formal ground for John's eventual petition of divorce was Sally's "gross neglect of duty." It is likewise suggestive that it was John—not Sally—who got custody of their children, an unusual divorce outcome in the 1950s. The official end of the marriage came on March 16, 1953. As it happened, however, Celia and Helen's problems were just beginning.

With no mother in the picture, John Barger was hard pressed to find care for his two daughters. When they were released from the orphanage in June 1952, he persuaded his sister, Anna Mulato, 53, to take them into her home in Mingo Junction, Ohio. Already coping with chronic high blood pressure, Anna soon found the two sisters too hard to handle. After she told John she couldn't take care of them anymore, he asked his brother Matthew and Matthew's wife, Mary, both 31 years old, to take them into their home in Cleveland. It seems to have been a temporary arrangement, for the girls were only with the Bargers for two months at their 1339 West 83rd Street home. In November 1952 Helen went back to live with Anna Mulato, and Celia was taken by John's sister, Susan Urzdich, 36, also living in Mingo Junction. Once again, the girls were too hard to handle: Anna Mulato's blood pressure wasn't getting any lower, and Susan Urzdich had her hands more than full with three boys of her own. In February 1953 the girls went back to the Bargers in Cleveland. John Barger, never heroic about assuming responsibility for what happened, would later insist that it was his ex-wife's idea that the girls live with them again.

The terms on which they returned were bitterly disputed—after the tragedy later that year. For the most part, Matthew and Mary insisted they had only taken the girls because John Barger pled so piteously to have them taken off his hands. John, on the other hand, would later recall that they begged for the children, especially as Mary Barger, owing to the consequences of several medical operations, could not conceive offspring of her own. Indeed, in a statement to Parma police—later repudiated at her trial—Mary admitted that she had only taken the girls on a second time after receiving written assurances from John G. Barger that she could keep them until they reached their majority because, as tender-hearted Mary put it, "I didn't want to become attached to them and have him take them from me." In all of her statements after the fact, however, Mary tended to downplay the material fact that John G. Barger also agreed to pay the Bargers $200 a month—most of his Air Force salary—to take care of his girls.

Whatever the motivation, the girls moved into the Bargers' West Side home in February 1953. We'll never really know what they were like before the awfulness began. Today, a half-century later, their pictures stare out at us, appealing girls with melting smiles, seemingly pleading to please and to be loved. It's clear, however, even discounting the lying Bargers, that there was more than sugar and spice in Helen and Celia's makeup. Chronically unwanted children, they had spent three years in an orphanage and then been shuttled from one reluctant relative to another before coming again to the Bargers. A number of witnesses could testify that their personalities were badly damaged by such experiences. Dr. Evelyn Stein, the girls' family doctor who treated them several times in 1953, thought they were "emotionally disturbed." Mrs. Dorothy Sullivan, the owner of the Barger flat on West 83rd, would testify that the girls were "afraid to talk." Anna Mulato said that they were "problem children," especially Celia, who was given to screaming and head-beating temper tantrums. As Mulato put it at Mary and Matthew's trial, Celia would "scream out of clear sky and throw her head against a pillow. I couldn't do anything for her." Susan Urzdich echoed Mulato's experience, stating that Helen and Celia were "too difficult to handle." She, too, also found Celia the greater burden, complaining, "[Celia] needed extra special care and demanded more attention than my three boys."

Whatever their merits or defects, Helen and Celia entered a special kind of hell the day they returned to the Bargers in February 1953. Mary Barger, already stressed out by the recent adoption of a two-year-old son, David, was in no mood to tolerate any misbehavior on the part of Helen and Celia. Matthew, a bricklayer who worked extended shifts at the Jones & Laughlin steel plant, was often absent from the home and, in any case, completely dominated by Mary. So almost all the discipline given the girls was devised and administered by Mary Barger. And what discipline it was . . . meted out by the homely, heavyset, 200-pound Mary.

The early 1950s were a different world from ours. Child abuse, as with wife-beating, was not acknowledged and dealt with as openly and effectively as it is nowadays. One could still hear the expression "spare the rod and spoil the child" uttered without apology, and children were often subject to levels of corporal punishment that went well beyond what would be legally or even socially acceptable today. It is clear, however, that Mary Barger transgressed even the lax punitive norms of her era from the day Helen and Celia entered her home.

We don't know the truth of Mary's assertions about the girls' behavior. According to Mary, Helen and Celia could—and frequently would—vomit and defecate just to spite her. Often refusing to go to sleep, they would scream uncontrollably and thrash to the point of hurting themselves by falling down and running into things. The screaming seems probable, but the more extreme and self-destructive behavior seems improbable at best. Landlady Dorothy Sullivan testified that the girls were forced to eat meals, so the vomiting may have been a natural reaction to their feeding. What isn't debatable is the fact that Mary Barger punished the girls with hideous, persistent, and remarkable ferocity. Both girls were beaten frequently during the six months they lived with the Bargers. The beatings began in the basement at 1339 West 83rd, where Mary, or sometimes Matthew, would take them so Mrs. Sullivan wouldn't hear their mistreatment. Matthew was a traditionalist, usually spanking them with his hands or using his belt. Mary, on the other hand, was a creative and sadistic abuser, slapping, kicking, pounding, and pummeling the girls over every part of their bodies. Sometimes she used a shoe, sometimes a board, sometimes a two-foot stick. By the time Mary got caught, Helen and Celia would be bruised and scarred on virtually every part of their small bodies.

But that wasn't even the worst of it. Mary Barger was a truly demented sadist, and it is clear that something had snapped in her angry, frustrated head. As the summer of 1953 came on, she began to devise new, ingenious punishments for the two girls. In these tortures, she was often aided by her niece, Shelva Jean Peterson, 16, who had come for the summer from Amsterdam, Ohio, to "help Aunt Mary" with the children. And how did Shelva Jean help? Well, one of the things she did was to assist Mary in bathing the girls. Acting on what she claimed was the advice of Dr. Evelyn Stein, Mary Barger had her husband procure 25-pound blocks of ice. Chopping it into chunks, she used it to concoct "ice baths," in which she forcibly immersed the girls when they had "tantrums" or could not go to sleep. "Watch Celia fight the water!" she would cackle, as she plunged the terrified girl under the water for interminable seconds. Sometimes, as an alternative chastisement, she would simply lock the girls in small, dark closets. Every night they were forced to sleep on the floor of a second-floor bedroom, without a mattress or pillow, just a sheet and blanket.

Things just got worse when the Bargers moved to 5588 West 24th Street in Parma on July 23, 1953. More frequent ice baths and beatings quickly ensued. But the Parma house had a bigger basement, and Mary knew just what to do with it. First, she sent Shelva to the nearby John Muir Elementary School playground at West 24th Street and Fortune Avenue. There, acting on Mary's instructions, Shelva collected stones of various sizes and brought them back to the basement. Taking the stones, Mary Barger mixed them with nutshells and spread them on the basement floor. What followed were repeated punishment sessions in which Mary would make the girls kneel on the stones until she was satisfied with their repentance.

One can imagine the mental condition of Helen and Celia

Barger as August 1953 arrived. Constantly beaten and tortured by their inventive aunt, they must have been in a traumatized psychological state like that of extermination camp victims. And they had no recourse or means of escape. Although somewhat reluctant, their cousin Shelva was a cowed accomplice to Mary's irrepressible sadism. As Shelva explained her complicity later, "I thought of calling the police but I didn't know, being in a strange city." And Matthew Barger left everything to his wife, punctuating her creative torments with beatings of his own. John Barger, the girls' father, was a distant presence who, in any case, had no inkling of their harsh treatment. Indeed, he visited the Barger home several times that year, and the girls were too traumatized to utter a word about the terror of their daily lives. Mary Barger would later claim—with no proof or corroborating evidence—that she wrote to John Barger "about 35 times," begging him to take his children back during the spring and summer of 1953. Whatever the truth, he did not, and the situation lurched toward its inevitable tragic climax.

That climax came on an early August afternoon in the Parma basement. Matthew was not home, and Shelva and Mary took Celia down to the basement for a punishment session. At some point during that session, Mary went berserk. Picking up a stone the size of a baseball, she began beating the kneeling Celia with it. She probably hit her 10 or a 12 times with great force. Mary may have blacked out then: 45 minutes later, she would later recall, she had no memory of the beating when a shocked Shelva told her what she had done. Even tolerant Matthew Barger thought this incident was a bit on the extreme side. When a frightened Mary Barger had him look at Celia's bruises, he ordered Mary to get her stone-and-shell "mess" out of the basement. But he did not call a doctor for the obviously badly injured Celia. He would later excuse this lapse by explaining that his job made a doctor visit inconvenient. And so the punishments continued for another two weeks. On at least one occasion Helen and Celia were burned on their legs with a hot iron, and Mary Barger burned both of the girls with lighted matches.

The end came on Tuesday, August 18. It's difficult to reconstruct exactly what happened that day. The Bargers lied about everything at their trial, particularly about the events of that day and the next. The only living witnesses, Helen Barger and Shelva Peterson, were both young, severely traumatized, and sometimes unreliable witnesses. But what follows is likely what must have happened . . .

One of the Bargers, perhaps both of them, beat Celia Barger that evening, either for vomiting up some chili or soiling her pants. When she and Helen would not—or could not—go to sleep, Mary Barger had a bright idea about how to make the girls tired enough to sleep. After Shelva got the girls dressed, about 10 P.M., the entire family went to the John Muir playground, already wreathed in darkness. Mary, standing at one end, commanded the girls to run to Matthew, standing at the other end. Then they had to run back to Mary, back to Matthew, back to Mary . . . and on and on in their run to death.

The 1950s *were* different. If you don't believe it, consider what happened next. About 11:45 P.M., at least an hour into the playground run, the Bargers' odd family tableau attracted the attention of Albert Mabin and Steve Kornajcik, two Parma police patrolmen cruising by in their police car. When the officers asked the Bargers why their children were running back and forth in a playground at 15 minutes to midnight, they explained that they were trying to make them sleepy. "Well, that's a good way to tire them out," said one of the patrolmen, and they got back into their patrol car and left. Painting an even more bizarre scene, one of the policemen would later state that the entire family was still dressed in their pajamas.

It isn't clear what happened after that. The children ran for some time—Cleveland newspaper headlines would later proclaim that Celia was "run to death." She may have been conscious when the Bargers left the playground; she may have collapsed there. Helen, the most trustworthy witness, told two different versions of the early morning events. But we do know that the same two Parma policemen, officers Mabin and Kornajcik, were driving on Broadview Road about 5 A.M. when they suddenly spotted the Bargers in their car. Mary and Matthew had Celia with them, and they were speeding north toward Pearl. The two policemen pursued them to their destination: Deaconess Hospital on Pearl Road.

Matthew brought Celia into the hospital at 5:15 A.M. Her hair was soaking wet—perhaps another nocturnal ice bath?—and nurse Lydia Fulkerson watched as Matthew casually tossed the limp Celia onto a table. He told Fulkerson that his niece was still breathing and needed a doctor to look at her. Fulkerson took a good look at Celia's body and told Matthew, "There's no use doing that anymore."

Fulkerson had seen enough in her brief examination of Celia's battered body to know what was going on. The corpse was a mass of bruises, abrasions, and suspicious-looking scars, so she asked Mary if she knew how the child had incurred such injuries. Mary replied that her injuries had resulted from a fall off a swing a few days before. When a persistent Fulkerson asked if she hadn't noticed the severity of her injuries while bathing Celia, Mary snapped that she didn't bathe her, she left that to Shelva. Minutes later, Mary and Matthew Barger were taken into custody and turned over to the Parma police. Several hours later, Helen and Shelva were taken into custody by authorities, who discovered more burns, bruises, and scratches on Helen.

Given their initial behavior after arrest, it's unlikely that the Bargers could have beaten the rap. Charged that very day with first-degree manslaughter, Mary only held out for 12 hours before signing a nine-page statement in which she confessed to everything: the beatings, the rocks and shells, the ice baths, the burning with the hot iron, and the assault with the rock. Later, talking to reporters, she nonetheless tried to justify her inhuman behavior, painting herself as the tormented victim:

> Maybe the fact that I couldn't have children of my own had something to do with this. They'd throw temper tantrums, they'd throw themselves down the stairs, beat their heads against the walls. They kicked me, they bit me, they vomited.

They lied. They never told the truth. Their father didn't care for the girls. I wrote the father in the Army, but I never heard from him. I probably would have beaten my own children if they'd done things like that. After I realized what I did to the girls I was sorry. But I knew I would do it again . . . I feel terrible about all of this. I just completely lost control of my temper. I suppose I do deserve punishment.

Perhaps unsurprisingly, Mary also mentioned that her father had beaten her when she misbehaved as a child growing up in Amsterdam, Ohio.

Charged with aiding and abetting manslaughter, Matthew Barger was initially more contrite and less defiant. "I know I'm done," he blurted to reporters, "I don't care what happens to me." Signing a statement in which he admitted spanking and beating the girls a bit, he blamed most of their rough treatment on his wife, repeatedly saying, "I don't know what happened. I don't know how it happened." At the same time he justified the ice baths, claiming they were done on the advice of a doctor. As for Mary's behavior, well, as he said, "She's a very good housekeeper, keeps a house spotless. Ask anyone . . . I never interfered with my wife. She said she was just straightening the kids out. The kids didn't seem to mind." In a more rueful moment he remarked, "I guess my mother was right when she told me on her deathbed not to marry my wife."

Even if the Bargers had denied their crimes, they could not escape the damning statements of Helen Barger and Shelva Jean Peterson. Speaking from the safety of the Cuyahoga County Detention Home, Helen detailed the months of torture that had climaxed in her sister's death. Her memory of the last scene at John Muir playground was chilling:

Aunt Mary and Uncle Matthew took us to the schoolyard and made us run to tire us out. We ran and ran and would try to stop, but they would make us run again. they wouldn't let us stop. We ran and ran all night. At 12 o'clock, 1 o'clock, 2 o'clock,

3 o'clock and I don't know how long until Celie fell down in the grass. She couldn't get up . . . I knew she was dead. I said, "What's wrong with Celie, Mommy," but she wouldn't answer me. Celie was dead but she was still mad at us. She said, "Don't call me Mommy. I'm not your mother." Aunt Mary and Uncle Matthew were scared then. I knew they were scared because Celie was dead.

Still showing signs of her profound disorientation, Helen expressed her love for "Aunt Mary and Uncle Matthew" and plaintively asked, "They won't be in jail a long time, will they?"

Shelva Jean Peterson supported virtually all of Helen's story, telling of the ice baths and how she had held the girls while Mary burned them with matches or a hot iron in the basement. "What else could I do?" she told reporters. "I was brought up to do what I'm told."

Matthew Barger was put in the Parma jail, while Mary was initially incarcerated in the Cleveland Central Police Station jail, as Parma had no facilities for female prisoners. Within a couple of days they found themselves in the Cuyahoga County Jail, with Mary on the seventh floor and Matthew on the sixth. Meanwhile, Air Force Sgt. John Barger had been notified of his daughter's death. Given compassionate leave from Stewart Air Force Base in Smyrna, Tennessee, he was on a plane to Cleveland the day after his daughter's death. Arriving at Cleveland Hopkins Airport, he was stunned to discover, after seeing a newspaper, that his daughter Celia had not died in an automobile accident, as he had thought. Reunited with Helen that evening, he insisted that he did not hold a grudge against Matthew or Mary but that he wanted them to get the full penalty of the law. Dumbfounded at his children's fate, he recalled his recent visits, insisting, "I visited my daughters four or five times since I placed them with my brother and sister-in-law. They seemed happy and well fed. I can't figure it out. My brother was always kind to even animals."

After a careful autopsy by assistant Cuyahoga County coroner Lester Adelson, Celia was laid out for view at the F. H. Cranium Funeral Home, 6204 Detroit Avenue, on Friday evening, August 21. About a thousand persons, both friends and strangers, showed up to pay their last respects to the little girl in the big headlines. She was dressed in white with a white veil, her reddish hair was visible, and she clutched a rosary in her hands. There were many floral tributes, many from sympathizers who wanted to remain anonymous. Sometime late that night, after the public had departed, Celia's mother, Sally, slipped in to see her daughter and to murmur, it was said, something about "my share of the blame." The next morning a solemn Mass of the Angels was offered over the body of Celia at Our Lady of Mount Carmel Church at West 70th Street and Detroit Avenue. Later, she was buried in Holy Cross Cemetery.

Bound over to the grand jury on August 31, 1953, in separate hearings before Parma municipal judge George P. Allen, the Bargers were soon out on bail, $10,000 for Mary and $5,000 for Matthew. As expected, Mary was charged with first-degree manslaughter and Matthew with aiding and abetting it. Hardly concealing his contempt for Mary, Judge Allen publicly complained that "the facts in this case indicate that Mrs. Barger should face a charge of second-degree murder, rather than manslaughter."

Four months later, in January 1954, the Bargers went on trial before a three-judge panel composed of Judges Joseph Arti, B. D. Nicola, and Edward Blythin (later to become infamous as the partisan judge at the first Sam Sheppard trial). Represented by attorneys Phillip Barragate and Hyman C. Wedren, the Bargers were determined to contest every shred of evidence and testimony in the case, and courtroom spectators were not disappointed by the trial's theatrics.

The state's case was blunt and simple. Assistant Cuyahoga County prosecutor Dennis McGuire carefully described the injuries suffered by Celia Barger over a period of months, which, he argued, caused her death. Assistant Cuyahoga County coroner Lester Adelson had found no fewer than 25 significant internal and external injuries to Celia's body, and McGuire read out Adelson's numbing catalog in court: many scrapes and bruises, a crushed kidney, a damaged heart, and hemorrhages in the areas of the chest, heart, throat, and thymus gland. Some terrible things had happened to this defenseless child, McGuire asserted, and the state was going to prove that Mary and Matthew had done them.

Not so, responded Phillip Barragate for the defense. Echoing the Bargers' claims that Celia had been a willful, explosive, and self-destructive child, Barragate told the jury that Celia's death had been her own fault:

> Shortly before her death she threw herself against an iron glider. The day before her death she threw herself down the basement steps from a landing and she landed on a tricycle. She died as a result of self-inflicted injuries.

Barragate also insisted, as per Mary Barger, that both children were in the habit of vomiting at will and throwing themselves against things to injure themselves. Summarizing his portrait of Mary and Matthew as loving foster parents, Barragate praised their charity in taking Helen and Celia into their home: "The Bargers took them in and treated them with kindness. But because of a lack of parental love the girls were rebellious and uncontrollable."

It was one thing to say such things; it was another to prove them. Barragate failed utterly at his thankless task. He could not shake Adelson's confident belief that Celia's injuries could not have been self-inflicted. He couldn't shake Adelson's assertion that Celia's death had resulted from being beaten with a rock in early August. Adelson was adamant in his conviction that Celia's death was caused by the crushed kidney and heart failure.

Barragate had little better luck with Shelva Peterson, who testified for the state. Although she recalled one instance of Celia's throwing herself to the basement floor, she flatly denied that she had witnessed Celia throwing herself against a glider or down the Barger basement stairs onto a tricycle. Nor did Barragate win any points for Mary in his questions about the rock-beating incident in the basement:

Barragate: How high did Mary Barger raise her hand?

Peterson: Over her head.

Barragate: Isn't that about four feet?

Peterson: I don't know. I can't measure in feet.

Worse yet, Shelva brought a plenitude of specific detail to add verisimilitude to her memory of the crucial events. She recalled how Celia was half-naked at the time Mary beat her with a rock. She remembered the color of the shoe Mary beat Celia with (a red loafer) and how Aunt Mary remarked that she could hit Celia and Helen "as often as she liked because the neighbors wouldn't be able to hear her."

Deaconess Hospital nurse Lydia Fulkerson followed Shelva on the stand, detailing Matthew's callous tossing of Celia's corpse and Mary Barger's evasive lies about the cause of her injuries. Then came Helen Barger, who calmly recalled the details of how she and her sister had been tortured and the macabre scene of their last night at John Muir playground.

Mary Barger got the chance to tell her side of the story on January 14, 1954. She didn't get very far that morning. Shortly after she took the stand, her lawyer interrupted her to tell her that the three presiding judges had just refused Barragate's motions for either a directed acquittal verdict or a reduction of the charge to assault and battery. Suddenly pitching forward, Mary Barger fell to the floor in what was later described as an "hysterical coma." Her sister Wilma rushed to her, slapping her cheeks in an effort to bring her out of it. Taken unconscious from the courtroom, Mary eventually revived and returned that afternoon and the next day to continue her version of the events. Characterizing the Barger children as willful demons, she reiterated her fiction that Celia had thrown herself into a glider "six or eight times." She repeated the tale that Celia had deliberately thrown herself down the basement stairs onto a tricycle, this time transposing the event to the last day of Celia's life. When asked why she didn't call a doctor after that incident, she replied that she didn't consider it an unusual occurrence. Crying almost constantly, Mary repeatedly denied that she had ever mistreated, must less tortured, her nieces. No, she had never burned the girls, although she admitted once lighting a match to frighten Helen. No, she had never made Shelva Jean hold the girls while she burned them. No, she had never hit them with anything but her hand or a loafer. Yes, she had once used an iron on the girls—but it was an unheated one. And yes, she had signed a nine-page statement on August 19, admitting virtually everything of which she was accused. But she had been abused by the Parma police, denied food for 12 hours after her arrest, and was never allowed to read the statement she had signed.

Mary's version of Celia's last night differed sharply from the versions offered by Helen and Shelva. No, Celia had not been beaten that evening. Mary's memory was that after Celia vomited, the girls were put to bed. They awoke about 11 P.M., so they were taken to the playground to run themselves sleepy. They returned home shortly after they were spotted by the police. Then, at 3 A.M., Celia awoke crying in pain. Mary could see that her stomach was bloated, so she had Shelva help give her an enema. When that didn't help, they gave her another, and when she lapsed into unconsciousness, Matthew drove them to the hospital.

Matthew Barger didn't fare any better on the stand than his wife. Crying so hard at one point that the trial had to be recessed, he repudiated the more damning parts of his signed confession and complained of his "third-degree" treatment by Parma police. He also accused them of trying to force him to put all of the blame on his wife. Initially denying he had ever laid a hand on either girl, McGuire's relentless cross-examination forced him to admit using a belt on them several times. But he insisted that he had only been following Dr. Stein's orders about the ice baths:

> Barger: She told us to throw them in ice water.
> McGuire: Did you throw them in ice water?
> Barger: No, I dunked them in ice water.
> McGuire: Did you put their heads under water?
> Barger: I don't remember.

The witnesses for the defense were hardly helpful to Matthew and Mary Barger. True, psychiatrist J. B. Cohn of Shaker Heights testified that he thought it was possible for Celia to have deliberately hurled herself down the Barger basement stairs. But he probably didn't burnish his professional credentials with his reply to McGuire's questions about the likely effects of the Bargers' disciplinary regime:

McGuire: Do you think a child who is put in a dark closet or dunked in ice-water, or who might have been beaten with a shoe could have temper tantrums?

Cohn: That would be difficult to answer because two of the three punishments you mentioned are ancient methods for dealing with temper tantrums.

Although he allowed that such punitive methods were "ancient" and "archaic," Dr. Cohn insisted that the ice water treatment could be interpreted as a form of "hydrotherapy." Mary Barger's sister, Wilma Eastman, followed Cohn on the stand. She testified that after Celia Barger died, Shelva had told her that she had cooperated with the Parma police only because they had threatened her with 10 years in prison if she didn't incriminate the Bargers.

The trial now recessed for several days. Testimony was needed from Matthew and Mary's relatives in downstate Ohio, and they were too ill to travel to Cleveland. So prosecutor McGuire and defense attorney Wedren journeyed southward to take depositions from Anna Mulato, Susan Urzdich in Mingo Junction, and Mary's parents, Mr. and Mrs. Sherman Dillon, in nearby Amsterdam. As expected, Mulato and Urzdich testified that the girls were behaviorally disturbed—but not given to intentionally injuring themselves, as claimed by the Bargers. Both aunts recalled Celia as needy, an "unruly child, so starved for affection that we fear we may have spoiled her." The Dillons, for their part, echoed the testimony of Wilma Eastman. Testifying about conversations they'd had with their granddaughter Shelva after Celia's death, they swore that she had told them she was "all mixed up" when questioned by the

Parma police and that they had threatened her with imprisonment
or a perjury charge if she did not play ball.

That was the end of the defense witnesses, as Hyman Wedren
informed the court upon his return, complaining that three Cleveland doctors had reneged on their promise to testify for the defense. Then came several state rebuttal witnesses to demolish
charges made by the Bargers during their lachrymose testimony.
Dr. Evelyn Stein flatly denied that she had prescribed ice baths for
Helen and Celia. Perhaps smarting from the refusal of his doctors
to testify in court, Barragate insinuated she had changed her testimony to mollify wrathful public opinion:

> Barragate: Could it be, doctor, that the unfavorable publicity
>   in this case has caused you to change your mind
>   that you told the Bargers to give ice baths?
> Stein: Absolutely not.

Genevieve Ball, the secretary to the Parma police chief who had
typed up Mary's August 19 confession, refuted her claim that she
had been under duress or unaware of what she was doing. Parma
police detective Virgil Costley, who had done much of the initial
investigative work, likewise denied coercing either of the Bargers
during their prolonged interrogations. Shelva Peterson also reap-
peared, to contradict assertions that she had been threatened or
manipulated by the police.

Closing arguments in the trial began the morning of January 25.
McGuire portrayed the Bargers as "medieval torturers . . . whose
minds were steeped with blind and brutal cruelty." Barragate's
closing rhetoric portrayed the Bargers as benevolent foster parents
and charged the state had failed to prove that Celia's presumed
fatal chest injury was caused by Mary hitting her with a rock. The
arguments last 140 minutes, and the judges retired to deliberate.

They returned after 2 hours and 40 minutes at 7 P.M. . . . with
a unanimous verdict of guilty for both Bargers. Speaking for the
court, Judge Arti stated that the evidence and testimony compelled

them to conclude that the Bargers had been responsible for a "combination of events that had caused the death of Celia Barger."

It was not one incident that took this child's life but rather a series of incidents, all of which contributed to her death. That they extended over a period of time there is no doubt.

Addressing the assertion that Celia's injuries had been self-inflicted, Arti cited Adelson's long list of grievous wounds and dismissed the Bargers' claims as "wholly incredible." Noting the defense lawyers' repeated claims that Helen and Celia had been "problem children," Judge Arti riposted, "However, gentlemen, even problem children are entitled to the protection of society from wrongful acts." He then revoked bond for both Mary and Matthew Barger and sentenced them to 1 to 20 years in Marysville Reformatory and the Ohio Penitentiary, respectively.

Predictably, Mary and Matthew didn't take the news with meek resignation. They heard the verdicts without flinching, and Mary was relatively subdued when asked if she had anything to say before sentence was pronounced: "I still say I am not guilty of hitting Celia with a stone, your honors, and I thank the Lord God, my supreme judge. He will take care of me from here on in." But to the press outside the courtroom she spluttered:

> We'll take this to the highest court we can go. We'll manage to get the money some way to fight it. I did not get a fair trial. One reason, the judges were prejudiced because of all the publicity since last August. As God is my judge I didn't do it.

Accusing the state witnesses of lying, she denounced Dr. Stein with particular venom:

> Dr. Stein lied all the way through. I've known her about 12 years. She operated on me five times. I will say she shook my hand and cried when she wished me the best of luck.

And, once again, Mary concluded by painting herself as the victim:

> I was never angry enough not to know what I was doing. I never lost my head with the children. If anyone was tortured it was Matthew and I during the past two weeks.

Matthew, as usual, played a relatively subdued second to his wife's starring role. Blaming the newspapers, he sourly whined:

> You guys built it up. I don't know what to say. You saw how the judges were. All I know is that I'm not guilty. I'm all mixed up. I didn't get much sleep.

Considering their crimes, the Bargers didn't pay a very heavy penalty for their bestial cruelties. Finally transferred to their respective prisons at the end of March 1954, they immediately began working for their release. Unsuccessful in their attempts to appeal their convictions, they soon focused their efforts on getting paroled. Mary's first parole bid was turned down only a year later, in February 1955. Three months later they lost the legal right to their adopted child, David, who had been put in the Parmadale orphanage after their conviction. Permanent custody of the boy—who, curiously, had never been harmed by either Mary or Matthew Barger—was given back to Catholic Charities in October 1955.

Matthew Barger won parole the day after Christmas in 1956, after serving less than two years of his 1-to-20 term. He was finally released on January 31, 1957. Mary, the guiltier of the two, remained in prison until she was paroled on March 31, 1960. If the Bargers are alive, they would be in their early 80s. Helen Barger, if alive, would be almost 60. And Celia Barger sleeps in Holy Cross Cemetery, forever five years old and forever knowing a peace she never knew in her life on earth. †

The Sins of the Father

The Neumeister Family Tragedy, 1911

It probably couldn't happen now. Some people even said it couldn't have occurred back in 1911—which is when it did happen in Cleveland. Several months before the Neumeister tragedy unfolded, Clyde Fitch's melodrama *The City* played at the Colonial Theater on Superior Avenue. Fitch's work related the star-crossed tale of Cicely Rand and George Hannock. Hannock, the secret and illegitimate son of respectable banker George Rand, uncomfortably resurfaces as an adult to blackmail his father. The father dies, telling his legitimate son, George Jr. the truth about Hannock. Hannock is confronted by Junior, who learns to his horror that Hannock has just married his sister Cicely—Hannock's own half-sister. The play ends predictably, at least for an Edwardian audience, with Hannock shooting at Rand and killing Cicely by accident.

Cleveland critics of the day found Fitch's story not so much improper as implausible. As *Plain Dealer* feature writer Sam B. Anson, who had seen the Cleveland production of *The City*, later confessed:

> If anybody had told us then that there was a possibility of real life actors participating in a scene such as that where George Rand Jr. tells Hannock that he is the elder George Rand's illegitimate son, born to the village dressmaker, and that consequently his love for Cicely Rand, whom he has married an hour before, is a love that cannot be—we'd laugh at him.

To say the least, Anson wasn't laughing when he wrote those words in the wake of the Neumeister tragedy, a horrifying event that demonstrated the cruel twin truths that art imitates life and that truth is stranger than fiction.

The Neumeister family's cruel destiny began its pitiless course in Kaiser Wilhelm I's Second Reich sometime in the mid-1880s. There, in some small and obscure German village, aspiring braumeister Leonard Neumeister fell in love—or at least in lust—with a comely girl named Margaretta Ott. As is the wont of smitten lovers, Leonard and Margaretta were, as Leonard later put it, "indiscreet," and the fruit of their indiscretion, a son named Hans, duly arrived. Leonard had previously offered to marry Margaretta, but she had refused him because she opposed his wish to live in Berlin, where he had a job offer and could perfect the beermaking craft he hoped to prosecute someday in America. After Hans arrived, Leonard decided to renew his offer, desiring to do the decent thing by Margaretta, even if it meant renouncing his dreams of Berlin. But just before he was about to speak to her, he heard "stories" about her from relatives. "They were not nice stories," he later recalled, and he decided to abandon both her and his native land. Before he left, however, he married an acceptable woman and fathered Fred, his first legitimate child.

Soon after Fred's birth in 1890, Leonard brought his family to America, where he labored hard and steadily prospered. Eventually settling in Cleveland, he worked his way up to the position of braumeister at the Pilsner Brewing Company plant at West 65th and Clark Avenue. Leonard's personal life likewise continued to advance. Another son, Alex, was born in 1896 and his only daughter, Anna, in 1893. His last child, William, was born in 1895. Shortly after his birth, his mother died. With four young children to rear, Leonard didn't grieve long before marrying again. His choice of Johanna was a fortunate one, and the children took immediately to their new mother in the Neumeister home at 7008 Hague Avenue on the West Side.

The years passed. Leonard probably didn't give a lot of thought to the offspring he'd left in Germany, what with his braumeister duties and his obligations to a family of five. But over the years he'd kept in touch with his relatives in the old country. As 1910 rolled around, he knew that his son Hans was still living, so he wasn't too surprised when he received a letter from Hans that spring. Hans had recently been told who his real father was, and a correspondence sprang up between father and son. Then, at the beginning of 1911, Hans was released from the German navy after fulfilling his military service requirement. He journeyed to America, arriving on the steamer *Ancoria* in Galveston in early 1911. Departing at once for Cleveland, he walked into the Pilsner brewery several days later and announced himself to his surprised father.

No one will ever know the exact motives the 25-year-old Hans entertained when he sought out his father. Had he for uncounted years nourished fantasies of hideous revenge on the parent who had abandoned him? Did he come to Cleveland specifically to annihilate the kind of loving, close family he had never enjoyed? Ostensibly, Hans's purpose in coming was to be close to his biological father. Whatever he told Leonard was convincing enough, for his father now took him into his home.

Illegitimacy was not the same in 1911 as it is now. With garden-variety Hollywood starlets parading their status as unwed mothers on prime-time television, it is hard to recall a time when illegitimate birth was a burning disgrace. It was a shameful secret for both Hans and his erring father, so they mutually decided to dissemble the sordid fact. Confiding the truth only to his wife, Johanna, Leonard introduced his son to his other children simply as "Hans Ott," a boarder who was coming to live with them.

The stage for the Neumeister tragedy was now fully set. Anna Neumeister, barely 18, was an innocent girl with little experience of the world or men. A devout member of St. Johannes Evangelical Church on West 44th Street, the pious Anna had been confirmed there just several years before. Perhaps recalling his own guilty missteps, Leonard had reared her very protectively, forbidding her to go to dances with young men and allowing her only to attend brewery dances where he was present. The maturing Anna had eventually rebelled against such constraints. At the age of 16, she demanded that she be allowed to get a job. Leonard refused to let her work in a store, so she went into domestic service. Her stint as a maid, however, ended sometime in 1910, when she returned home to care for her ailing stepmother. Anna had not yet returned to work when her life was brightened by the arrival of the handsome new boarder, Hans Ott.

Hans must have known what he was doing. A self-acknowledged, irreligious "freethinker," he knew that Anna was his half-sister. So, too, in due time, did Anna's brothers, who apparently figured out Hans's true identity by themselves. Only Anna didn't know. Moving into the Neumeister home in January 1911, Hans quickly ingratiated himself with the impressionable Anna.

Stepmother Johanna was the first to have an inkling of Hans's malignant attraction to Anna. But she said nothing to her husband, hoping that their budding intimacy was only a warm friendship. Leonard, for his part, remained, as he later admitted, "a blind old fool." He was impressed with the well-educated, personable Hans, and Hans further gratified him by soon getting steady work as a baker. Then, on Friday, March 31, Johanna found Hans and Anna furtively embracing in the living room.

The horrified Johanna sent Anna to her room, while Hans, without a word, picked up his hat and left the house. Fearful of her husband's rage, Johanna kept silent for twenty-four hours. Then, on Saturday evening, she told Leonard what she had witnessed. As

she had foreseen, he flew into a rage. Summoning Anna, he told
her the awful truth and banished Hans from the house forever.

Although obviously stunned, Anna said nothing when her father revealed Hans's identity and expelled him. The next morning she attended church as usual, spending several hours praying

---

*Stepmother Johanna was the first
to have an inkling of Hans's
malignant attraction to Anna.*

---

on her knees and listening raptly to a squad of girls preparing for
confirmation. Dressed in white, the girls sang a hymn beseeching
God to be a good shepherd and to keep them from sin. The hymn
also beseeched God to "take them to himself" if they could not
keep their purity.

Sometime after Sunday-afternoon dinner, Anna confronted her
parents. Weeping copiously, she demanded that Hans be allowed to
return to the house. She told Leonard and Johanna that she loved
Hans and couldn't live without him and that if he had to go, she
would go with him. Leonard didn't believe her, and their stormy
exchange ended with her going to her room. Sometime during the
next several hours, she disappeared from the house.

It was later surmised that Anna stole away from her home to
keep a prearranged rendezvous with Hans. Together, they walked
the West Side streets for hours, eventually ending up at Edgewater
Park. They were seen there about 10 P.M. by Cleveland city councilman Lyman O. Newell and his brother Will, standing by the latter's boat livery at the foot of West 58th Street. No one knows what
they said to each other—but that didn't stop at least one Cleveland
journalist from later reconstructing their colloquy. Writing in the
Cleveland News, one yellow scribe related Hans's presumed avowal
and Anna's appalled response:

Sunday, she left and sought him out. He told her then, "I am your half-brother. I've known it all along and yet I've gone on loving you and making love to you and letting you learn to love me."

Anna fled from him, shame overcoming her.

Maybe she did, maybe she didn't. No one saw the two together after 10 P.M. Sunday night. But early Monday morning, about 5:30, a watchman at the Hill Clutch Company plant at the foot of West 65th Street saw a young woman walking up and down the Edgewater Park beach in an agitated manner. Her behavior suggested a potential suicide, and the watchman summoned park policeman William O'Brien. They searched for the girl for some time but found no trace of her. Then, sometime after 7 A.M., a man named Peter Stible rented a boat from Newell's boathouse and rowed out into Lake Erie. A short distance from shore, he espied a dark object floating in the water. Rowing to it, he realized it was a body and lifted it into his boat. Minutes later, Patrolman O'Brien put in a call for the dead wagon at A. R. Nunn's morgue, 11604 Detroit Avenue.

Anna's body remained unidentified for some hours. The only clue to her identity was a gold ring on one finger with the initial "A." But a worried Leonard Neumeister had already reported Anna missing to the 10th Precinct police station at 2061 West 53rd Street the night before. About noon on Monday Leonard learned from the police that a drowned woman's corpse lay at Nunn's morgue. Leonard and his son Fred went there and identified Anna immediately. Leonard then left to break the news to the rest of the family, while Fred departed with a .44-caliber pistol and the announced intention of shooting Hans Ott on sight. Fred, recently returned from a stint as a Texas cowboy, was determined to avenge his sister's honor and death in timely Wild West fashion.

Fred was already too late. Early that same morning, about a half hour after Anna drowned herself, Cleveland police officer Thomas J. Murphy had come across a young man lying on the sidewalk of West 58th Street, just three blocks from the fatal beach.

The young man was obviously in a bad way, and he asked Murphy to take him to St. John's Hospital. Hans Ott was dead by the time Murphy got him to St. John's, and a newspaper reporter brought the news of Hans's death to the Neumeister home late that night.

What killed Hans Ott? Leonard Neumeister's judgmental neighbors and friends thought they knew: it was God's righteously punishing hand that struck Hans dead on the street for his premeditated and primal sin. But Cuyahoga County and Cleveland officials were not so certain. Anna's death, clearly, was due to drowning, and Coroner Max A. Boesgner issued a quick verdict of suicide. But Deputy Coroner Robert C. Droege's autopsy of Hans's corpse found no trace of a toxic agent and none of the physical evidence invariably left by the era's most popular suicidal agents: Rough-on-Rats, bichloride of mercury, and oxalic or carbolic acids. Boesgner, however, let it be known that he thought it was an unidentified but lethal narcotic. More he could not say, as he was not legally or fiscally empowered to conduct more definitive chemical tests that might identify the agency of Hans's demise.

There were also ambiguous aspects of Anna's death that provoked questions. Had she and Hans concerted their suicides together? Was it planned as a double drowning—only to have Hans change his mind after Anna had leapt into the Lake Erie waves? Or—as the unforgiving Fred Neumeister eventually insisted—had Hans simply murdered Anna by pushing her into the lake and then committed suicide in more comfortable fashion several blocks away? No one knew, although the Reverend Carl Weiss, Anna's pastor, thought he knew what had pushed Anna over the edge. Weiss had noticed her fervent orisons at his church that Sunday, and it was his smug, expressed conviction that it was the sight of his confirmation girls, clad in virginal white, that had brought home to Anna the depth and infamy of her sin. Indeed, the Reverend Weiss went further, opining publicly that the unknown female who had repeatedly telephoned his rectory on Monday morning, asking where she could find the Creed, must been the conscience-stricken Anna. (Devotees of such tales may uncharitably recall the Reverend Weiss as the cowardly divine who figured in the saga of "Blinky" Morgan, Cleveland's greatest desperado of the 19th century. Present in the same railroad car where Morgan murdered Cleveland police detective William Hulligan, Weiss had become temporarily famous in Cleveland's newspapers as "Rev. Under-the-Seat Weiss" for his craven behavior on that occasion.)

Whatever the whisperings of his neighbors and the certitudes of the clergy and press, there was nothing left for Leonard Neumeister but sorrow and regret. Although he was urged to let Hans lie in a pauper's grave, his paternal instinct belatedly triumphed. After a brief service over Hans's remains at McGorray's undertaking establishment at 3038–42 Lorain Avenue on Wednesday, April 5, Hans's coffin was interred in West Park Cemetery. That same afternoon the Reverend Weiss conducted funeral rites for Anna at her father's home. Her corpse was then interred beside her mother in the Monroe Avenue Cemetery.

Except for a *Plain Dealer* feature story several weeks later, the Neumeister sensation was soon forgotten. But the shocking question at the center of this tragedy remains: Did Hans Ott deliberately set out to make his half-sister Anna fall in love with him? Was it all a malevolent design of the freethinking youth to revenge himself on his neglectful father? Or was Hans as much a victim as Anna, the unwitting, vulnerable victim of Cupid's cruel and inexplicable darts? Whatever his intentions, the fact remains that he knew Anna was his half-sister—and she didn't. The fact that he nevertheless pursued the relationship, whatever his motives, is evidence enough of the evil that lurked in the heart of this truly misbegotten young man. †

A Second Shot at Life

The Gothic Tale of Eula Dortch, 1965

Are some people just no damn good? Are some persons rotten to the core, incapable of redemption or rehabilitation? Mankind has struggled with this question for all of recorded history without coming to a final conclusion. Most correctional institutions have struggled too, alternating between sheer punishment and hopeful rehabilitation. Various cultural voices have argued for the redemptive outlook, as in the sublime figure of Victor Hugo's Jean Valjean or the sentimental melodrama of Jimmy Valentine. But a skeptical public has, more often than not, put little faith in giving criminals a second chance. This author's own annals of Cleveland woe offer instances of persons who committed terrible crimes and lived to regret them in later lives of repentance: Joe Filkowski, Velma West, and "Big Jim" Morton come to mind. (The Joe Filkowski saga is recounted in "Stand by Your Man," *The Corpse in the Cellar*, 1999; the Velma West tragedy is told in "Twelve O'Clock Girl in a Nine O'Clock Town," *The Maniac in the Bushes*, 1997, and in this volume; and the "Big Jim Morton" story is told in "Gangster's Gangster," *The Killer in the Attic*, 2002.) Those same annals, however, also furnish tales of thorough evildoers who never learned their lessons, pursuing wickedness right up to their unlamented deaths: monsters like Jiggs Losteiner, Henry Hagert, and John Leonard Whitfield. (For the Jiggs Losteiner saga, see "High Noon at Bedford," *They Died Crawling*, 1995; and for the Hagert saga, see "When Monsters Walk," *The Killer in the Attic*, 2002.) No one seems able to predict the fates of once fallen souls. It is with these suitably sobering thoughts in mind, therefore, that we begin the cautionary tale of Eula Mae Dortch.

Many and many a year ago . . . and in a galaxy far, far away . . . lived a woman named Eula Dortch. Actually, it was 1965, and the place was the East Side of Cleveland, 927 East 129th Street, to be exact. It was a three-story frame house, and it was there that Eula dwelt with her husband John, 34, and their seven children. They lived in imperfect amicability, sorry to say, for the word in the neighborhood was that John Wesley Dortch beat his wife during their not infrequent quarrels. She would later claim that he used both his hands and feet in assaulting her during their bouts of domestic infelicity.

Perhaps it was the stress of their hard lives: Eula toiled at Lutheran Hospital as a nurse's aide for only $45 a week, while John labored as a machinist at Wood, Spencer & Company and took other jobs on the side. Or maybe it was just the pressure of too many children and too many bills to meet over the 13 years Eula and John had been wed, not to mention their hard journey from Jackson, Mississippi, to the mean streets of Cleveland in 1954.

Perhaps, too, it was the times. The 1960s were tumultuous and unprecedented times for African American Clevelanders like the Dortches. As with many of their Glenville neighbors, they were involved in the struggle to obtain better and unsegregated schools for their children. In the fall of 1964 Eula jumped into the fight over the new Stephen E. Howe Elementary School. It was a complex controversy, but the crux of it was that many Glenville African Americans like Eula believed the new school was too far away for their children to walk to and had been sited to perpetuate segregated schools for the black residents of Glenville. (The United States Supreme Court would eventually validate that interpretation in its historic 1976 ruling ordering the desegregation of Cleveland schools.) In September 1964 Eula and like-minded neighbors organized the Hazeldell Parents Association (Hazeldell was the former neighborhood elementary school) and boycotted Howe Elementary. There is no reason to doubt Eula's idealism or sincerity in that cause: the *Cleveland Call & Post* would subsequently dub Eula a "Joan-of-Arc" in the fight against inconvenient, inferior, and segregated Cleveland schools. But by January 1965 Eula had given up on the public schools and transferred her children to a Catholic parochial school.

In retrospect, she had also given up on her husband John. On the morning of January 7 Eula was working at a little business called the Hazeldell Variety Shop, a small shop she operated with a friend at 805 East 125th Street. The friend's husband had left a handgun at the store, a .35-caliber Walther automatic pistol. Eula asked her friend if she could borrow the gun, saying that her husband John was going to drive to Detroit and needed it for protection on the highway. The friend agreed to loan her the gun, and Eula put it in her purse and left the store sometime that afternoon.

When Eula got home, she found John alone in the house, her children being looked after during her work days by a neighborhood woman named Mrs. Thomas. We only have Eula's version of what happened next. She told the cops that as soon as she came in the side door of the house, John started arguing with her. She didn't remember later what it was all about, but she did recall that he threatened to kill her. She drew the gun from her purse and pointed it at him. Then he sat down on the couch in the living room, repeating several times his threat to kill her as soon as she fell asleep. Suddenly, he got up from the couch, and she thought she saw something in his hand. She fired one shot. It hit him in the chest, and he went down. He lay there moaning for 45 minutes until he died.

At this juncture the Dortch tragedy evolved from a mundane domestic killing into a tale of unique gothic freakishness. Many women are mistreated by their husbands, and some of them eventually turn on and even kill their tormentors. But Eula Dortch was no common woman, and what she did now was breathtakingly bizarre. After calming down for about an hour, she decided that she just couldn't face the disgrace to herself and her family potentially ensuing from John's death. So she decided not to tell anyone about it and to hide the evidence.

Laboriously hauling the late John down to the basement, Eula dragged him into the fruit cellar, a 10-by-5-foot concrete-floored room in the southeast corner of the basement. Then she brought in a posthole digger and a sledgehammer and went to work. All that afternoon and part of the next day, she hammered away at the four-inch-thick concrete. Her plan was to bury John underneath it, but by the time she got through the four inches she was tired.

Not just tired of pounding at the concrete, but tired of the sight and smell of John Wesley Dortch. So, sometime on the morning of January 8, she decided to forget about it. There was already a hasp on the fruit cellar door, so she walked over to the Eddy Road Hardware store at 12424 Arlington Avenue and purchased a Slaymaker padlock from owner Ben Asnien. Returning home, she placed a beige bedspread over John's corpse and padlocked the door.

It's quite possible that if Eula Dortch had stayed out of other kinds of trouble, no one would ever have known what happened to John Dortch. She told her children and relatives that John had gone to Detroit to take another job. They believed her story, as did Henry Berghaus, the Wood, Spencer & Company manager she called right after killing John to tell him about the Detroit job. Everyone believed Eula, even her sister Elizabeth Cobb and Elizabeth's husband, Joseph. Week by week, Eula kept up the fiction of John's life in Detroit, telling everyone of his telephone calls and the support money he faithfully sent back. (Sometimes Eula varied the fiction, boasting that John had inherited a legacy from an aunt.) As

January passed into February, February gave way to March, and March waned toward April, Eula's daring and improvised murder cover-up plan seemed to be working on every front. As Cleveland police homicide bureau chief Lieutenant Carl Delau, not a Eula Dortch admirer, later put it: "It could have been a perfect crime. I

She told her children and relatives that John had gone to Detroit to take another job. They believed her story.

---

wonder how many persons have disappeared like this before, and were never heard of again."

But, as Bob Dylan once astutely remarked, "To live outside the law, you must be honest." Eula had not quite thought out the long-term aspects of killing her husband, and her lack of foresight now led to her downfall. If she didn't miss the personality or the physical abuse of the late John Wesley, she certainly did miss his weekly paycheck from Wood, Spencer & Company. Her $45 per week wage at Lutheran Hospital didn't go very far in covering the demands of seven kids and a mortgage. So Eula Dortch decided to steal.

For the hard-pressed Eula, it must have seemed an irresistible opportunity. Back in the fall of 1964, when she was involved in the boycott of Howe Elementary, she had been elected second vice-president of the Hazeldell Parents Association. With the responsibilities of that office came access to the organization's checking account. Sometime later that fall, the association officers were told to transfer any checking funds left into a savings account. This they duly did, but Eula hung on to some of the blank checks from the defunct account. After the money from John's paychecks ceased in January, she began forging and cashing the checks at local stores. By the end of March she had cashed checks worth $1,000 on the nonexistent account.

The end came at the close of March. Following a parade of bouncing checks, local businesses and banks contacted the Cleveland police. They arrested Eula Dortch on the evening of Tuesday, March 29, 1965. She was arrested at her home and taken away to the city jail, pending a charge of forgery. Some years ago this author talked with one of the Cleveland detectives who arrested Eula that evening. He regrets to this day the fact that he and his partner did not search Eula's home when they arrested her. It could have been the crime scoop of their career. Later investigators of matters at the Dortch house would be praised and promoted for what they found; for the arresting officers, it was simply a case of might-have-been.

Actually, it was hardly brilliant police work that broke the Dortch case. Eula had left home in haste, and Mrs. Thomas, who normally minded the Dortch children, became aware that the seven kids were now left completely unsupervised in their East 129th Street home. She called Elizabeth Cobb, Eula's sister, the next day and shared her concern. That evening, Elizabeth and her husband Joseph went over to Eula's house to search for John Dortch's address or telephone number in Detroit.

When they didn't find any information about John after several hours of searching, they decided to try the only unsearched area—the basement. Eventually, having run out of options, Joseph Cobb got a screwdriver and took the hasp off the fruit cellar door. They opened it . . . and found what was left of John Wesley Dortch. Undisturbed by anyone since January 7, his corpse was in an advanced state of decomposition. His eyes were gone, as were his penis and testicles. He was still wearing black shoes, black-and-white socks, gray Oxford pants, a red, white, and black sport shirt, a white tee shirt, and white jockey shorts. There were two dried bloodstains underneath the body.

Initial public shock over the grisly find in Eula's fruit cellar was soon displaced by disagreement over the character of Eula Dortch and her deserved fate. Surprisingly, it was only the minority opinion that Eula Dortch was an inhuman monster deserving harsh judicial treatment. Lieutenant Carl Delau succinctly voiced that judgment soon after he toured the crime scene and interviewed Eula in jail:

> This woman was calm, cool, scheming, and cunning. She showed no signs of regret in this killing. She kept a dirty, filthy house, and it's unbelievable that nobody smelled the foul odors outside of her house at 927 East 129th Street. She told of frequent beatings, but she never went to the prosecutor's office and she never went to a hospital. They quarreled that night while he was sitting down, and when he stood up she shot him . . . she just didn't like her husband. She called his job right away—he was getting ready to go to work, and told them he was gone to Detroit. Then she went down and picked up his pay check. She smashed up the concrete but never got to dig the grave.

Delau's skeptical opinion was hardly the majority view. From the moment Eula's arrest was blazoned forth by the Cleveland media, her version of the crime dominated interpretations of the crime. They didn't used the term "battered woman syndrome" or talk about traumatic stress disorders in the 1960s, but the times they were a-changing toward those kinds of things. Eula herself was the most forceful and articulate analyst in explaining her seemingly unbelievable behavior. Describing her 13 years of marriage as "hell," she justified her actions by invoking notions of self-defense, motherly love, and idealistic visions of a better, higher life:

> You wonder why? For myself I could stand anything, any physical harm. For my children I could not . . . John had a different philosophy in life. It was for material things. I wanted more from life, more from my children . . . I have no self-pity for myself, but I could not stand to hurt my children more.

Referring to John's murder and macabre burial only as the "incident," she told *Plain Dealer* reporter Doris O'Donnell that she hid the body to avoid disgracing her family:

I realized and knew what I had destroyed, and I thought of John's family and mine and the children, and I could not face reality. But I was relieved when everything ended.

Following her arrest, Eula was charged with forgery on April 1. The next day she was charged with second-degree murder. On April 4, accompanied by her attorney, Glenville councilman George Forbes, she waived preliminary examination before municipal judge Hugh P. Brennan and was bound over to the grand jury. Bond was set at $5,000, and she remained in jail.

By the time Eula Dortch came to trial in late June, the groundswell of support for this supposed abused wife and struggling mother was almost universal throughout the Cleveland community. Many Clevelanders had decided it was a shame about Eula Dortch and that maybe the late John Dortch had deserved what he got. *Plain Dealer* columnist J. F. Saunders spoke for all of Eula's pitying champions in a column published just before her case came to trial:

> In 1952, Eula Dortch was the radiant bride of a young man she had known through all of her teen years and had grown to love with deepening affection. She was then 19 . . . She had seven children and they were her life. She involved herself in all of their interests, gave freely of her time to helping solve community problems [no mention of check forging here!] and became an officer in an association seeking to improve the educational environment of neighborhood children. All this time Eula Dortch was aware that her marriage was a mistake but she could not bring herself to concede defeat. She had seven compelling reasons for her resolve to maintain the struggle even after the battle had been lost. And then in a sudden climax of supreme despair and distraught tension Eula Dortch picked up a small gun and shot her husband of 13 years, killing him with a single squeeze of the trigger. The castle came tumbling down. The dream exploded.

Warming to his theme, Saunders pleaded that Eula deserved a second shot at a decent life:

> Society has treated Eula Dortch cruelly and is not through with her. A year in prison can destroy this sensitive, patient, and devoted mother who withstood as long as she could the tortures of a married hell to give her children a chance at a normal life. Her crime was an impulsive act of passion committed in a moment when endurance had run out and reason had deserted a mind that could absorb no more of the punishment that astonished her attorney in its magnitude and terror. Eula Dortch is not a criminal and no imprisonment can inflict upon her suffering that could match the agony that was hers in seeing her children's world collapse. A way must be found to restore her to those children.

The pleas of J. F. Saunders and many other voices were not in vain. On June 18, 1965, Eula Dortch stood trial before Judge Hugh A. Corrigan in Cuyahoga County Common Pleas Court. After listening to her version of her unhappy marriage, Prosecutor Lloyd Brown accepted her plea of guilty to a reduced charge of first-degree manslaughter. Judge Corrigan then sentenced her to a term of 1 to 20 years in Marysville Reformatory. He also sentenced her to 1 to 20 years on the check forging charge, to be served concurrently. Giving thanks that her seven children were being reared properly by her sister, Eula Dortch vowed to get an education while she was in Marysville. And, as J. F. Saunders had so passionately hoped, a way was found to restore Eula Dortch to her seven children. In 1967 Ohio authorities decided to give her a second shot at life and released her after only two years. Three years went silently by.

Early on the morning of January 7, 1970—five years to the day after John Dortch died—police got a call to come to the Montgomery Brothers Market, a grocery at 8425 Euclid Avenue. What they found when they got there wasn't pleasant. Entering through the east door, they found the body of a young black male about five feet from the door. He was lying on his stomach, and on the other side of the door was the body of a middle-aged black female. In the rear of the store, by the beer cooler, lay the body of another young black male. They were all dead from recent gunshot wounds.

The story told by brothers Robert and Jack Montgomery was a straightforward and blunt narrative. An hour earlier, they had been working in the store with clerk Calvin Hill. Robert was behind the meat counter by the entrance when a black female entered the store. As she walked past the meat counter, he noticed a large .38 Colt revolver sticking out of the woman's waistband. She browsed around the store for a few minutes and then asked Robert what time the store closed. He told her in about 15 minutes, and she went out the front door. She returned to the store several minutes later, accompanied by two young black males. One of them headed for the beer cooler, and the other one stood by the door. The black female walked up to Robert at the meat counter, pulled out her gun, and said, "Don't move!"

Robert and Jack Montgomery had worked very hard to open their business in the heart of one of Cleveland's ghettoes. The two brothers worked 12-hour days, seven days a week, and were still paying off the Small Business Administration loan that had helped them start up the business. So when Robert heard the woman and saw the gun, he knew what to do. Ducking behind the counter, he ran to the rear of the store. Picking up a shotgun he kept there for such conversations, he sprinted back to the meat counter as the woman tried to run out of the store. Even as Robert's Ithaca Model 37 shotgun roared, Jack's .38 Iver-Johnson revolver thundered from over by the beer cooler.

She never had a chance. As Jack Montgomery later remarked, "It's suicide to try and rob this store." The black female robber and her two accomplices didn't know that both Montgomery brothers were armed. More important, they didn't know that the store was equipped with a special antitheft device that allowed the brothers to lock the exit door from the inside by pressing a button. Even if the trio had made it to the door, they would have been cut down by the six shots and two shotgun loads fired, respectively, by Jack and Robert Montgomery. By the time the brothers stopped firing, there was nothing for the police to do but pick up the bodies and identify them.

It wasn't difficult to discover who they were. One of the black males was 18-year-old Joseph Moore, address unknown; the other black male was Tommy Lee Perkins, 20, of 20103 Longbrook Road in Warrensville Heights. The families of the two young men were outraged at the celerity with which police prosecutor Clarence Rogers ruled the killings "justifiable homicide." They pointed out that neither of the two men were armed and that it couldn't be proven that they were acting in concert with the black female when she pulled the gun at 12:55 A.M. According to their grieving relatives, Joseph and Tommy Lee were just innocent bystanders, caught in the wrong place at the wrong time.

It's possible—but not too likely—that such assertions were true. Yet no one ever entertained any doubts about the female gunman of the supposed robber trio. The woman lying dead on the floor of the Montgomery Brothers meat market was, of course, our old friend Eula Dortch. Whatever the truth about the death of her husband, it remains an indisputable fact that Eula Dortch hadn't made much of her second shot at a decent life. Many people don't—and it would be well to remember Eula's cautionary tale the next time you hear someone whining about letting "reformed" killers out of prison because they have "paid their debt to society." As my brother's astute sister-in-law Laurie has oft remarked, "With some people, *once* is a pattern." So it proved with Eula Dortch, truly one of the most cold-blooded and gothic killers in the annals of Forest City woe. †

ORIGINAL PUBLICATIONS

The following stories originally appeared in the author's previously published books:

From *They Died Crawling*, 1995: "She Got Her Money's Worth: Eva Kaber, Lakewood's Lady Borgia, 1919"

From *The Maniac in the Bushes*, 1997: "'Twelve O'Clock Girl in a Nine O'Clock Town': The Red Rage of Velma West, 1927," and "Medina's Not-So-Merry Widow: Martha Wise's Deadly Crying Game, 1925"

From *The Corpse in the Cellar*, 1999: "The Incredible Vanishing Killer: Cleveland's 'Black Widow,' 1922," "Medina's Wickedest Stepmother: The Garrett Tragedy, 1887," "'Step Aside, Daddy, and I'll Fill Him Full of Lead': The Insouciant Mabel Champion, 1922," "'This Is My Last Day!': The Strange Death of Minnie Peters, 1906," "Assassin from Nowhere: Christina Lipscomb's Terrible Secret, 1908," and "The Phantom Flapper Killer: The Mystery of Margaret Heldman, 1928"

From *The Killer in the Attic*, 2002: "A Most Unquiet Grave: The Sarah Victor Scandal, 1868," and "Three Distaff Poisoners: Elsie Bass, 1917; Anna Kempf, 1928; Dorothy Kaplan, 1956"

From *Death Ride at Euclid Beach*, 2004: "Seduced and Abandoned: Jennie, a Girl of the Cleveland Streets, 1871," "A Second Shot at Life: The Gothic Tale of Eula Dortch, 1965," and "'Straighten Them Out': The Celia Barger Horror, 1953"

PHOTO CREDITS